THE RECEPTION OF JESUS IN THE FIRST THREE CENTURIES

7

Editors

Chris Keith, Helen Bond and Jens Schröter

EARLY CLASSICAL AUTHORS ON JESUS

Margaret H. Williams

t&tclark

LONDON • NEW YORK • OXFORD • NEW DELHI • SYDNEY

T&T CLARK
Bloomsbury Publishing Plc
50 Bedford Square, London, WC1B 3DP, UK
1385 Broadway, New York, NY 10018, USA
29 Earlsfort Terrace, Dublin 2, Ireland

BLOOMSBURY, T&T CLARK and the T&T Clark logo
are trademarks of Bloomsbury Publishing Plc

First published in Great Britain 2023

A catalogue record for this book is available from the British Library.
Library of Congress Cataloging-in-Publication Data
Names: Williams, Margaret, 1947- author.
Title: Early classical authors on Jesus / Margaret H. Williams, University of Edinburgh, UK.
Description: London ; New York : T&T Clark, 2023. | Includes bibliographical references and
index. | Summary: "Margaret Williams examines how classical writers saw and portrayed Jesus. The
volume shows how each of the early classical writers who mentions him (the historian Tacitus; the
biographer Suetonius; the epistolographer Pliny, the satirist Lucian and the philosopher Celsus) takes
a different view of Jesus and presents him in a different way." -- Provided by publisher.
Identifiers: LCCN 2022010925 (print) | LCCN 2022010926 (ebook) | ISBN 9780567683151 (hb)
| ISBN 9780567683168 (epdf) | ISBN 9780567683199 (epub)
Subjects: LCSH: Jesus Christ. | Classical literature--History and criticism.
Classification: LCC BT198 .W475 2022 (print) | LCC BT198 (ebook)
| DDC 232--dc23/eng/20220608
LC record available at https://lccn.loc.gov/2022010925
LC ebook record available at https://lccn.loc.gov/2022010926

ISBN: HB: 978-0-5676-8315-1
         PB: 978-0-5677-0865-6
       ePDF: 978-0-5676-8316-8
      eBook: 978-0-5676-8319-9

Series: The Reception of Jesus in the First Three Centuries, volume 7

Typeset by Trans.form.ed SAS

For Peredur, with my gratitude and love.

CONTENTS

PREFACE

The origins of this monograph lie in the four short chapters (5,000 words apiece) that I contributed to the award-winning, three-volume work, *The Reception of Jesus in the First Three Centuries*, published in 2020 by Bloomsbury T&T Clark. In the aftermath of my submission of those chapters on, respectively, Lucian, Pliny the Younger, Suetonius and Tacitus, it was suggested to me by the chief editor of that work, Chris Keith, that the expansion of this material into a full-scale monograph would be a worthwhile project for me to undertake. For what had become very clear to him was that my views on, and handling of, the earliest 'pagan' sources relating to Jesus were very different from those generally found in the scholarly literature. This was largely because I was approaching them as a classicist, not as an Historical Jesus specialist, let alone as a mythicist – the two types of scholar traditionally most concerned with this small but important (because non-Christian and theoretically independent) body of evidence.

But what is their approach and why is mine different? Both Historical Jesus specialists and mythicists, though having very different, indeed diametrically opposed, preoccupations, have one important thing in common – they focus almost exclusively on the factual content of the various classical testimonia for Jesus. While the former are keen to maximize that content, even to the extent of sometimes convincing themselves that reference is being made to 'Jesus' when almost certainly it is not, the latter are unrelenting in their determination to discount the content altogether. Ideologically committed to proving that Jesus never existed as a creature of flesh and blood but is simply an invented figure for whom a plausible back-story was made up by his devotees, the mythicists routinely argue that the early classical evidence relating to him, none of it to be dated before the early second century CE, has been so corrupted through Christian fabrication in one form or another (e.g. myth-making, rumour-mongering or textual interpolation) that it has no value whatsoever.

Given this narrow preoccupation with the factual, it is hardly surprising that relatively little attention gets paid by these scholars to the language of the Jesus material, all of it composed, it is important to note, by highly educated individuals, each of whom had been thoroughly trained in the art of persuasion (rhetoric) and so were adept at the choice, placement and general manipulation of words. Nor is much made of the literary conventions that shape the various types of writing in which their comments on Jesus occur – a key factor in evaluating any piece of classical evidence.

And a third area that enjoys only the most cursory of treatments is context. Indeed, such context-setting as there is generally consists of little more than a few biographical details and the odd date (sometimes wrongly given because recent classical scholarship in this area has been ignored). Virtually no attention is paid to the social, cultural and even the political factors which underlie these literary compositions and so very likely influence both the amount of coverage given to Jesus and the character of it.

Yet all of these things, language, genre and context, surely need to be examined as thoroughly as possible if the full potential of the early classical evidence for Jesus is to be realized.

Hence my preoccupation with these matters in this monograph. It seems to me that how and why our various authors chose to portray Jesus is arguably more important than their capacity to produce hard, supposedly pure and unsullied facts about him. It should be noted at this point that, besides the four writers mentioned above – namely, Pliny, Tacitus, Suetonius and Lucian – the late second-century Platonist and anti-Christian polemicist, Celsus also receives extensive treatment in this work.

The five classical authors covered in this study have all been the subject of immense scholarly interest for over several centuries, with the consequence that the bibliography generated by each of their respective oeuvres is vast. Although I have endeavoured in my research for this monograph to read as widely as possible, total coverage of such a mass of scholarship – and it continues to grow apace – clearly is an impossibility for anyone. I can only hope that I have not overlooked any work of such a character that it renders this one redundant.

In the course of working on this project I have been fortunate to receive support of various kinds from a number of individuals: my colleagues here in the School of Divinity at the University of Edinburgh, most notably Helen Bond and Matthew Novenson; Sarah Blake, the Commissioning Editor for the T&T Clark division of Bloomsbury Publishing and Lucy Davies, Editorial Assistant at the same; and last, but far from least, my husband Peredur, who has ever been ready to listen, discuss, criticize and encourage during the period when I toiled over what must have seemed at times to be a never-ending project. To all of them I extend my warmest thanks.

At one stage in the composition of this work when I was despairing at the slowness of my progress, Todd Still, a New Testament scholar on study leave in the UK from Baylor University in the USA, sought to cheer me up with these words: 'Better a good book, Margaret, than a quick book'. Well, *Early Classical Authors on Jesus* definitely has not been 'a quick book', as Sarah Blake, generous granter of several extensions to the deadline for the submission of my manuscript, will testify. Whether it comes to be considered 'a good book' will be for readers to decide. However, if I succeed in getting classicists to take a fresh look at the Jesus material in their sources and theologians and mythicists to consider more seriously the literary aspects of the evidence for Jesus provided by 'pagan' Greek and Latin writers, then I shall be satisfied that my labours will not have been in vain.

Margaret H. Williams
Edinburgh, 22nd February 2022

ABBREVIATIONS

ABD	*Anchor Bible Dictionary*. Edited by David Noel Freedman. 6 vols. New York: Doubleday, 1992.
Add.	Addenda
AE	L'Année épigraphique
AIPHOS	Annuaire de l'Institut de philologie et d'histoire orientales et slaves
AJP	*American Journal of Philology*
ANRW	*Aufstieg und Niedergang der römischen Welt*
BJRL	*Bulletin of the John Rylands Library*
BMCR	*Bryn Mawr Classical Review*
CGL	*Cambridge Greek Lexicon*
CIG	Corpus Inscriptionum Graecarum
CIIP	Corpus Inscriptionum Iudaeae/Palaestinae
CIL	Corpus Inscriptionum Latinarum
CJ	*The Classical Journal*
CPh	*Classical Philology*
CQ	*Classical Quarterly*
CR	*Classical Review*
CRAI	Comptes-rendus de l'Académie des Inscriptions et Belles-Lettres
CW	*Classical World*
EDCS	Clauss/Slaby Epigraphic Database
G&R	*Greece and Rome*
GRBS	*Greek, Roman and Byzantine Studies*
HSCP	Harvard Studies in Classical Philology
HTR	*Harvard Theological Review*
ILS	Hermann Dessau. *Inscriptiones Latinae Selectae*. 3 vols. Berlin: Weidmann, 1892–1916.
JBL	*Journal of Biblical Literature*
JECS	*Journal of Early Christian Studies*
JEH	*Journal of Ecclesiastical History*
JQR	*Jewish Quarterly Review*
JRS	*Journal of Roman Studies*
JSNTSup	Journal for the Study of the New Testament Supplement Series
JSOT	*Journal for the Study of the Old Testament*
JSP	*Journal for the Study of the Pseudepigrapha*
JThS	*Journal of Theological Studies*
LACTOR	London Association of Classical Teachers
LCL	Loeb Classical Library

LSJ	Liddell, Scott, Jones – *A Greek-English Lexicon*, 9th edn. Oxford: Clarendon, 1968.
LXX	Septuagint
NEB	New English Bible
NovT	*Novum Testamentum*
NTS	*New Testament Studies*
NTTS	New Testament Tools and Studies
OCD[3]	*Oxford Classical Dictionary*. 3rd edn. Oxford: Oxford University Press, 1996.
OGIS	*Orientis Graecae Inscriptiones Selectae*
OLD	*Oxford Latin Dictionary*
OWC	Oxford World's Classics
PCPhS	Proceedings of the Cambridge Philological Society
Rev.Phil.	*Revue de Philologie*
RHPhR	*Revue d'histoire et de philosophie religieuses*
RIB	*The Roman Inscriptions of Britain*, I. Edited by R. G. Collingwood and R. P. Wright. Oxford: Clarendon, 1965.
SAPERE	Scripta Antiquitatis Posterioris ad Ethicam Religionemque Pertinentia
SBFLA	Studi Biblici Franciscani Liber Annuus
SCI	Scripta Classica Israelica
SJLA	Studies in Judaism in Late Antiquity
SR	*Studies in Religion/Sciences Religieuses*
STAC	Studien und Texte zu Antike und Christentum
s.v. /s.v.v.	*sub voce, sub vocibus*
Symb.Osl.	*Symbolae Osloenses*
TAPA	*Transactions of the American Philological Association*
TAPS	*Transactions and Proceedings of the American Philosophical Society*
TynBul	*Tyndale Bulletin*
TZ	*Theologische Zeitschrift*
VC	*Vigiliae Christianae*
VT	*Vetus Testamentum*
WBC	Word Biblical Commentary
WUNT	Wissenschaftliche Untersuchungen zum Neuen Testament
YCS	*Yale Classical Studies*
ZAC	*Zeitschrift für antikes Christentum*
ZKG	*Zeitschrift für Kirchengeschichte*
ZNW	*Zeitschrift für die Neutestamentliche Wissenschaft und die Kunde der älteren Kirche*

Chapter 1

ANOTHER BOOK ON JESUS?

1.1. *Introduction*

Why another book on Jesus? That surely is a legitimate question for any would-be reader of this volume to raise, given the non-stop stream of publications, popular and scholarly, printed and electronic, about the individual commonly, even if not entirely accurately, credited with having been the founder of Christianity. Surprisingly, an answer to this question can easily be given: despite this plethora of works about Jesus, no monograph, so far as I am aware, covers precisely the topic to be explored here – namely, the various ways in which he is perceived, presented and pressed into service by the earliest pagan authors to note his existence.[1] It is a curious fact that scholars engaged in the writing of ancient history pay scarcely any attention to the references to Jesus in their classical sources. Gibbon in his famous analysis of the rise of Christianity all but ignored Christ himself.[2] A similar disregard is to be seen in the works of both latter-day writers of ancient history and commentators on classical texts.[3] Yet the fact that Jesus was the inspiration behind a religious movement that was to transform the classical world and an individual who continues

---

1. When used by classicists and ancient historians such as myself, the term pagan carries no negative connotations. It simply has proved to be the least cumbersome way of referring to writers of the Graeco-Roman period who were neither Jewish nor Christian. Although occasional attempts have been made to use as substitutes for pagan more neutral-sounding terms such as polytheistic, these alternatives have never really caught on.

2. His only reference comes in his quotation of Tacitus, *Annals* 15.44. See Edward Gibbon, *The History of the Decline and Fall of the Roman Empire*, ed. J. B. Bury, 7 vols (London: Methuen, 1906), 2:85.

3. For some examples, see Jan N. Bremmer, 'Why Did Jesus's Followers Call Themselves "Christians"?', in *Maidens, Magic and Martyrs: Collected Essays*, 1 (Tübingen: Mohr Siebeck, 2017), 3–12 (3).

to exert enormous influence over a significant part of our own world's population surely makes the first pagan references to him inherently interesting. These are – providing, of course, that we can be sure of their authenticity – among the earliest pieces of independent testimony for one of the most important figures (many would say the most important) to come out of the ancient world.[4]

In the course of this study we shall be meeting Jesus under a number of different names and in a number of different guises – as an object of worship, a common criminal, a lawgiver, a sophist, a religious charlatan, an Egyptian-trained sorcerer, a self-declared god, a beggarly social outcast, an encourager of apostasy, a leader of sedition and even an existential threat to the Roman Empire. Different writers had different agendas and the result is this array of depictions. Our principal concern here will be to try and understand those agendas and to see how they affected their portrayals of Jesus. Throughout this study particular attention will be paid to the language in which these various depictions of Jesus are couched. Our authors, being elite and male, were all highly educated individuals and therefore thoroughly trained in the art of rhetoric (persuasive oratory). Consequently they took immense care over both their choice of vocabulary (*delectus verborum* being a very serious matter indeed[5]) and the placement of their words.

The classical authors with whom we shall be working, all of them active at some point during the second century CE, fall into two distinct groups. In the first, we have three of the best known Latin prose writers of the early Roman imperial period. The first to produce evidence relating to Jesus is the Roman senator, Pliny the Younger, now best known for his ten-book collection of literary and official letters.[6] His three references to Christus (Pliny appears not to know the name Jesus) occur in his

---

4. The only significant pieces of independent evidence to pre-date them are to be found in two passages written by the Jewish historian, Flavius Josephus – namely, *Antiquities* 18.63-64 and 20.200. Since they are not of pagan authorship, they are not considered in this volume. For a recent assessment of the first of these passages, the so-called *Testimonium Flavianum*, see Jan Willem van Henten, '*Testimonium Flavianum*', in *The Reception of Jesus in the First Three Centuries*, ed. Chris Keith, Helen K. Bond, Christine Jacobi and Jens Schröter, 3 vols (London: Bloomsbury T&T Clark, 2020), 1:365–9.

5. R. H. Martin and A. J. Woodman, eds, *Tacitus: Annals Book IV* (Cambridge: Cambridge University Press, 1989), 20.

6. Detailed bibliographical information relating to both Pliny and each of the other authors under consideration in this volume will be provided below in the chapter(s) in which they and their testimony concerning Jesus are discussed.

celebrated letter to the emperor Trajan about the worshippers of Christ in Pontus (now northern Turkey), the eastern half of the province of which, at the time of writing (*ca.* 110 CE), he was the governor.[7] Next in date comes the testimony commonly attributed to his friend, fellow senator and slightly older colleague, the historian, Cornelius Tacitus. It is in the course of his graphic account of the sadistic punishments inflicted by the emperor Nero upon the Christians of Rome in the aftermath of the 'Great Fire' of 64 CE that Tacitus's much discussed thumbnail sketch of Jesus (likewise referred to as Christus) occurs.[8] Whether Pliny's young protégé, Suetonius Tranquillus, the erudite author of (among many other works) the biographies of Rome's earliest emperors, should also be regarded as a source for Jesus is still a live issue. Most scholars, especially those approaching this text from a theological or ecclesiastical background, are keen to see in his brief reference to a Claudian rabble-rouser called Chrestus [*sic*] an allusion, albeit rather garbled, to (Jesus) Christ himself.[9] Not all, however, are convinced of this identification. The whole question, notwithstanding the 'oceans of ink' that have already been spilled over it,[10] remains open and is still worth discussing afresh, especially as evidence not generally considered in connection with it can be brought to bear upon it.

The composition of the second group of writers is more certain. It consists of two authors only, both of them from the eastern, predominantly Greek-speaking part of the Roman Empire, and both of them active during the latter part of the Antonine period – more specifically, the reign of Marcus Aurelius (161–180 CE). One is Lucian of Samosata, the well-known belletrist whose large, lively and extraordinarily varied body of works is notorious for its sustained mockery of the gods, among them 'the crucified sophist' – a mocking description, so it is generally assumed, of Jesus.[11] The other is the utterly obscure but, for us, extremely important individual, the anti-Christian polemicist, Celsus. Author of the first, and indeed the only, detailed pagan critique of Jesus and his cult to come down to us, Celsus is now known purely through the quotations from his work made by the learned third-century Christian scholar and apologist, Origen of Alexandria. Fortunately those quotations (generally, and here also, assumed to be accurate) are so extensive that it has proved to be entirely

7. For the letter itself and Trajan's reply, see Pliny, *Ep.* 10.96 and 97.

8. Tacitus, *Annals* 15.44.3.

9. For the reference itself, see Suetonius, *Div. Claud.* 25.4.

10. Erich S. Gruen, *Diaspora: Jews amidst Greeks and Romans* (Cambridge, MA: Harvard University Press, 2002), 39.

11. See Lucian, *De morte Peregrini* (On the Death of Peregrinus) 11-13. At no point does Lucian actually identify Jesus by name.

feasible to attempt reconstructions of Celsus's work as a whole. This was a Platonizing treatise that went by the name *Alethes Logos* (literally, True Word).[12]

To this list of five, many scholars would add Mara bar Serapion, author of a letter in Syriac replete with classical allusions in which reference is made to a 'wise king' (=? Jesus), wrongfully killed by the Jews.[13] Although this 'wise king' almost certainly is to be identified as Jesus,[14] such are the uncertainties surrounding this text that including it in a monograph such as is envisioned here seems unwise. In the first place, there is no consensus about when this letter was written: dates proposed for it range from the first to the sixth century CE.[15] Also problematic is its authorship: although most scholars believe that the writer was a pagan,[16] a minority argue that he was a Christian.[17] And as if these unresolved issues were not enough, recently it has been proposed that the passage in the letter possibly alluding to Jesus is a Christian interpolation (*ca.* 400 CE) into an earlier pagan letter (*ca.* 200 CE)[18] – all of which makes its exclusion here the only prudent course of action.

12. Extensive bibliography relating to both Origen's eight-book refutation of Celsus, the *Contra Celsum*, and the various attempted reconstructions of the *Alethes Logos* will be supplied in Chapter 8 below.

13. See, for instance, Craig A. Evans, 'Jesus in Non-Christian Sources', in *Studying the Historical Jesus: Evaluations of the State of Current Research*, ed. Bruce Chilton and Craig A. Evans, NTTS 19 (Leiden: Brill, 1994), 455–7; Robert E. Van Voorst, *Jesus Outside the New Testament* (Grand Rapids: Eerdmans, 2000), 53–8; Paul Eddy and Gregory A. Boyd, *The Jesus Legend* (Grand Rapids: Baker Academic, 2007), 173–5.

14. Steve Mason, 'Griechische, römische und syrische Quellen über Jesus', in *Jesus Handbuch*, ed. Jens Schröter and Christine Jacobi (Tübingen: Mohr Siebeck, 2017), 160 – 'Obwohl Jesus nicht namentlich genannt wird, ist es schwerlich möglich einem anderen als ihm…zu identifizieren'.

15. Kathleen McVey, 'Mara bar Serapion', in Keith et al., eds, *The Reception of Jesus*, 3:72.

16. In addition to the authorities listed in n. 13 above, note Fergus Millar, *The Roman Near East 31 BC–AD 337* (Cambridge, MA: Harvard University Press, 1993), 507.

17. E.g., Pieter W. Van der Horst, 'Consolation from Prison: Mara bar Sarapion and Boethius', in *Studies in Ancient Judaism and Early Christianity* (Leiden: Brill, 2014), 209–19. The earliest proponent of this view was the first translator and editor of this text, William Cureton. For his edition, see *Spicilegium syriacum: Containing Remains of Bardesan, Meliton, Ambrose and Mara Bar Serapion* (London: Rivington, 1855), xiii–xv.

18. Kathleen E. McVey, 'The Letter of Mara bar Serapion to his son and the Second Sophistic: Palamedes and the "Wise King of the Jews"', in *Syriac Encounters:*

1.2. *The Early Classical Sources for Jesus:*
Their Paucity and Lateness

From the foregoing remarks it will already have become abundantly clear that the number of surviving classical authors who might possibly have something to say about Jesus is very small and the date of even the earliest of their testimonies comparatively late. Jesus's death at the hands of the Roman authorities is generally reckoned to have taken place around 30 CE.[19] Yet the first mention of him in a classical text occurs only some eighty years later. Pliny's famous letter to the emperor Trajan about the Christians in which the name Christus crops up three times can be dated no earlier than 110 CE and could have been written slightly later (in either 111 or 112 CE).[20]

To the conspiratorially minded, this long gap between the generally accepted date for Jesus's death and his first mention in a classical text is highly suspicious. Consequently, they use this long interlude, plus the fact that none of the early pagan testimonies for Christ can be shown to be indisputably of an archival/documentary origin, to argue that Jesus is no more than a Christian fabrication uncritically accepted by the three Latin authors involved. Had such an important figure truly existed as a creature of flesh and blood, so their argument goes, then he would have been attested in pagan sources (and indeed in Christian sources too) very much earlier than is the case.[21] But such suspicions are ill grounded: both

Papers from the Sixth North American Syriac Symposium, ed. Maria Doerfler, Emanuel Fiano and Kyle Smith (Leuven: Peeters, 2015), 305–25 (especially 316–22).

19. John P. Meier, *A Marginal Jew: Rethinking the Historical Jesus*, 5 vols (New York: Doubleday, 1991), 1:89.

20. That *Ep.* 10.96 was written fairly late in Pliny's governorship of Bithynia-Pontus is agreed. The problem is that we do not know precisely when that governorship, assumed to have lasted around eighteen months, began. If it commenced in the autumn of 109 CE, as argued powerfully by Sherwin-White, then Pliny's long missive about the Christians should be dated to the autumn of the following year. See A. N. Sherwin-White, *The Letters of Pliny: A Historical and Social Commentary* (Oxford: Clarendon, 1966), 80–1. He is followed by, *inter alios*, Fergus Millar, 'Trajan: Government by Correspondence', in *The* Epistles *of Pliny*, ed. Roy Gibson and Christopher Whitton (Oxford: Oxford University Press, 2016), 419–41 (435). Some scholars, however, prefer to see either 110 or 111 CE as the start-date of Pliny's governorship. For an excellent, succinct discussion of all the issues, see Wynne Williams, *Pliny the Younger: Correspondence with Trajan from Bithynia* (Warminster: Aris & Phillips, 1990), 13.

21. For some examples of this typical mythicist thinking, see Arthur Drews, *The Christ Myth*, trans. C. Delisle Burns, 3rd edn (London: T. Fisher Unwin, 1910),

the absence of first-century pagan testimonies to Jesus and their paucity in the second can be explained very easily without having to hypothesize either Christian fabrication or a lack of critical awareness on the part of Pliny and his two friends and contemporaries.

1.3. *The Low Survival Rate of Pagan Texts*

In the first place, it cannot be emphasized too strongly just how little has survived of the known literary output of the Greeks and Romans. Literary activity being a key marker of high social status, unsurprisingly we find the elite of Graeco-Roman society engaging in it to the full. This is best illustrated by the nine books of Pliny's personal correspondence. It takes no more than a quick scan of them to appreciate the importance elite Romans attached to literary composition (*litterae*) and the amount of leisure time (*otium*) they were prepared to devote to it.[22] Not only are there more letters on literary topics than on any other subject[23] but we see Pliny himself, when not engaged in forensic matters or actively participating in public life, toiling tirelessly over the polishing and preparation for 'publication' (i.e., declamation before a select audience consisting of friends and acquaintances) of the various speeches he has delivered in one public arena or another – the Senate House, the law courts, the council chamber of his home town of Comum.[24] Nor was he averse to trying his hand occasionally at other forms of composition such as poetry. And no less assiduous in their literary endeavours were many of his friends. Numerous examples can be cited of their engagement with historiography and poetic compositions of one type or another.[25] Indeed, such was the enthusiasm of

231–5; the numerous monographs of G. A. Wells on the ahistoricity of Jesus – e.g., *The Historical Evidence for Jesus* (Buffalo: Prometheus, 1982), 15–18; *Did Jesus Exist?*, 2nd edn (London: Pemberton, 1986), 10–16 and 60, and the various publications of Richard Carrier – e.g., *On the Historicity of Jesus: Why We Might Have Reason for Doubt* (Sheffield: Sheffield Phoenix Press, 2014).

22. On the subject of *otium litteratum* ('lettered leisure') generally, see Roy K. Gibson and Ruth Morello, *Reading the Letters of Pliny the Younger: An Introduction* (Cambridge: Cambridge University Press, 2012), Chapter 6 (*Otium*: How to Manage Leisure).

23. Shown clearly by the preponderance of literary entries in the index on aspects of social life at P. G. Walsh, *Pliny the Younger: Complete Letters* (Oxford: Oxford University Press, 2006), 371–2.

24. For the full list, see Walsh, *Pliny the Younger*, 371, under 'publications of Pliny: speeches'.

25. See Walsh, *Pliny the Younger*, 371, under 'publications of others'.

the elite for writing and proclaiming poetry that it became a prime target for the contemporary satirist, Juvenal.[26]

What is significant for us about all this activity, however, is not its extent but its very tiny footprint. Almost all of the works to which Pliny makes reference have vanished without a trace and that applies even to his own. Most of his poetry has been lost – a lucky escape for us, if the two examples of his work that he quotes are at all typical.[27] Of his numerous speeches, only one has come down to us – an extended version of the panegyric that he delivered before the emperor Trajan in 100 CE on the occasion of gaining the consulship.[28] Regarded as a model of its kind, it attained classic status in antiquity and so managed to survive.[29]

Pliny's writings are not unique in their low survival rate. Suetonius has suffered just as grievously. Out of the long list of works accredited to him,[30] only his Lives of the Caesars (*De vita Caesarum*) have survived more or less intact. Of the remainder, we have, with two exceptions,[31] little more than their titles and the odd citation. Tacitus's various works we are lucky to have at all, the survival of each one being dependent on a single manuscript. Even then we have only portions of his two major compositions. Of his masterpiece, the *Annals*, a year-by-year history of the period 14–68 CE and the locus of his material on (Jesus) Christus, we have roughly a half. Of his *Histories*, an account of the civil wars of 68–69 CE and the Flavian dynasty 70–96 CE, we have the narrative only as far as the start of 70 CE – a huge loss, as it was in the final years of the Flavian period in the latter part of Domitian's reign (81–96 CE), a time through which Tacitus himself lived, that Jews, Christians and their respective sympathizers at Rome (and possibly elsewhere too) became the

26. See the opening lines (1-14) of his first satire. Translation to be found at *Juvenal: The Satires*, trans. Niall Rudd, Oxford World's Classics (Oxford: Oxford University Press, 1992), 3.

27. See *Ep.* 7.4.6 and 9.11.

28. For text and translation, see Betty Radice (trans.), Pliny, *Letters and Panegyricus*, LCL, 2 vols (London: Heinemann, 1969), 2:317–547.

29. *OCD*[3], *s.v.* panegyric (Latin). On the afterlife of Pliny's *Panegyricus*, see Roger Rees, 'Afterwords of Praise', in *Pliny's Praise: The* Panegyricus *in the Roman World*, ed. Paul Roche (Cambridge: Cambridge University Press, 2011), 175–88.

30. For a comprehensive list, see Andrew Wallace-Hadrill, *Suetonius: The Scholar and His Caesars* (London: Duckworth, 1983), 43.

31. For these, see Robert A. Kaster, *C. Suetonius Tranquillus: De grammaticis et rhetoribus* (Oxford: Oxford University Press, 1995) and Jean Taillardat, *Suétone*: Περὶ βλασφημιῶν. Περὶ παιδιῶν. *extraits byzantins* (Paris: Les Belles Lettres, 1967).

objects of imperial suspicion, harassment and punishment.[32] Since some of these victims were of the highest social standing (two were actually members of the ruling dynasty[33]), it is surely inconceivable that Tacitus will have failed to mention them or to make some allusion to the cult with which they were accused (quite possibly maliciously) of being involved. That this was 'Christianity' is highly probable.[34]

These examples of low survival could be multiplied many times over. Here it will be sufficient to remark that not a single one of the many histories known to have been composed between 30 CE and the time of Tacitus has come down to us.[35] Particularly to be regretted is the loss of the annalistic history of Pliny the Elder, since that work could well have been Tacitus's source for his material on Christ and his devotees in the Rome of Nero.[36]

Nor is it just formal histories written during the first century that have not been preserved. None of the memoirs known to have been produced by members of Rome's ruling elite, some of them governors of Rome's eastern provinces and so quite likely to have had dealings with Christians, have come down to us.[37] Also lost is the work (genre uncertain) that a certain Antonius Julianus composed about the Jews.[38] If, as several scholars believe,[39] he is the same man as Marcus Antonius Julianus, referred to by Josephus as the procurator of Judaea at the time of the First

32. Margaret H. Williams, 'Domitian, the Jews and the "Judaizers": A Simple Matter of *Cupiditas* and *Maiestas*?', *Historia* 39 (1990): 196–211 = *Jews in a Graeco-Roman Environment* (Tübingen: Mohr Siebeck, 2013), 95–110.

33. Dio, *Roman History* 67.14.1-2 who names among Domitian's many victims Flavius Clemens and Flavia Domitilla.

34. So argued by Marius Heemstra, *The* Fiscus Judaicus *and the Parting of the Ways*, WUNT 2/277 (Tübingen: Mohr Siebeck, 2010), 117–18 with whose interpretation of the evidence I broadly concur.

35. For a comprehensive list of these lost works, see T. J. Cornell, *The Fragments of the Roman Historians*, 3 vols (Oxford: Oxford University Press, 2013), 1:xii–xiii.

36. See Gerd Theissen and Annette Merz, *The Historical Jesus: A Comprehensive Guide* (London: SCM, 1998), 83; Birgit van der Lans and Jan N. Bremmer, 'Tacitus and the Persecution of the Christians: An Invention of Tradition?' *Eirene. Studia Graeca et Latina* 53 (2017): 229–331 (301 n. 9).

37. For some examples, see Ronald Syme, *Tacitus*, 2 vols (Oxford: Clarendon, 1958), 1:296–7.

38. For the solitary reference to the work of this writer, see Menahem Stern, *Greek and Latin Authors on Jews and Judaism*, 3 vols (Jerusalem: Israel Academy of Sciences and Humanities, 1974–84), 1:458–61 (no. 201).

39. For these authorities, see Stern, *Greek and Latin Authors*, 1:458. For a dissentient view, see Barbara Levick in Cornell, *Fragments*, 1:631.

Jewish War,[40] then it is not out of the question that he could have made some mention in that work of Jesus and his devotees. Their leader in Jerusalem, Jesus's brother James, had, after all, been executed there not that long before Julianus took up his post in Judaea.[41]

1.4. *The Narrowness of Elite Interests*

That some references to Jesus could well have been lost through the non-survival of the great bulk of classical writings is, then, highly likely. However, even if the survival rate of texts had been higher, it may be doubted, given the well-known biases of Greek and Roman writers, whether the material on Jesus would have been vastly greater. It is an incontrovertible fact that, in general, Greek authors of the early imperial period were more interested in celebrating their glorious past than in dwelling upon their inglorious present,[42] and the main focus of most Roman prose-writers of the early imperial period tended to be on Rome itself, its elite citizens and their political concerns, the most important of which was their relationship with the emperor. Their subjects in the provinces, by contrast, were of little interest to them and so receive relatively little attention in their works. Although authors of Roman annalistic histories, on account of the conventions of that genre, were obliged to offer some coverage of events external to Rome itself (generally the frontier wars and provincial revolts in which the elite played a prominent part), little attention is paid in that coverage, on an individual level at least, to Rome's opponents – whether foreign enemies or internal rebels. The number of provincials, for instance, singled out for mention by name in Roman rebellion narratives is incredibly small. The few provincial subjects who are so identified almost invariably enjoy high social status. A good example is Boudicca, the leader of the British uprising against the Romans during the reign of Nero in 60/61 CE. The only rebel actually to be named in narratives of that uprising, she was, as their authors are keen to stress, of royal status.[43] Tellingly, the only history of a Roman province

---

40. Josephus, *War* 6.238.
41. Josephus, *Ant.* 20.200.
42. E. L. Bowie, 'Greeks and their Past in the Second Sophistic', in *Studies in Ancient Society*, ed. M. I. Finley (London: Routledge & Kegan Paul, 1974), 166–209 remains fundamental. See also Jason König, *Greek Literature in the Roman Empire* (London: Bristol Classical Press/Duckworth, 2009), 8 (their obsession with the past) and 28 (their pride in 'the glorious heritage of classical Greece').
43. Tacitus, *Annals* 14.31.1; Dio, *Roman History* 62.2.2.

that has come down to us was written by a provincial. I am, of course, referring to Josephus, the first half of whose life was spent in a province (Judaea) as a subject of Rome, not as one of her citizens.[44]

Given such a lack of interest by elite Roman writers in their provincial subjects, it should come as no surprise to learn that the latter's religious practices likewise tend to be regarded with indifference. Even when the more easily transferable provincial cults manage to become established in Rome itself as the result of immigration, Roman writers show little interest in them. Not only do they have very little to say about these so-called alien superstitions (*externae superstitiones*), but the few comments that they do venture to make often reveal a quite astonishing level of ignorance. Take the Jewish cult, for instance. Although there had been a substantial and conspicuous Jewish presence in Rome from at least the early 50s BCE,[45] Roman writers throughout the early imperial period remain remarkably ill-informed about them and their cult. To quote Gruen on this point: 'In fact, they (*sc.* Jews) had too little importance even for Roman intellectuals to undertake any serious research or enquiry about them. The latter seem satisfied with superficial appearances and impressions; hence they retailed shallow, half-baked, and misinformed opinions. Why bother to do more?'[46] And unlike early Greek writers about the Jews who display quite a positive interest in the founder of their distinctive socio-religious system, the lawgiver Moses,[47] Roman writers display very little interest in him at all: for Pliny the Elder, uncle and adoptive father of Pliny the Younger, he was simply a magician.[48]

With Roman writers displaying these kinds of attitudes, the chances of a man of artisanal status, as Jesus allegedly was, receiving much notice from them would appear to be exceedingly slim. Had he raised a rebellion against Rome, conceivably he might have gained the odd notice from

44. For Josephus's enfranchisement by the emperor Vespasian in the aftermath of the First Jewish War and his subsequent domicile in Rome, see Tessa Rajak, *Josephus: The Historian and his Society*, 2nd edn (London: Duckworth, 1983, 2002), 194–5.

45. Cicero, *Pro. Flacc.* 28.66 – a speech delivered in 59 BCE.

46. Gruen, *Diaspora*, 52.

47. For a survey of the evidence, starting with Hecataeus, see Louis H. Feldman, 'Reflections on Jews in Graeco-Roman Literature', *JSP* 16 (1997): 39–52 and *Jew and Gentile in the Ancient World: Attitudes and Interactions from Alexander to Justinian* (Princeton: Princeton University Press, 1993), 233–87. In both these works, Feldman either downplays or ignores altogether most of the admittedly very slight Roman evidence relating to Moses.

48. Pliny, *NH* 30.11 – 'There is yet another branch of magic, derived from Moses...and the Jews'. For Tacitus's only slightly less cursory treatment, see *Histories* 5.3-4.

Roman historians, notwithstanding his lowly social status. That is how 'a certain Simon' (*Simo quidam*) managed to secure a mention from Tacitus in his brief overview of Jewish history at *Histories* 5.9-10. Although only a slave,[49] Simon had exploited the power vacuum in Judaea following the death of Herod the Great in 4 BCE to stage a coup serious enough to require intervention by troops loyal to Rome and the Herodian dynasty.[50] Jesus, however, clearly had done nothing comparable. According to Tacitus, Judaea was at peace during Tiberius's reign, the time when Jesus was executed.[51] No reason, then, to mention him at all in an historical survey aimed at an elite, metropolitan Roman readership.

Given this situation, with Greek writers fixated on the classical past and Roman writers concerned mainly with warfare and metropolitan politics, the surprising thing about Jesus is not how little he is mentioned by classical authors but how much. I know of no other Roman subject of comparable social status who figures as much as he does in their writings.

1.5. *Pagan Testimonies for Jesus:* *Familiarity and Under-exploitation*

Much of the material to be studied in this monograph will already be familiar. The three Latin texts with which our study will begin (Pliny, *Ep.* 10.96; Tacitus, *Annals* 15.44 and Suetonius, *Div. Claud.* 25.4) are among the best-known and most intensively discussed prose passages in the whole of early Roman imperial literature. Besides generating in each case an immense and continuously expanding scholarly bibliography, they also feature regularly in a wide swathe of textbooks designed primarily for use by students. Besides handbooks concerned with the Historic Jesus[52] and the early history of the church,[53] these include sourcebooks on the Roman Empire in general[54] and particular aspects of it – e.g., religion in

49. We owe this detail to Josephus. See *War* 2.57 and *Ant.* 17.273.

50. For a brief account of this attempted coup, see Josephus, *War* 2.57-59 and *Ant.* 17.273-76.

51. Tacitus, *Histories* 5.9.2 – *sub Tiberio quies* ('under Tiberius, all was quiet').

52. See, for instance, Theissen and Merz, *Historical Jesus*, 79–84; Van Voorst, *Jesus*, 23–53; Eddy and Boyd, *Jesus Legend,* 175–7 and 179–84; *Jesus Handbuch*, 159–65.

53. E.g., J. Stevenson, *A New Eusebius: Documents Illustrating the History of the Church to AD 337*, rev. W. H. C. Frend (London: SPCK, 1987), nos. 2; 3; 16 and 17.

54. E.g., A. H. M. Jones, eds, *A History of Rome Through the Fifth Century*, 2 vols (New York: Harper & Row, 1970), 2: nos. 168–69; Naphtali Lewis and Meyer Reinhold, eds, *Roman Civilization: Selected Readings*, 2 vols, 3rd edn (New York: Columbia University Press, 1990), 2:137–40 and 551–3.

the Roman world,[55] Gracco-Roman views of Jews and Christians[56] and Jews in the Graeco-Roman world.[57]

Under-exposure, then, is not something from which the early pagan texts referring to Jesus/Christus/Chrestus can be said to suffer. Although the material on him in Lucian and Celsus figures far less frequently in sourcebooks, substantial extracts from both Lucian's *On the Death of Peregrinus* and Celsus's *Alethes Logos* are now to be found (that was not always the case) at least in those with a strong Christian focus.[58] However, despite the ready availability of these materials for study, surprisingly little has been made of the treatment in them of Jesus himself, compared with that given to his followers, the Christians.[59] Given the availability of such a promising body of evidence, why has it not evoked a more substantial scholarly response and why has an historico-literary study of the kind envisaged here not been undertaken? Is it because some of the testimonia appear at first sight to be rather slight? Cook, for instance, bemoans the lack of information supplied by Pliny about Christus,[60] and Bond, while conceding that Pliny supplies 'a number of interesting details about Christians in Bithynia [*sic*]', claims that he is 'completely silent regarding Jesus'.[61] Or might there be more substantial reasons for this state of affairs?

Among the possible reasons that spring to mind, the first is the enduring influence of the convention noted at the beginning of this chapter whereby both ancient historians and classicists tend to give Jesus a wide berth, the belief having become deeply ingrained that he is the

---

55. Mary Beard, John North and Simon Price, *Religions of Rome*, 2 vols (Cambridge: Cambridge University Press, 1998), 2:11.11a-d.

56. Molly Whittaker, *Jews and Christians: Graeco-Roman Views* (Cambridge: Cambridge University Press, 1984), 104 and 147–53.

57. E.g., Stern, *Greek and Latin Authors*, 2: nos. 294; 307 and 375.

58. See, for instance, Stevenson/Frend, *New Eusebius*, nos. 106-117; Whittaker, *Jews and Christians*, 178–85, 187–9. Brief discussions only of Lucian and Celsus at Eddy and Boyd, *Jesus Legend*, 177–8.

59. Two notable examples of this are Robert L. Wilken, *The Christians as the Romans Saw Them* (New Haven: Yale University Press, 1984) and John Granger Cook, *Roman Attitudes toward the Christians*, WUNT 261 (Tübingen: Mohr Siebeck, 2011). Granted that their main preoccupation is, as their respective titles proclaim, with the Christians, it is striking how little either has to say about Jesus himself.

60. See *Roman Attitudes*, 207.

61. Helen K. Bond, *The Historical Jesus: A Guide for the Perplexed* (London: Bloomsbury, 2012), 38.

intellectual property, as it were, of the theologians.[62] To appreciate the weight still exerted by that convention one has only to consider the way in which many university libraries continue to be organized – 'Jesus' books tending to be placed, as here in Edinburgh, in divinity libraries, and the classical/ancient history materials elsewhere. To be sure, the last twenty-five years have seen moves by scholars in both these areas of academic endeavour to bridge this divide. An early and deliberate effort to do so is to be seen in the monograph written by the ancient historian Helga Botermann on Claudius's Jewish edict, a work in which Suetonius's Chrestus evidence bulks large.[63] That work was written with the express intention of closing the gap between ancient history and theology.[64] And increasingly we see classicists also giving serious consideration to Christian literature. General surveys of classical literature of the Roman imperial period, as well as publications of a more specialist nature, both illustrate this trend. An instance of the former is König's *Greek Literature in the Roman Empire*: in the sections of this work devoted to novelistic narratives, philosophy, miscellanism and biography numerous examples from Christian literature are to be found[65] – a development that would have been unthinkable a generation earlier. Another striking example is Hägg's monograph on ancient biography. This contains a whole chapter on the gospels.[66] Nothing, however, illustrates more clearly how strongly the wind is blowing in this direction than the deliberate decision of the editors of the recently published *Cambridge Greek Lexicon* (April 2021) to include in this intended replacement for Liddell and Scott's now very dated and never revised *Intermediate Greek Lexicon* (1889) significant amounts of early Christian material.[67]

---

62. On the general lack of co-operation between theological scholars on the one hand and ancient historians on the other during much of the twentieth century, see Miriam T. Griffin at *Latomus* 59, no. 3 (2000): 694 (review of Botermann's *Judenedikt*, for details of which see next note).

63. Helga Botermann, *Das Judenedikt des Kaisers Claudius: Römischer Staat und Christiani im 1. Jahrhundert* (Stuttgart: F. Steiner, 1996), 50–102 (= Section III).

64. Botermann, *Das Judenedikt*, 24 – 'Dazu muss ich versuchen, gewissermassen in meiner Person den Dialog zwischen Religions- und Altertumswissenschaftlern zu führen, der in den letzten Jahrzehten zu kurz gekommen ist'.

65. König, *Greek Literature*, 24–5 (novels); 63–5 (philosophy); 72–3 (miscellanism); 92–3 (biography).

66. Tomas Hägg, *The Art of Biography in Antiquity* (Cambridge: Cambridge University Press, 2012), 148–86 (= Chapter 4).

67. Much was made of this decision by the Editor-in-Chief of the new lexicon, Professor James Diggle, at its official launch (via Zoom) on 6 May 2021.

Much, however, remains to be done, as Ash's recent commentary on Tacitus, *Annals* 15.44, just to give one example, shows.[68] Although the author clearly is aware of the controversial nature of this chapter, most notably the possibly anachronistic nature of the Christian material in general and the suspected inauthenticity of the sentence relating to Christus in particular,[69] she does not engage with either of these issues. Symptomatic of her lack of interest in Christus is the fact that the latter's name fails to make it into any of her indices, unlike that of Pontius Pilate, the man on whose authority 'Jesus' was put to death. As for the portrayal of Christus and the language in which that portrayal is couched, about these matters she has very little to say – surprising omissions indeed in a commentary so sensitive to linguistic usage.

But even if classicists and ancient historians by convention pay very little attention to the pagan references to Jesus/Christus, one would not expect theologians to behave similarly. Yet we find that they do. Why is this?

One powerful reason, I suspect, is the distaste, verging sometimes on revulsion, with which scholars with a Christian agenda traditionally have regarded most of the pagan material to be discussed in this volume. Lucian's satire on Jesus and his devotees in *On the Death of Peregrinus* has been found particularly repellent. Indeed, the vociferous objections to it by Christian scholars and commentators can be traced all the way back to antiquity itself. Thus we find the author of the entry on Lucian in the tenth-century CE encyclopedia, the Suda, for instance, not only denouncing 'the filthy brute' as a blasphemer, a slanderer and an atheist but grimly predicting that because of his foul comments about Jesus 'in the next world he will inherit eternal fire with Satan'.[70] In the sixteenth century, so offensive did the Papal authorities find Lucian's work that by the end of it they had placed his entire oeuvre on the Index of Banned Books (*Index Librorum Prohibitorum*).[71] Protestant scholars, of course,

---

68. Rhiannon Ash, ed., *Tacitus, Annals Book XV* (Cambridge: Cambridge University Press, 2018).

69. See her brief introduction to chapters 42–45 ('Deviant Reconstruction') at *Annals XV*, 194.

70. For this translation, see Paul Turner, *Lucian: Satirical Sketches* (Harmondsworth: Penguin, 1961), 7. On the abuse heaped upon Lucian by ancient Christian scholars, especially for his scurrilous treatment of Jesus in *On the Death of Peregrinus*, see Mark J. Edwards, 'Lucian of Samosata in the Christian Memory', *Byzantion* 80 (2010): 142–56.

71. Christopher Robinson, *Lucian and His Influence in Europe* (London: Duckworth, 1979), 98.

will not have been affected by that prohibition. Their freedom of action notwithstanding, their distaste for Lucian's scurrilous treatment of both the Christians and Jesus himself was such that for a very long time his work was largely omitted from sourcebooks relating to early Christianity.[72] Nor has this censorship of pagan material disparaging of Jesus altogether ceased. It is noticeable that in the latest edition of Bettenson, for example, the total ban on pagan material critical of Jesus remains in force.[73]

A similar reluctance to engage with uncongenial material may account for the relatively little attention given by Christian scholars to Celsus's extensive attack on Jesus. Although the bibliography generated by Origen's *Contra Celsum* is huge, that monumental work of early Christian apology being of enormous interest particularly to Patristic scholars, the number of publications which focus to any extent on Celsus's treatment of Jesus, as opposed to other aspects of his treatise (e.g., the identity of Celsus's Jew), is remarkably small.[74]

But a disinclination to engage with what is regarded as distasteful, impious even, is not the only reason for the under-exploitation of the pagan material relating to Jesus by theologians. New Testament scholars in general traditionally have paid only scant attention to the classical source material relating to him.[75] Although Historical Jesus specialists have no option but to consider it, the unreasonable demands they routinely make of it inevitably result in its not being taken very seriously. By insisting that the pagan testimonies relating to Jesus, if they are to be viewed as serious evidence, must (a) contain nuggets of pure, independent information about him, ideally of an archival nature, and (b) not be based on Christian testimony, either written or oral, they effectively set up them

---

72. See, for instance, B. J. Kidd, *Documents Illustrative of the History of the Church*, 2 vols (London: SPCK, 1920 and 1923); and Henry Bettenson, *Documents of the Christian Church* (London: Oxford University Press, 1943). On the efforts of, first, Stevenson (1957) and then Frend (1987) to change that state of affairs by including examples of anti-Christian pagan polemic in the sourcebook intended to be a replacement for Kidd – namely, *A New Eusebius* – see their respective prefaces to the first and revised second edition of that handbook.

73. See Henry Bettenson, *Documents of the Christian Church*, rev. Chris Maunder (Oxford: Oxford University Press, 1999).

74. For a rare exception, see Eugene V. Gallagher, *Divine Man or Magician? Celsus and Origen on Jesus*, SBL Dissertation Series 64 (Chico, CA: Scholars Press, 1982).

75. On their entirely understandable privileging until relatively recently of canonical Christian texts over all other types of evidence for Jesus, see Van Voorst, *Jesus*, 2–3.

up to fail. For reasonable as these requirements might seem to the modern reader ignorant of ancient literary values and compositional practices, they are in fact virtually impossible to meet. Classical writers, as will be explained in detail in Chapter 4, operated along completely different lines from those of modern scholars. Not only were their views of the relative merits of oral and documentary evidence diametrically opposed to our own, but they regarded the consultation and citation of archival source material as neither essential nor even particularly desirable. And no less unreasonable is it to insist that the classical testimonies relating to Jesus must be free of all Christian input. For who, if not Christians, could supply non-Christians with information about their beliefs and practices? Even the court records and police reports that are held up as models of independence and neutrality ultimately will have been derived from Christian testimonies.

No surprise, then, given the unsurmountable objections routinely raised by Historical Jesus specialists against the classical source material relating to Jesus, that most of it gets given very short shrift. Apart from Tacitus who, somewhat illogically, tends to be regarded as 'an important source'[76] and so gets granted relatively generous treatment,[77] the other classical writers who make reference to Jesus, all of them frequently classified as 'sources of minimal value',[78] are generally dealt with in a couple of short paragraphs each. Some are not considered to deserve even as much as that. On a few occasions, we even find Celsus, whose well informed, detailed critique of Jesus is based largely on Christian sources, being disregarded altogether.[79]

No less severe in their treatment of the classical references to Jesus are the mythicists. Given their urgent need to consign these unwelcome testimonies to the dustbin of history, unsurprisingly we find them imposing on them the same stringent, utterly unreasonable requirements as the Historic Jesus specialists. Where they differ from the latter, however, is in

---

76. For this evaluation of Tacitus, see Evans, 'Jesus in Non-Christian Sources', 464–6, followed by Eddy and Boyd, *Jesus Legend*, 167. Tacitus, however, produces no new information about Jesus. Further, his source, though much discussed, remains unknown. Conceivably, it could have been both oral and Christian. See Meier, *A Marginal Jew*, 1:91.

77. Eddy and Boyd, *Jesus Legend*, 179–84 give more space to Tacitus than to our other four authors combined.

78. See, for instance, Evans, 'Jesus in Non-Christian Sources', 457–62 and Eddy and Boyd, *Jesus Legend*, 175–8.

79. Notwithstanding the title of Theissen and Mertz's handbook – namely, *The Historical Jesus: A Comprehensive Guide* – Celsus finds no mention in it.

their much greater readiness to declare material interpolated and therefore inauthentic – a highly convenient but rather questionable way of disposing of unwelcome pieces of evidence.[80]

Such then are the main reasons for the under-utilization of the pagan testimonies relating to Jesus by, respectively, classicists, ancient historians, *Neutestamentler*, Historical Jesus specialists and mythicists. However, the considerations that fettered each of these groups need not bind us. There seems to be no good reason why I, primarily a classicist and ancient historian, should regard Jesus as somehow off-limits and handle him differently from those other rare provincials who happen to make the odd, brief appearance in the pagan literature of the early Roman imperial period. Nor is there any good reason for treating the classical source material for Jesus in the narrow, anachronistic manner adopted in particular by Historical Jesus specialists and mythicists. Their obsession with extracting from it 'real facts of history'[81] not only is doomed to failure for the reasons indicated above but it has some truly unfortunate consequences too. Not the least of these is the neglect of subjects that are worth exploration in their own right – namely, the specific context of each piece of pagan testimony and the highly sophisticated, literary character of the material as a whole. Too often these texts are treated as if they had no context, neither the authors themselves nor the social and political factors that may have influenced their writings receiving anything more than the most perfunctory and, on occasion, inaccurate of notices.[82] As for the literary character of the pagan testimonies for Jesus, that tends to be totally disregarded.

Yet the accidents of survival have put at our disposal a substantial body of evidence, both epigraphic and literary, that makes the exploration of such issues entirely feasible. And because that evidence spans the greater part of the second century CE, a time of immense change for both Christianity in particular and the Roman Empire generally, it becomes possible for us both to track the increase in elite knowledge about Jesus and to see how attitudes towards him and the literary treatment of him changed during that period.

---

80. See, for instance, Richard Carrier, 'The Prospect of Christian Interpolation in Tacitus, Annals 15.44', *VC* 68 (2014): 264–83. For trenchant criticism of this 'scholarship of convenience', see Bart D. Ehrman, *Did Jesus Exist? The Historical Argument for Jesus of Nazareth* (New York: Harper Collins, 2012), 55, 59, 118, 133.

81. Drews, *Christ Myth*, 232.

82. The mis-spelling, for instance, of quite a few classical proper nouns in Eddy and Boyd's *Jesus Legend* – e.g., Pythagoras (174, twice), Suetonius (176), Samosata (441), hardly instils confidence in their mastery of classical source material.

In order to illustrate these processes, it is essential that the evidence is handled chronologically. Thus our study will commence with Pliny the Younger, whose testimony dates from the high point of Trajan's rule (*ca.* 110 CE), and will end with that of Celsus in the final years of Marcus Aurelius's deeply troubled reign (the late 170s CE).

Chapter 2

PLINY AND CHRISTUS (I):
SETTING THE SCENE

The first reference to Jesus (or rather, to Christus) in a classical source occurs in Pliny's celebrated despatch to the emperor Trajan from the province of Bithynia-Pontus (*Ep.* 10.96). Sent just a few months before Pliny's presumed death in office *ca.* 111 CE,[1] this unusually long and carefully crafted missive is among the last letters from his pen to receive publication.[2] Few classical texts have generated as much discussion or as extensive a bibliography as this particular epistle. Providing, as it does, the first pagan testimony for the socio-religious practices of the early Christians and for the status of their cult in law, it is, without question, a source of enormous historical value. But despite having received so much scholarly attention on these two particular matters,[3] almost nothing has been written about the specific references contained within it to the originator of the so-called Christian superstition – i.e., Christus himself. Wilken, for instance, does not discuss the references at all in his classic work on Roman views of Christians, despite devoting a whole chapter to this Plinian letter.[4] Cook, in his extensive analysis of this text in his recent monograph on Roman attitudes towards Christians, largely confines himself to regretting that Pliny tells us so little about Christ.[5]

---

1. For this common assumption, see Wynne Williams, *Pliny the Younger*, 13 – 'His sudden death is the simplest way to explain the sudden interruption in the corre-spondence'. However, this widely held view has recently been challenged. See, for instance, Greg Woolf, 'Pliny's Province', in Gibson and Whitton, eds, *Epistles of Pliny*, 442–60 (447–8).

2. For the dating of Pliny's Bithynian correspondence, see Millar, 'Trajan: Government by Correspondence', 439–41.

3. For the extensive bibliography on both of these subjects, see Cook, *Roman Attitudes*, Chapter 4 ('Trajan and the Christians').

4. Wilken, *The Christians as the Romans Saw Them*, 1–30.

5. Cook, *Roman Attitudes*, 207.

Yet the very fact that Pliny does say so little, so late in his life about Christ and, what is more, goes to such lengths to stress his ignorance about his cult and its devotees, surely are matters worth pondering. One might reasonably expect a man whose entire career had been pursued in the public domain at Rome to have been better informed about a subject which, if our sources are to be believed, had become an extremely sensitive political issue at an earlier stage of his life. In the 90s CE, when he was already a public figure, indeed a legal figure, of some prominence at Rome, allegations of involvement in 'Christianity' had played a crucial part in the ruination of a number of elite Romans, some of them of extremely high standing in Roman society. The Christian historian, Eusebius, is quite unequivocal on this point: viewing the emperor at that time, Domitian, as a persecutor second only to Nero, he claims at *Hist. eccl.* 3.17 that he 'executed great numbers of men distinguished by birth and attainments and ruined a whole lot more either by banishing them or confiscating their property'. Although it is hard to document these sweeping claims at all adequately, Eusebius's conviction, one shared by many Christians, that Domitian was a persecutor is unlikely to be totally without foundation. Various Christian texts, widely believed to be Domitianic in date, can be adduced to support this notion.[6] Nor is this the only evidence for the unwelcome prominence 'enjoyed' by the cult of Christ in the Rome of the 90s CE. A passage in the *Roman History* of Cassius Dio (67.14.1-2) can be interpreted along broadly the same lines.[7]

Given, then, that 'Christianity' very likely was quite a hot topic in the Rome of the 90s CE, Pliny's insistence in his letter to Trajan upon his ignorance of the subject is very striking. What might be the reason for this? Was it just a rhetorical ploy – a way of flattering Trajan and getting him to reveal his superior knowledge about the cult? As Pontifex Maximus and so official head of Roman state religion, Trajan could be assumed to be well informed on the subject (or at least to be able to command the expertise of those who were knowledgeable).[8] Or was it simply that it had

6. For full discussion of some of these, most notably 1 Peter, Revelation and Hebrews, see Heemstra, *Fiscus Judaicus*, Chapters 4–6.

7. For this interpretation of Dio's reference to Domitian's punishment for 'atheism' of individuals who had 'drifted into Jewish ways', see Heemstra, *Fiscus Judaicus*, 117–18 and G. K. Beale, *The Book of Revelation: A Commentary on the Greek Text* (Grand Rapids: Eerdmans, 1999), 8–9. On Judaizing as 'a form of Christian faith that promoted Jewish observance without the necessity of circumcision', see Paul Foster, 'The Epistles of Ignatius of Antioch', in *The Writings of the Apostolic Fathers*, ed. Paul Foster (Edinburgh: T&T Clark, 2007), 91.

8. On this point, see Pliny, *Ep.* 10.68.

not occurred to Pliny, unquestionably a deeply conservative and snobbish individual, to inform himself about a newfangled, alien cult whose devotees at that time, notwithstanding the alleged involvement in it of certain Roman grandees,[9] were drawn largely from the non-elite parts of society? Or had calculations of a political nature been the main driver of what appears to be a distinctly ostrich-like attitude on his part towards the cult of Christ? 'Christianity' was, after all, an illegal cult.[10] Of that much Pliny clearly was aware.[11] Was it simply too dangerous to be seen to have any knowledge of it?[12]

In order to figure out the factors likely to account for Pliny's apparent lack of curiosity and ignorance about the cult of Christ it will be appropriate at this point to examine in some depth his background and life-experiences prior to his departure to Bithynia-Pontus *ca.* 109 CE. On both of these topics we are unusually well informed. Thanks to the publication of a considerable selection of letters from his voluminous correspondence with friends, family members and the emperor Trajan, we know more about him and his take on life than any other private Roman individual of the early imperial period. Nor are these letters our sole source of information about him. Several inscriptions relating to him have been discovered either in or near his home town in northern Italy.[13] These turn out to be invaluable since they contain information not found (because deliberately suppressed?) in the letters that he carefully revised and edited prior to placing them in the public domain.

9. See Dio, *Roman History* 67.14.3-4, where three such individuals are singled out for naming.

10. When and by whom the cult of Christ was ruled illegal remain highly disputed, as does the precise form taken by the ruling itself. However, Tertullian's view (*Nat.* 1.7) that the responsibility for it lay with Nero appears to be gaining increasing scholarly support. For a useful recent discussion, see John Granger Cook, '*Chrestiani, Christiani,* Χριστιανοί: A Second Century Anachronism?', *VC* 74 (2020): 237–64 (249–52).

11. Walter Ameling, 'Pliny: The Piety of a Persecutor', in *Myths, Martyrs, and Modernity: Studies in the History of Religions in Honour of Jan N. Bremmer*, ed. Jitse Dijkstra, Justin Kroesen and Yme Kuiper (Leiden: Brill, 2010), 271–99 (295) – 'From the start, he (*sc.* Pliny) recognized the mere *nomen Christianum* as a convictable fact: confessing to the *nomen* was seen as a guilty plea, preventing any defence and rendering further investigation unnecessary'.

12. On the very real danger of guilt by association under Domitian, see Thomas E. Strunk, 'Domitian's Lightning Bolts and Close Shaves in Pliny', *CJ* 109, no. 1 (2013): 88–113 (95–9).

13. For the most important of these texts, see Appendix 1, A, nos. 1-3.

2.1. *Background and Early Influences*

Born in either 61 or 62 CE[14] in the town of Comum (modern Como) in Transpadine Gaul, an area in the far north-west of Italy renowned for its cultural conservatism,[15] Pliny belonged to the landowning, and therefore the economically and politically dominant, class of that region. Unsurprisingly, both his father's family, the Caecilii, and his mother's, the Plinii, were stalwart supporters of the Principate, the quasi-monarchical system of government established by Augustus in 27 BCE on the ruins of the old Roman Republic. Although wealthy municipal families like theirs had been qualified to participate in the running of the Roman state since 49 BCE,[16] the civil wars of the 40s and 30s BCE and the collapse of the Roman governmental system during that period had made that virtually impossible. However, with Augustus's decisive victory at Actium in 31 BCE and his re-establishment of the state on a new footing four years later, 'job' opportunities on a hitherto unimaginable scale now became available. As the new system bedded down and steadily expanded, so the number of government positions correspondingly increased. And who better qualified to fill many of those posts than men from families such as theirs – wealthy, ambitious and, as events were to show, extremely able?

Among the various individuals from the Transpadana who in due course took advantage of the many opportunities offered by the rule of the Caesars and so became the virtual backbone of the early Principate, was Pliny's father, Lucius Caecilius Secundus.[17] Already a magistrate in Comum (a *quattuorvir iure dicundo*) and a priest (*pontifex*) in one of the local cults, he now substantially enhanced his social standing by securing the position of *praefectus fabrum* (prefect of engineers) in the Roman army. Although by this stage in the history of Rome (the middle of the first century CE) the post was well on the way to becoming little more than a sinecure,[18] it remained a source of considerable prestige,

14. For a detailed discussion of the date, see A. R. Birley, 'Pliny's Family, Pliny's Career', in Gibson and Whitton, eds, *Epistles of Pliny*, 51–66 (51).

15. For the Transpadana, the area between the Alps and the river Po, as 'domicile and paragon of the ancient ways', see Syme, *Tacitus*, 2:616.

16. On the ruling of Julius Caesar that made that possible, see *OCD*³, *s.v.* Gaul (Cisalpine).

17. For other notable Transpadani of the early Principate, see G. E. F Chilver, *Cisalpine Gaul: Social and Economic History from 49 B. C. to the Death of Trajan* (Oxford: Clarendon, 1941), 86–95 (the Julio-Claudian age).

18. J. B. Campbell, *The Roman Army 31 BC–AD 337: A Sourcebook* (London: Routledge, 1994), 56.

especially among ambitious members of the equestrian order, the social class to which both Lucius Caecilius Secundus himself and his brother-in-law, Gaius Plinius Secundus (generally known as Pliny the Elder), belonged.[19]

The significance of this honour to Caecilius Secundus is shown by his reaction to obtaining it: on the inscribed foundation plaque of the temple for the imperial cult which he went on to commission for the town of Comum, pride of place was accorded the title *praefectus fabrum*.[20] Not only did it head the list of Caecilius's public offices but the reader's attention was also directed to the means by which this honour had been attained: it had been through the recommendation of no less exalted a figure than a Roman consul.[21] Although Caecilius himself did not live long enough to see the completion of this temple for the worship of the Eternity of Rome and of the Augusti (*Aeternitate Romae et Augustorum*), his teenage son, our Pliny, did. His first recorded act, as can be seen from the final line of the inscription on the foundation plaque, was to oversee the dedication of this magnificent, richly decorated, colonnaded structure.[22]

The way in which Pliny's father behaved in respect of Rome clearly made a deep and lasting impression upon his young son. Throughout his life our Pliny likewise made a point of cultivating the 'great and good' of imperial Rome – and with even greater success. His membership of the ancient priestly college of augurs, for instance, a highly coveted socio-religious honour conferred upon him by Trajan in 103/4 CE, was entirely

19. The qualification for membership of this class, which comprised the lower echelon of the Roman governing elite, was a minimal annual income of 400,000 sesterces. For the upper echelon, the senatorial order, the census qualification was roughly double that – a minimal annual income of 1,000,000 sesterces. Given that the annual income of a legionary soldier (and legionaries were a well-paid section of the populace) was 900 sesterces, it can be seen that both the Caecilii and the Plinii were seriously rich.

20. For an illustration of this plaque with its high-quality lettering, see Geza Alföldi, 'Ein Tempel der Herrscherkultes in Comum', in *Städte, Eliten und Gesellschaft in der Gallia Cisalpina: Epigraphisch-historische Untersuchungen* (Stuttgart: Franz Steiner, 1999), 211–19, Tafel 5.1 and 2.

21. For a translation of this inscription, see Appendix 1, A. no. 1a.

22. For this inscription, see Appendix 1, A, no. 1b. The dedication itself probably took place late in Vespasian's reign, sometime between 77/78 CE, the time when Pliny came of age, and 79 CE, the year in which he was adopted by his maternal uncle and so changed his name from Caecilius Secundus to Gaius Plinius Caecilius Secundus. See Alföldi, 'Ein Tempel', 216.

due to the persistent advocacy on his behalf by the three-times consul, Sextus Julius Frontinus (*Ep.* 4.8.3), at that time one of the most respected men in the state (*Ep.* 5.1.5).[23]

Also of lasting influence with our Pliny was his father's deep commitment to the imperial cult. Throughout his life Pliny was to prove to be a staunch upholder of the worship of the Caesars. On an honorific inscription found near Comum, it is recorded that he was, among other things, a priest (*flamen*) in a local cult of the deified emperor, Titus.[24] From the emperor Nerva he sought and gained permission to build a temple of the imperial cult at Tifernum in Umbria, the town closest to his large estate in that part of Italy (*Ep.* 10.8.1-2). Interestingly, this shrine was not purely for the worship of dead, deified emperors any more than the temple Pliny had dedicated to the Eternity of Rome and the Augusti some twenty years earlier in Comum. From his correspondence, first, with Nerva, and subsequently with Trajan, we can see that Pliny went to great trouble to ensure that their respective statues were installed within this new shrine in the company of those of earlier emperors.[25] Although Trajan clearly was somewhat reluctant to be an object of religious devotion during his lifetime, nonetheless he acceded to Pliny's request, interpreting it, correctly, as an expression of the latter's loyalty: 'You may erect my statue in the place you desire (though I allow honours of this kind very sparingly), for I do not wish to appear to have limited the scope of your devotion (*pietas*) to me' (*Ep.* 10.9).

A final example of Pliny's life-long commitment to the imperial cult is to be seen in the loyalty test that he applied, when governor of Bithynia-Pontus, to lapsed Christians in the Pontic part of his province. In order to ensure that these individuals really had renounced the worship of Christus and so had ceased through their atheism to be a threat to the well being of the empire, he required them not only to join with him in an invocation of

---

23. For Frontinus's distinguished career under the Flavians, Nerva and Trajan, see *OCD*[3], *s.v.*, Iulius Frontinus, Sextus. Other distinguished consulars to whom Pliny was indebted were Verginius Rufus (*Ep.* 2.1.8) and Julius Servianus (*Ep.* 10.2).

24. For this inscription, see Appendix 1, A, no. 2. For a thorough discussion of the likely location of the cult (the town of Vercellae near Comum) and the probable date of Pliny's appointment to the priesthood of it (first half of the 80s CE), see Ameling, 'Pliny: The Piety of a Persecutor', 281–3.

25. *Ep.* 10.8.1 and 4. Although Pliny takes care to point out to Trajan that his statue is to be for adornment only (*exornare* = to decorate), worshippers at the temple surely are unlikely to have observed that rather fine distinction.

the gods of Rome but also to make an offering of wine and incense to a statue of the reigning emperor that he had had installed in the courtroom for that very purpose.[26]

2.2. *Pliny's Maternal Uncle as an Exemplar*

Pliny's father, however, was not his sole model. A far more influential exemplar, in that he presided over Pliny's welfare during his crucial teenage years (*ca.* 75–79 CE), was his maternal uncle, Pliny the Elder. A workaholic who managed both to have an impressive public career and, simultaneously, to be an immensely prolific author,[27] he made it his particular care to show his young charge, by personal example, how to fashion a successful career at Rome, and how to cope with the almost inevitable ups and downs of political life there. The latter he was eminently qualified to do as his own career had not been a smooth, unbroken success. Despite starting promisingly under Claudius (three successive officer posts in the army in Germany[28]) and ending on a very high note under the joint-rule of Vespasian and Titus (*Ep.* 3.5.7), it had come to a complete standstill under Nero. Even worse, during the latter's final years, he had come to believe that his very life might be in danger. That he had both survived the tyranny of Nero and gone on to enjoy immense success under the Flavian dynasty was entirely down to the political skills that he had spent a lifetime acquiring and honing. It was these that he was determined to pass on to his ward.

---

26. *Ep.* 10.96.5. Precisely when this ritual was turned into a loyalty test in the courtroom is not known. For arguments that it was probably of Domitianic origin, see M. P. Charlesworth, 'Some Observations on the Ruler-Cult, Especially in Rome', *HTR* 28 (1935): 5–44 (32–4), who very reasonably connects it with Domitian's insistence that he be addressed as *Dominus et Deus* (Master and God). As a private ritual, it already existed in early imperial times. See Cook, *Roman Attitudes*, 179, citing Ovid, *Pont.* 4.9.105-12. In this passage, written in 16 CE, we see the exiled Ovid offering incense and prayers to the images in his *lararium* (private shrine) of the deified Augustus (died 14 CE), the reigning emperor, Tiberius, and also various living members of the imperial family – namely, Tiberius's mother, Livia, and his sons, Drusus and Germanicus.

27. For a listing of his uncle's numerous works and a full description of his workaholic ways, see Pliny, *Ep.* 3.5. For his career, see Ronald Syme, 'Pliny the Procurator', *HSCP* 73 (1969): 201–36.

28. For a detailed discussion of these, see Syme, 'Pliny the Procurator', 204–8.

2.3. *Lessons in Political Survival from the Elder Pliny*

So what were these skills? The first was the critical importance of commending oneself to and ingratiating oneself with the ruling family. Useful, indeed necessary, as it was to secure the backing of the 'great and good',[29] in the final analysis what really mattered was imperial favour, since it was the emperor who was the fount of all patronage. Early evidence for the Elder Pliny's appreciation of this basic fact of political life and for his possession of the instincts that were to make him such a consummate courtier in the early Flavian period is supplied by his decision, while still a youngish army officer on the Rhine frontier, to write a comprehensive history of Rome's wars with the Germanic tribes from the time of Julius Caesar down to that of the reigning emperor, Claudius (*Ep.* 3.5.4). Germany, as he cannot have failed to notice, had a special significance for that emperor: not only was Germanicus (Conqueror of the Germans) one of Claudius's names[30] but such was the pride that the latter felt in the conquest of the German tribes by his revered father, Drusus, under Augustus that he celebrated it frequently on his own coinage, especially in the early years of his reign.[31]

That the decision to write about the German wars was a deliberate act of flattery on the Elder Pliny's part can be seen from the story that he put about that he was doing so at the bequest of the ghost of Claudius's father, Nero Drusus. The latter, so the Elder Pliny alleged, had appeared to him in a dream, pleading with him to undertake this work 'so that he might be delivered from the injustice of oblivion (*orabatque ut se ab iniuria oblivionis adsereret*)'.[32] Obviously this claim could never be substantiated. For the Elder Pliny, however, it would have served its purpose if it managed to gain circulation in elite and court circles.

As far as our Pliny is concerned, all this, of course, will have been mere history, Claudius's reign having ended some years before his own life began. Of far greater impact will have been his uncle's conduct during the time when he was actually living under the latter's roof. That will

---

29. On the Elder Pliny's friendship with the influential governor of Upper Germany, the consul, Pomponius Secundus, see Pliny, *Ep.* 3.5.3.

30. To be seen in many public inscriptions – e.g., *ILS* 210 (Rome; 47–48 CE) – *Pro salute Ti. Claudi Caesaris Aug. Germanici* = For the well being of Tiberius Claudius Caesar Augustus Germanicus.

31. For an illustration of one of these *De Germanis* ('Victory over the Germans') coin-types, see Josiah Osgood, *Claudius Caesar: Image and Power in the Early Roman Empire* (Cambridge: Cambridge University Press, 2011), 61, fig. 20.

32. *Ep.* 3.5.4.

have been in the second half of the 70s CE, when, 'barely a teenager' (*Ep.* 6.6.3), he was studying Latin rhetoric with Rome's greatest teacher of that subject, Quintilian, and Greek rhetoric with the distinguished sophist, Nicetes of Smyrna.[33] At that time his uncle was once again domiciled in the capital, having completed several successful tours of duty in the western provinces as a financial administrator for the Flavians.[34] During the period when the two resided together, Pliny will have observed that his uncle, largely as a consequence of his long-standing friendship with the emperor Vespasian's older son, Titus,[35] was now in such high favour with the ruling dynasty that he had become a regular member of the emperor's advisory council and was a welcome daily visitor at the palace (*Ep.* 3.5.7-9). Nor can he have failed to notice the dividends that accrued to him from such close relations with the ruling family. Before the decade was over, Pliny the Elder was to be seen holding at least one (and perhaps more) of the most important administrative jobs open to men of his social (i.e., equestrian) status, the command of the Roman fleet based in the Bay of Naples.[36] For our Pliny, able to observe the final stages of his uncle's stellar career at such close quarters, the lesson offered by the latter's successes could hardly have been clearer – in order to get on in imperial Rome and have a public career of any distinction, it was absolutely essential to curry favour with those who mattered, most notably the emperor, and to do the latter's bidding as diligently as possible. No surprise then to see him, from the moment he embarked upon his own public career *ca.* 81 CE, tirelessly ingratiating himself with the emperor of the day and conscientiously applying himself to whatever administrative tasks that ruler assigned him.[37] As a result, our Pliny, although a man of

33. For Quintilian, see *OCD*[3], *s.v.*, Quintilian; for Nicetes, see Philostratus, *Lives of the Sophists* 1.19.

34. On the likely locations of Pliny's various procuratorships, see Syme, 'Pliny the Procurator', 211–15. On the immense integrity with which he administered them, see Suetonius's *Vita Plinii* (Life of Pliny), in the Loeb Suetonius (rev. 1998), vol. 2:486–7 – '*procurationes quoque splendidissimas et continuas summa integritate administravit*'.

35. They had been fellow officers in Germany. See Pliny, *NH*, Praef. 3.

36. On his command of the fleet, see *Ep.* 6.16.4. For the suggestion that earlier he might have been in charge of the fire service at Rome, see Syme, *Tacitus*, 1:61.

37. For full details of Pliny's career, see the 'Great Comum' inscription at Appendix 1, A, no. 3. For an attempt to date the tenure of his various offices, see the timeline in Gibson and Morello, *Reading the Letters*, 266–9. Pliny's silences and obfuscations about his career under Domitian mean that several of the offices held during the latter's reign, most notably the praetorship, cannot be dated with total certainty.

rather modest ability, prospered greatly at Rome. Qualified to embark upon a senatorial rather than an equestrian career as his financial resources were considerably greater than those of his uncle,[38] he was able over the course of some twenty years to make it to the very top of Roman society – the first in his family to do so.

2.4. *Pliny's Career under Domitian*

Hard as Pliny tried to hide this fact, his most spectacular progress as a politician actually occurred under the hated tyrant, Domitian. In the course of the latter's reign (81–96 CE), Pliny went – and with unusual rapidity – from being the most junior of judicial functionaries, a member of the Board for Ten for Judging Lawsuits,[39] to presiding over the department of state that handled army pensions, the *Aerarium Militare* (Military Treasury).[40] Were it not for certain chance epigraphic survivals, however, we would not know this. In his letters, Pliny omits to mention many of the positions he had held – some because they were not very important but others because it was too embarrassing to admit that he had been beholden to Domitian for them.[41]

In getting such a long way up the greasy pole and so expeditiously, Pliny owed much to the interventions of Domitian with whom he clearly was something of a favourite. As the emperor's candidate for the quaestorship, the junior magistracy which ensured automatic entry to the senate, Pliny was a shoo-in. To quote Walsh, 'he escaped the formality of an election'.[42] The praetorship, the magistracy second in importance

---

38. On Pliny's vast wealth, much of it derived from family legacies, see Richard P. Duncan-Jones, 'The Finances of a Senator', in Gibson and Whitton, eds, *Epistles of Pliny*, 89–106 (= Chapter 4).

39. As a *decemvir stilitibus iudicandis*, Pliny took turns with the other *decemviri* to preside over the court which dealt with civil cases. See Walsh, *Pliny the Younger*, xiii.

40. For the creation of this institution by Augustus in 6 CE, see Alison E. Cooley, *Res Gestae Divi Augusti: Text, Translation, and Commentary* (Cambridge: Cambridge University Press, 2009), 179–80 (commentary on *Res Gestae* 17.2). For a useful discussion of this poorly documented post, see Christopher Whitton, 'Pliny's Progress: On a Troublesome Domitianic Career', *Chiron* 45 (2015): 1–22 (16–19).

41. On his suppression of the fact that he owed his position at the Military Treasury to Domitian, see Sherwin-White, *Letters of Pliny*, 75 and Gibson and Morello, *Reading the Letters*, 34–5.

42. Walsh, *Pliny the Younger,* xiii – an inference from an allusive remark of Pliny's at *Ep.* 2.9.1.

only to the consulship, he was able to run for a full year early, thanks to Domitian's waiving of the age-qualification (*Ep.* 7.16.2). Having served his term as praetor, he was speedily shoe-horned into the post of prefect of the Military Treasury. Many ex-praetors are known to have had to wait years for such a promotion.[43] When the political weather changed with Domitian's fall from power (September 96 CE), Pliny had the nerve to claim that he had been 'utterly hated by the worst of emperors'.[44] The inscriptional evidence gives the lie to this.[45]

2.5. *Pliny's Career under Nerva and Trajan*

Domitian's fall from power had no noticeable impact upon Pliny's political progress. Nerva had long approved of him[46] and it was with his blessing and presumably that of his co-emperor, Trajan,[47] that Pliny was given the job of presiding over the Treasury of Saturn (*Aerarium Saturni*), Rome's ancient exchequer (98–100 CE). Only three things now were wanting to make Pliny's career complete – (i) Rome's highest magistracy, the consulship; (ii) membership of one of Rome's ancient and prestigious priestly colleges and (iii) the governorship of a province. These he duly obtained from Trajan – the consulship in 100 CE, the augurate in 103/4 CE and the governorship of Bithynia-Pontus *ca.* 109 CE.

The importance to Pliny of the first two honours is shown not only by his shameless bragging about them in his correspondence[48] but also by the prominence accorded them in public inscriptions.[49] With the third honour, his governorship of Bithynia-Pontus, special emphasis is placed

---

43. Syme, *Tacitus*, 1:83.

44. *Panegyricus* 95.4.

45. See Appendix 1, A (intro).

46. *Ep.* 7.33.9 with Sherwin-White's commentary *ad loc.*

47. During his brief joint reign with Nerva (Oct. 97–Jan. 98 CE), Trajan seemingly never set foot in Rome, his first visit occurring only in late 99 CE. See Paul Roche, 'Pliny's Thanksgiving: An Introduction to the *Panegyricus*', in Roche, ed., *Pliny's Praise*, 1–28 (15).

48. See, for instance, *Ep.* 3.18 (the consulship) and *Ep.* 4.8.5, where he boasts that he acquired his augurate at a younger age than his idol, Cicero.

49. On the positioning of the titles consul and augur in the 'Great Comum' inscription (Appendix 1, A, no. 3) and the large size of their lettering, see Ameling, 'Pliny: The Piety of a Persecutor', 285 n. 68. For Pliny's likely composition of this text, see Werner Eck, 'Rome and the Outside World: Senatorial Families and the World they Lived in', in *The Roman Family in Italy: Status, Sentiment, Space*, ed. Beryl Rawson and Paul Weaver (Oxford: Oxford University Press, 1997), 73–99 (98–9).

in the 'Great Comum' inscription on the fact that Pliny had been hand-picked by the emperor himself for that position. Normally the governors of that province were selected by the senate and by lot. Pliny's proven competence as an administrator, particularly in fiscal matters, made him the obvious choice to sort out that troubled area, many of whose problems were financial.

The reasons for the comparative ease with which Pliny, clearly a safe pair of hands, managed to acquire these and other honours from Trajan can easily be deduced from his correspondence with the latter, a judicious selection of which comprises the tenth book of his letters. Partly it was by commending himself to the emperor (10.13), partly by getting some of his more influential patrons to exert themselves on his behalf[50] and partly by flattery. Pliny omitted no opportunity, whether the emperor's accession to power (10.1), some victory in battle (10.14) or his granting to Pliny of some minor request (10.10), to indulge in sycophancy of the most toe-curling kind. In behaving in this manner, clearly he was following in the footsteps of his uncle, who, through a combination of competence and cultivation of the great, had carved out for himself a career of considerable distinction.

2.6. *Additional Lessons in Political Survival from the Elder Pliny*

The necessity of being both a conspicuously loyal and a solidly competent imperial servant was not the only lesson, however, that our Pliny learned from his uncle. The Elder Pliny's career, as noted above, had not been a seamless success – under Nero it had come to a complete standstill. Why that happened is a matter of conjecture. Possibly men from the Transpadina, a part of Italy renowned for 'still keeping and preserving much of the modesty, frugality, and indeed the rusticity of old',[51] simply were not welcome in the decadent, luxury-obsessed Rome of Nero.[52] Whatever the reason, there can be no doubt that the Elder Pliny's career stalled and he knew that he was out of favour.

---

50. E.g., Julius Servianus (*Ep.* 10.2.1). For this powerful Trajanic and Hadrianic courtier, see John Crook, *Consilium Principis: Imperial Councils and Counsellors from Augustus to Diocletian* (Cambridge: Cambridge University Press, 1955), 170 (no. 191). For the advocacy of Sextus Julius Frontinus on Pliny's behalf, see *Ep.* 4.8.3 and n. 23 above.

51. Pliny, *Ep.* 1.14.4 – *quae multum adhuc verecundiae frugalitatis atque etiam rusticitatis antiquae retinet ac servat.*

52. For the Elder Pliny's own deep disapproval of luxury, see *NH* 33.145-50.

So how had that junior ex-army officer coped with that setback? His response had been to do nothing that might attract unfavourable attention from the authorities. Consequently, we find him busying himself as a lawyer and devoting his leisure hours (*otium*) to the production of literary works on topics so bland that no objection could possibly be raised against them – a three-book manual on rhetoric in which 'he trained the orator from the cradle and brought him to perfection' (*oratorem ab incunabulis instituit et perfecit*) and the even duller sounding eight-book linguistic treatise on ambiguity (*dubii sermonis octo*).[53]

In playing safe like that, the Elder Pliny was once again showing the soundness of his political instincts. As a consequence, he emerged unscathed from the tyranny of Nero's final years – something that not all members of the equestrian class managed to do.[54]

That our Pliny heeded well this second lesson of his uncle's is clear from his own conduct particularly during the closing years of Domitian's reign when the latter's rule degenerated into a comparable despotism. He too tried to keep a relatively low profile, focusing on his work at the Military Treasury and on his legal practice. It was then, according to the poet Martial, that he established his reputation as an authority on inheritance law.[55] Again, like his uncle, he took great care not to write anything that might get him into trouble. In fact, so scared was he of offending the notoriously suspicious Domitian, who had begun to execute the authors of works which displeased him,[56] that he refrained from putting any written matter at all into the public domain. In consequence, every single one of Pliny's published works, his epistolary 'autobiography', his poetry and the revised versions of his various speeches, belongs to the period after Domitian's downfall when freedom had once again been restored to Rome.

2.7. *The Limitations of the Elder Pliny's Exemplary Behaviour*

Adequate as these self-preservation tactics had been for the Elder Pliny, they were not sufficient for his nephew, the situation in which the latter found himself being rather different from that faced by the former. As

53. Pliny, *Ep.* 3.5.5. On these (now lost) works, see Walsh, *Pliny the Younger*, 312.

54. For *equites* who got caught up in the unsuccessful Pisonian conspiracy, for instance, see Miriam Griffin, *Nero: The End of a Dynasty* (London: Batsford, 1984), 166 and Tacitus, *Annals* 15.48; 50 and 70.

55. Martial, *Epigrams* 10.19.14-17 – a poem written in 94 CE.

56. Suetonius, *Domitian* 10.1 and 3-4; for the public burning of their manuscripts, see Tacitus, *Agricola* 2.

a senator of some standing, a man of praetorian rank, our Pliny was far more exposed politically than his uncle had been during the tyranny of Nero. Although attendance at meetings of the senate was not compulsory, absence without good reason was fraught with danger, especially if the senate was sitting as a court of law and was trying people whom the emperor deemed a threat and wanted to eliminate.[57] History had shown that in such circumstances non-attendance could easily be construed as political disaffection and punished accordingly.[58]

A second complicating factor for our Pliny was the very different character of Domitian's despotism from that of Nero. Whereas Nero had merely been brutal and murderous,[59] Domitian, a self-proclaimed Master and God,[60] was nothing less than a complete control freak. Determined to use his position as Pontifex Maximus, head of state religion, to enforce correct religious behaviour, and the office of *censor perpetuus* (censor for life) to police public morals,[61] he did so with increasing zeal from the mid-80s CE onwards.[62] Noting this development, professional informers (*delatores*) were not slow to supply Domitian with people to punish. The result was an explosion of allegations of impropriety of one kind and another.[63] In such a situation no one was safe, not even members of the

57. On the operation of the senate under Domitian and the way in which the senae tors were cowed into collusion with his malign designs, see Tacitus, *Agricola* 45 and Pliny's sad admission at *Ep.* 8.14.9: 'On becoming senators we took part in these evils (e.g., the condemnation of fellow-senators who had fallen foul of the emperor) and continued to witness and endure them for many years, until our spirits were blunted, broken and bruised with lasting effect'.

58. See Tacitus, *Annals* 14.12 and 16.21-22 and 33-34 for the condemnation and enforced suicide of Thrasea Paetus a generation earlier precisely on that ground.

59. Suetonius, *Nero* 33-34 provides numerous examples of his *saevitia* (savagery/ cruelty).

60. Apparently his self-designation as *Dominus et Deus* occurred in 86 CE. See Jerome, *Chronicle*, the year 2102 after Abraham = 86 CE. For undated references to Domitian as 'Master and God', see Dio, *Roman History* 67.4.7 (epitome of Zonaras) and Martial, *Epigrams* 10.72.

61. The coin evidence shows that Domitian's assumption of this highly unpopular office (the elite in particular resented any imperial oversight of their morals) occurred late in 85 CE. See Brian Jones, *The Emperor Domitian* (London: Routledge, 1992), 106–7.

62. Illustrated most starkly by the increasing harshness with which he punished errant Vestal Virgins and their lovers (Suetonius, *Domitian* 8.3-4). For full discussion and bibliography, see Jones, *The Emperor Domitian*, 101–2 and 218 n. 11.

63. For a graphic account of delatorial activity under Domitian, see Tacitus, *Histories* 1.2.2-3.

imperial family, two of whom, Flavius Clemens and Flavia Domitilla, were brought low on charges of a religious nature.[64] Whether those charges were true or false is immaterial. Quite likely the principal reason for those prosecutions anyway was political.[65] Whatever the truth of the matter, the fate of Clemens, Domitilla and the many others accused of 'atheism' (*atheotes*) showed that allegations of a religious nature could be brutally effective in terminating careers, ruining livelihoods and even costing lives.

Given such a situation, the necessity for extreme caution in the area of cult becomes clear. No surprise, then, to find Pliny adopting such an ostrich-like attitude towards 'Christianity' and insisting that he knew almost nothing about it. Its illegal status meant that any hint of interest in it, let alone involvement, could invite delation, confiscation of property and even death. And even though the chances of wrongful accusation and conviction for Christianizing will have diminished under Nerva and Trajan, both of whom made a point of reining in the delators,[66] neither emperor legalized the cult of Christ. Hence to affect to be ignorant about it was the only safe and sensible thing for a politically ambitious man like Pliny to do.

Although it had not been difficult for Pliny to practise this kind of self-censorship while in Rome, in the province to which Trajan sent him *ca.* 109 CE that was not be the case. There he found himself having to deal with a whole range of issues which previously he had been able to ignore. Nor could he confine his social interactions almost exclusively to like-minded members of the elite, as he had done in Italy. In Bithynia-Pontus he found himself compelled to deal with people of all kinds, among them Christians and their accusers. Habituated through the example set by his workaholic uncle to apply himself conscientiously to whatever task was assigned to him, Pliny did not duck the challenge presented by the Christian problem. Consequently, we find him trying for the first time

---

64. Dio, *Roman History* 67.14.2. For the view that their alleged 'atheism' is to be seen as Christianity, see Heemstra, *Fiscus Judaicus*, 117–18 and the other authorities cited in n. 7 above.

65. Williams, 'Domitian, the Jews and the "Judaizers"', 107–8 – 'Often the real grounds for such proceedings do not surface in the sources. Instead what we are given is often the more piquant and emotive top-up charges'. On the influence of 'factional or some other non-religious animosity' in the bringing of charges of 'Christianity', see Gary J. Johnson, 'De conspiratione delatorum: *Pliny and the Christians Revisited*', *Latomus* 47, no. 2 (1988): 417–22.

66. Dio, *Roman History* 67.1.2 (Nerva); Pliny, *Panegyricus* 34.1, where Trajan's clampdown is described as the removal of a cancer.

to find out what this relatively new religious movement with its slightly sinister reputation[67] might be about and what the devotees of Christus might actually be doing. How he went about this task will form the subject matter of the next chapter.

---

67. Pliny is aware that disgraceful practices (*flagitia*) are associated with it. See *Ep.* 10.96.2.

Chapter 3

PLINY AND CHRISTUS (II):
INVESTIGATING THE CULT OF CHRIST

3.1. *The General Context*

Around 109 CE (the date cannot be fixed any more precisely[1]) Pliny was sent to Bithynia-Pontus by the emperor Trajan to sort out the many problems besetting that province. Bithynia-Pontus was in a mess. Maladministration by Roman governors, coupled with incompetence and corruption at the municipal level, meant that 'many things there stood in need of correction'[2] – not least, the financial administration of many of the province's cities (*Ep.* 10.18.3).

To the emperor and his advisers, Pliny must have seemed the ideal person for sorting out this mess. In the first place, he had extensive administrative experience, especially in the area of finance. As we saw in the previous chapter, at an earlier stage of his career he had presided over two government finance departments – the Military Treasury, which dealt with the retirement pay of army veterans, and the Treasury of Saturn, which handled more general fiscal matters. Even before that, at the very start of his public career, he had gained basic financial know-how by being required as part of his military service to audit army accounts.[3] Secondly, he was a highly trained lawyer unlikely to be fazed by the challenges

---

1. On the problem of establishing the exact start-date of Pliny's provincial governorship, see Chapter 1 n. 20.

2. *Ep.* 10.32.1 – *multa in ea emendanda.*

3. Before embarking on the *cursus honorum* (course of honours), the ladder of public offices at Rome that culminated in the consulship, it was customary for all would-be senators to do a stint in the army. Pliny's 'national service' was spent as a junior officer in Syria with the Legio III Gallica. See Appendix 1, A, nos. 2 and 3. In his case, his duties were largely financial, as can be seen from his comments at *Ep.* 7.31.2 – 'My orders from the consular legate [i.e., the Roman governor in Syria]

arising from the different legal statuses, and so the different legal rights, of the individuals and cities under his control.[4] Thirdly, he will almost certainly have been better informed than many of his senatorial colleagues about the current state of Bithynia-Pontus: in recent years he had twice led for the defence in trials before the Senate of governors charged with maladministration in that province.[5]

How seriously Pliny interpreted his special brief can be seen from the very first letter he sent to Trajan on taking up his post in Bithynia-Pontus: no sooner had he arrived than he wrote to the emperor to assure him that he had already started to review 'the expenditure, revenues, and debtors of the city of Prusa (modern Bursa)', discovering in the process that 'many sums of money are for various reasons being held back in private hands, and, again, some are being disbursed on wholly illegal outlays'.[6] But that was only for starters. Pliny was determined to carry out to the letter his instructions to wage war on waste and to introduce efficiency and probity into local government. Soon other cities in the western half of his province, the focus of his attention in his first year in office, came also to feel the impact of this ultra-conscientious trouble-shooter.[7]

Sorting out municipal finances, however, though of great importance, was not Pliny's sole duty. As with Roman provincial governors every-where, his prime responsibility was the maintenance of law and order.[8] Another area where he was expected to be proactive was that of cult. For unless the gods were kept happy by the performance of the tradi-tional rituals and the proper maintenance of their temples, then the well being/safety (*salus*) of the Roman state and its ruler would be at risk.[9] Hence Pliny's punctiliousness, right from the outset of his governorship

were to audit the accounts of the cavalry and infantry units [i.e., the auxiliary forces attached to his legion]'.

4. For the various statuses of the cities with which Pliny had to deal, see Williams, *Pliny the Younger*, 11–13.

5. For the trial of Julius Bassus in 103 CE, see *Ep*. 4.9; for that of Varenus Rufus in 106/7 CE, see *Ep*. 5.20; 6.5 and 13; 7.6 and 10.

6. *Ep*. 10.17A.3.

7. For his activities in Nicomedia and Nicaea, the principal cities of Bithynia, see *Ep*. 10.37-40. For his cancellation of the all-expenses-paid annual diplomatic trips enjoyed by the richer citizens of Byzantium, see *Ep*. 10.43-44. Byzantium, though not in Bithynia itself, was nevertheless part of Pliny's province.

8. Hence his many letters on issues relating to that subject – e.g., *Ep*. 10.19, where the issue was the proper custody of state prisoners, and *Ep*. 10.29 – how to deal with slaves recruited illegally into the army.

9. For an excellent discussion of the governor's religious duties, see Ameling, 'Pliny: The Piety of a Persecutor', 289–91.

(*Ep.* 10.17A), in doing everything that was required of him in the area of cult and then assuring the emperor that all the prescribed rituals had been carried out.

What is striking about Pliny's correspondence with Trajan during his time in Bithynia-Pontus is the large proportion of letters concerned purely with cultic matters, an aspect of the correspondence that generally gets overlooked.[10] Whereas references to 'religion' are extremely rare in the personal letters published in Books 1-9, and, where they do occur, are largely concerned with Pliny's benefactions to temples,[11] nearly one-fifth of the communications between Trajan and Pliny during the latter's provincial governorship are concerned purely with cultic matters. Of these letters, the majority are brief reports about Pliny's enactment of the prescribed vows, prayers and sacrifices on occasions such as the emperor's birthday (18 Sept.), the anniversary of his accession (28 Jan.) and the opening of the year on 3 January.[12] These rituals were always performed publicly in the presence of the provincials and, if they were on hand, the Roman military too.[13]

In a few letters, however, we see him dealing with religious matters of a less routine type – in one instance, a request relating to the re-location of family tombs (*Ep.* 10.68-69); in another, the proposed re-siting of an entire temple (*Ep.* 10.49); and in yet another (*Ep.* 10.70) the problem of developing for secular purposes a site on which a shrine to the emperor Claudius might once have stood.[14] In handling matters of this kind, Pliny was doing nothing unusual: in cases such as these the provincials were

10. As, for instance, by Williams, whose discussion of the powers and functions of provincial governors is limited to the military, the judicial and the administrative. See his *Pliny the Younger*, 6.

11. See, for instance, *Ep.* 3.6 (his gift of a costly bronze statue to a temple in Comum); *Ep.* 4.1.3-6 (his construction, entirely at his own expense, of a whole new temple at Tifernum-on-Tiber); *Ep.* 9.39 (his re-building, again at Tifernum, of the ancient Temple of Ceres and his commissioning for it of a splendid new cult statue).

12. *Ep.* 10.17A and 88 (Trajan's birthday); 52 and 102 (his accession); 35 and 100 (Roman New Year).

13. See *Ep.* 10.52 and 53; 100 and 101, where Trajan replies to Pliny as follows: 'I was glad to learn from your letter that the day of my accession was celebrated under your direction with due joy and ritual correctness (*religione*) by our fellow soldiers and the provincials'.

14. Pliny, who clearly is very keen to promote the development of this site is less than transparent on this point and Trajan picks him up on this (*Ep.* 10.71), thereby providing an interesting insight into his own religiosity: 'But you did not make it clear enough whether the shrine to Claudius had actually been erected in the peristyle. If it had, the ground remains consecrated to him, even if the shrine itself has collapsed'.

obliged to consult the governor and to secure his permission before taking any action.[15] Sacrilegious acts had to be avoided at all cost. The ultimate responsibility for ensuring that none took place rested with the Roman governor.

Unsurprisingly, given Pliny's ingrained conscientiousness, the traditional character of his piety[16] and his legal cast of mind, we see him dealing with such matters invariably with great thoroughness. Not only are the legal and religious implications of each proposal given extremely (excessively?) careful consideration[17] but imperial endorsement for each of Pliny's decisions is sought as well. Pliny was greatly concerned about possible infringements of Roman pontifical (i.e., sacred) law. Trajan, as *pontifex maximus* and the head of college of pontifices (*collegium pontificum*), could be relied upon to have access to the best advice available.[18]

Such conspicuous diligence cannot have gone unobserved by Pliny's provincial subjects. Before his first year in office was out he must have gained a formidable reputation for being not only a stickler for probity in financial and administrative spheres but a staunch upholder of traditional religion too. Consequently, there should be no surprise that when, in the second year of his governorship, Pliny turned his attention to the eastern, Pontic part of his province,[19] his pagan subjects there thought it worth their while to try and press this new governor into taking decisive action against the worshippers of Christ. Increasingly concerned about the negative impact of this upstart religious movement upon both the economy and the traditional cults of their region,[20] they thought that

15. See Ameling, 'Pliny: The Piety of a Persecutor', 291.

16. His re-building of the Temple of Ceres at Tifernum (n. 11 above) had been on the advice of the soothsayers (*haruspicum monitu*). On the ancient (originally Etruscan) art of *haruspicy* (literally, gut-gazing), see R. M. Ogilvie, *The Romans and Their Gods* (London: Chatto & Windus, 1969), 65–7 and Plate II (relief from the Louvre of a *haruspex* examining the entrails of a sacrificed animal.

17. On occasion, Trajan appears to have regarded Pliny's behaviour as excessively cautious. See *Ep.* 10.50 and 69.

18. This point is underlined by Pliny at *Ep.* 10.68.

19. Consisting of no more than the coastal strip between Amastris and Amisus, now the flourishing Black Sea ports of Amasra and Samsun in modern Turkey, Pontus functioned in Pliny's time 'as a mere adjunct to the Bithynian part of the province'. See Millar, 'Trajan: Government by Correspondence', in Gibson and Whitton, eds, *Epistles of Pliny*, 436.

20. Precisely where in Pontus Christian activity had caused such anxiety that it had been decided to invoke the law against them is nowhere revealed. For discussion,

by bringing formal charges against its devotees they might get the new governor to deal with this blight on their society once and for all. How Pliny handled this challenge is the subject of his celebrated letter to Trajan about the Christians.

3.2. *The Correspondence between Pliny and Trajan about the Christians*

Pliny's letter to Trajan about the Christians of Pontus, the longest and most closely argued communication in his entire correspondence with that emperor,[21] is easily the most important surviving early classical document relating to the Christian movement. Besides being the first pagan text to mention Christus,[22] it supplies invaluable evidence for both the legal status and the cultic practices of the Christians around the beginning of the second century CE. Hence its frequent citation and discussion by both ancient historians and scholars interested in the development of early Christianity, and the enormous bibliography that it has generated.[23]

What has attracted far less attention, however, is Pliny's portrayal of Christ himself. Admittedly Pliny has very little to say on the subject, his focus mainly being on Christ's adherents and how best to deal with them, but it is surprising nonetheless how little discussion there has been of his brief references to Christ. Cook, for instance, in his recent, extremely long and detailed treatment of Pliny's letter (nearly one hundred pages) does

see Sherwin-White, *Letters of Pliny*, 693–4, who favours Amastris, largely because it became 'the chief Christian centre of Pontus later in the century'. Williams, *Pliny the Younger*, 139 regards Amastris and Amisus as equally possible locations for the hearings conducted by Pliny. The offences themselves could, of course, have occurred anywhere in that part of the province.

21. Only two other letters, *Ep.* 10.58 and 81, begin to approach it in length. The length of *Ep.* 10.96 is no argument, however, for doubting its authenticity, as some have done. See, for instance, L. Hermann, 'Les interpolations de la lettre de Pline sur les chrétiens', *Latomus* 13, no. 3 (1954): 343–53 (345). For powerful arguments against Christian interpolation, see Murray J. Harris, 'References to Jesus in Early Classical Authors', in *Gospel Perspectives: The Jesus Tradition Outside the Gospels*, 5, ed. David Wenham (Sheffield: JSOT, 1984), 346. For powerful arguments for the authenticity of Pliny's text and a comprehensive refutation of Hermann, see Sherwin-White, *Letters of Pliny*, 691–2.

22. For the slightly earlier (90s CE) references to Jesus by the Jewish historian, Flavius Josephus, see Chapter 1 n. 4.

23. For extensive references to this, see the footnotes at Cook, *Roman Attitudes*, 138–229.

not engage at all with what Pliny actually says about Christus. He confines himself to regretting that the information supplied by him on this subject is so limited: 'It would be good to know exactly what Pliny knew of Christ besides the fact that Christians would not curse him and that they did like to sing antiphonal hymns to him as to a god'.[24]

But even though Pliny has little specific to say about Christus that does not mean that we can deduce nothing about the founder of 'Christianity' from his famous letter. By paying attention not only to what he tells us about Christus but also to the information he supplies about the latter's adherents, we find ourselves able to sketch, at least in outline, a portrait of him. That picture turns out to be far from unfavourable, an unexpected outcome given Pliny's clear contempt for Christianity itself, a movement that he describes, in a clear echo of Livy's highly influential account of the suppression of the Bacchic cult in 186 BCE,[25] not only as a plague (*contagio*) but as 'a debased sort of superstition' (*superstitio prava*).[26] That paradox needs to be explained. Before we can attempt to do that, however, we need, first, to set out the evidence and then see what can be gleaned from it about Christus.

Given the importance of this Plinian material, his letter on the Christians will be set out in its entirety. The translation offered here is my own. In those places where it is desirable for the sake of the argument to know precisely what Pliny wrote, I have supplied the requisite Latin words in brackets. Since there will be reference also in the discussion below to Trajan's reply to Pliny, my translation of that text is given here as well.

3.3. *Pliny's Letter to Trajan*

It is my regular practice, my lord, to refer to you all matters about which I am doubtful, for who is better able to deal with my irresolution or to instruct my ignorance?

I have never been present at trials of Christians (*cognitionibus de Christianis interfui numquam*). Consequently, I do not know what and how

24. See Cook, *Roman Attitudes*, 207.

25. On the so-called Bacchic conspiracy, see Livy, *History of Rome* 39.8-22.

26. For *contagio*, compare Pliny, *Ep.* 10.96.9 with Livy 39.9.1; for *prava* (crooked, debased, degenerate, perverse), compare Pliny, *Ep.* 10.96.8 with Livy 39.16.6. Besides these and other verbal allusions to the Livian narrative, Pliny clearly sees himself as a latter-day Spurius Postumius Albinus, the energetic consul whose vigorous actions in 186 BCE, which included the interrogation of lapsed initiates (Livy 39.12), saw the effective suppression of the alien, morally reprehensible superstition that had been brought to his notice. This is not the only case of Pliny presenting himself as an old-style Roman magistrate. See also *Ep.* 1.23.

far anything is usually punished or investigated. I have been altogether unsure as to whether there should be any discrimination on grounds of age; whether the young (literally, the tender) should be treated differently from the more mature (literally, the more robust); whether a pardon should be granted for repentance (*paenitentiae venia*) or if those who were Christians should derive no benefit from desisting (i.e., from apostasizing); whether it is the name itself (*nomen ipsum*) which is to be punished, even if it is untainted by crime, or the crimes associated with the name (*flagitia cohaerentia nomini*).

In the meantime I have taken this line with those denounced to me (*deferebantur*) of being Christians. I interrogated them as to whether they are Christians. Those admitting it I interrogated a second and a third time, threatening them with punishment. Those who persisted, I ordered to be led away (i.e., to be executed). For I was in no doubt that, whatever the nature of their admission, their pertinacity and inflexible obstinacy ought to be punished. There have been others, similarly out of their minds (*similis amentiae*), who, because they are Roman citizens, I have designated for despatch to Rome for trial.

As usually happens, now that I have begun to handle the matter accusations are becoming widespread and more types (of accusation) have occurred. An anonymous pamphlet (*libellus sine auctore*) has been placed in the public domain containing many names. Those who denied that they were or had been Christians I thought should be formally dismissed once they had, following my lead, invoked the gods and had made offerings of wine and incense to your statue, which I had ordered to be brought into court for this very purpose along with the images of the gods, and, moreover, had cursed the name of Christ (*male dicerent Christo*). For it is said that those who are truly Christian can be forced to do none of these things.

Others who had been named by an informer (*ab indice nominati*) first said that they were Christians and then denied it; they admitted that they had indeed been Christians but had stopped, some of them three years earlier, some several years before that and some even twenty years ago. All of them too worshipped your statue and the images of the gods and cursed Christ (*Christo male dixerunt*). And they affirmed that this was the sum total of their guilt or error – namely, that they had been accustomed to come together before dawn on a fixed day and to sing a hymn antiphonally to Christ as if to a god (*carmen Christo quasi deo dicere secum invicem*), and to bind themselves by oath (*sacramento*), not for any criminal purpose, but that they would not commit either theft or robbery or adultery, nor would they break faith (*fidem fallerent*) or refuse to return a deposit when called upon to do so. They said that when they had done these things it had been their custom to depart and to come together again for the taking of food – food, however, that was of a common and harmless kind (*cibum promiscuum et innoxium*); however, they had stopped doing this after my edict in which, in accordance with your instructions (*secundum mandata tua*), I had banned political societies (*hetaerias*). As a result of this, I believed it to be all the more necessary to discover the truth by putting two slave-women (*ancillae*) who are termed deaconesses (*ministrae*) to the torture. I found nothing but a perverse sort of cult carried to extremes (*superstitionem pravam et immodicam*).

For that reason I have deferred the trials and have hastened to consult you. For the matter seems to merit consultation, particularly on account of the number of those at risk; for many of all ages and all ranks and of both sexes are being enticed into danger and will continue to be enticed. For the contagion caused by that superstition (*superstitionis istius contagio*) has pervaded not only towns but even villages and rural areas. But it seems that it can be stopped and corrected. For it is generally agreed that the temples which until very recently had been deserted have begun to be frequented and the sacred rites which for a long time have been in abeyance are being performed again and the flesh of sacrificial animals, for which until recently purchasers were very rare, is now on sale everywhere. From this it is easy to infer that large numbers of individuals could be put straight [literally, emended] providing that room is made [i.e., an opportunity is created] for repentance (*paenitentiae locus*). (*Ep.* 10.96)

3.4. *Trajan's Reply to Pliny*

You have followed the appropriate course of action, my dear Secundus, in dealing with the cases of those formally denounced to you as Christians. For it is impossible to lay down a general rule which would establish a fixed routine. These people are not to be sought out (*conquirendi non sunt*); if formal charges are laid against them (*deferantur*) and those charges are proved, they must be punished, but in such a way that anyone who denies that he is a Christian, and makes it clear that he is not by worshipping our gods,[27] then he is to obtain pardon for his repentance (*veniam ex paenitentia impetret*), even though (he was) suspected in the past. But pamphlets published anonymously should have no place in any accusation. They set the worst sort of example and do not reflect the values of our age. (*Ep.* 10.97)

3.5. *Pliny's Portrayal of Christus*

Limited as Pliny's direct comments on Christus are, they are extremely important as they picture Jesus in a manner not found in any other classical text of the period. Uniquely, Pliny presents him in a wholly

27. It is to be noted that Trajan does not require the performance of ritual acts before his own statue/image. For his restraint in this area, see *Ep.* 10.9 and *Panegyricus* 52.3.

positive way – a figure of god-like stature whose followers venerate him to such a degree that they are willing to submit to the death penalty for his sake rather than blaspheme his name (*Christo male dicere*).

Pliny, unlike Tacitus, whose thumbnail sketch of Jesus will be analysed below (Chapter 5), does not offer any specific information about the background of Christus.[28] However, the language he uses to describe the manner in which Christians venerate him (*carmen Christo quasi deo dicere secum invicem* = 'they sing a hymn antiphonally to Christ as if to a god') seems to imply that Pliny thought that he had originally been mortal rather than divine. As Murray Harris has correctly observed:

> If Pliny had regarded Jesus as a god comparable to Asclepius or Osiris, he would have written *Christo deo*, 'to the god Christ'. The intervening word *quasi* ('as if') highlights the distinctiveness of Jesus in relation to other known gods. In what did that distinctiveness consist? In the fact that, unlike other gods who were worshipped, Christ was a person who had lived on earth.[29]

This elevation of Christus, originally a human being, to godlike status would not have struck Pliny as at all untoward. He lived in a society where individuals whose conduct during their lifetime had been judged especially meritorious often were granted divine status posthumously. Indeed, Pliny had personal experience of this social practice and its reverse, *damnatio memoriae*, the condemnation of memory. As a student in Rome at the time of Vespasian's death in 79 CE, almost certainly he will have witnessed the elaborate rituals that accompanied the apotheosis of that emperor.[30] At some point after the death and deification of Vespasian's successor, the emperor Titus (81 CE), Pliny actually became one of his priests (*flamen*).[31] Finally, as a senior member of the Senate at the time of both Domitian's assassination in September 96 CE and the death of his successor Nerva only eighteen months later, almost certainly

---

28. At *Annals* 15.44.4, Tacitus speaks of 'Christianity' originating in Judaea and thus clearly implies that Christus was a Jew.

29. Harris, 'References to Jesus', 346–7. See also Theissen and Merz, *Historical Jesus*, 81: '[Pliny] seems to know that the one worshipped in the cult was a man; this is indicated by the formulation '*carmen...quasi deo dicere...*'., which suggests that Pliny sees Christ only as a quasi-god, precisely because he was a man'.

30. For a later description of these rituals, see Dio's eye-witness account at *Roman History* 75.4.2-5.5 of the apotheosis of the emperor Pertinax (193 CE).

31. *CIL* 5.5667 = *ILS* 6727. For this text, see Appendix 1, A, no. 2. For the likely location of this cult, see Ameling, 'Pliny: The Piety of a Persecutor', 281–3.

he will have been party to the decisions of that body, first, to obliterate the memory of the former[32] and subsequently (Jan. 98 CE) to elevate the latter to the gods.[33]

Nor, as Pliny would have known well, was divine status conferred only upon deserving rulers. Revered private individuals might be the object of cult too. From reading the work of his uncle and adoptive father, the Elder Pliny, he will have known, for example, of the divine status accorded the philosopher and teacher, Epicurus. Worshipped as a founder-hero (ἥρως κτίστης) in various parts of the Roman world, Epicurus was not only offered sacrifices on his birthday but was the object of regular cultic devotion, meetings for that purpose being held on the twentieth day of every month.[34]

But it is not just the divine status acquired by Christus that enables Pliny to present the Christians' 'founder-hero' as an altogether positive figure. The information he relays about the behaviour of his worshippers, all of it the testimony of one-time Christians, has that effect too. From these apostates Pliny had discovered (*Ep.* 10.96.7) that at their regular community meetings the Christians bound themselves by oath (*sacramento*) to refrain from crimes such as theft, robbery and adultery and from anti-social acts such as breaches of trust (*fides*). Since the clear implication of that solemn act was that the Christians' god likewise will have regarded those offences with abhorrence, Christus emerges as upholding values that Pliny himself, not to mention all upstanding Romans, held dear! Of all Roman values, *fides* (faith/trust) was probably the most important.[35]

Further contributing to the positive image of Christus is Pliny's description of the communal activities of the Christians in his province. Their main religious ritual, antiphonal hymn-singing in their god's honour, was a feature of Roman religious practice too and so entirely acceptable.[36] The best attested example of a Roman antiphonal hymn is

32. For a description of the almost unseemly glee of the senators on that occasion, see Suetonius, *Domitian* 23.1. On the smashing of Domitian's statues on that occasion, almost certainly witnessed by Pliny himself, see *Panegyricus* 52.4-5.

33. On the apotheosis of Nerva, see Pliny, *Panegyricus* 10.5–11.3.

34. Pliny the Elder, *Nat.* 35.5. On the cults of Epicurus, see Diskin Clay, *Paradosis and Survival: Three Chapters in the Epicurean Philosophy* (Ann Arbor: University of Michigan Press, 1998), 75–102.

35. At Rome, Fides was worshipped as the personification of good faith. See *OCD*[3], *s.v.* Fides.

36. See Cook, *Roman Attitudes*, 203–4 for some examples of Roman ritual singing.

the *Carmen Saeculare* (Centennial Hymn).[37] Written by the poet Horace for Augustus's great festival of national renewal, the Centennial Games, in 17 BCE, its verses were sung for the most part antiphonally, the semi-chorus of youths taking those addressed to Apollo and the semi-chorus of maidens those for his sister Diana.[38]

Likewise, the social activities of Christian groups in the province did not give any cause for alarm. In obedience to Trajan's ban on associations (*hetaeriae*[39]), they had given up holding their communal meals. Even when those meals had taken place, the food consumed at them had been entirely innocuous.[40] Christus, Pliny seems to be implying, did not require his worshippers to participate in any of the disgraceful practices (*flagitia*) commonly associated by outsiders with his cult.[41]

This portrayal of Christus and his followers in the central part of the letter, though pleasingly positive from a Christian perspective, is decidedly puzzling given that Pliny clearly was of the view that adherence to Christus smacked of insanity[42] and that the Christian superstition itself

37. For the text and a translation of this hymn, see James Michie, *The Odes of Horace* (Harmondsworth: Penguin, 1964), 267–73.

38. For the most likely division of the verses between the boys and the girls, see Tenney Frank, 'The Carmen Saeculare of Horace', *AJP* 42 (1921): 324–9.

39. The translation offered above for *hetaeriae* – namely, political societies – reflects the Romans' main fear of associations. Whatever their ostensible purpose, there was always a risk that they would be used for political ends – and those against Rome!

40. *Ep.* 10.96.7 (*promiscuum et innoxium*). On an unusual diet as prima facie evidence for involvement in superstition (*inter argumenta superstitionis*), see Seneca, *Moral Epistles* 108.22.

41. Generally it is assumed that Pliny is hinting here at cannibalism and incest. Later in the second century, well after Pliny's time, those allegations against Christians did indeed become common. See Bart Wagemakers, 'Incest, Infanticide, and Cannibalism: Anti-Christian Imputations in the Roman Empire', *G&R* 57 (2010): 337–54. It is questionable, however, whether they should be read back into texts of early second-century date. See Cook, *Roman Attitudes*, 47 and 213 on the dangers of over-interpreting the word *flagitia* both here and at Tacitus, *Annals* 15.44.2. The clear influence upon both these authors of Livy's 'Bacchanalian' narrative should also be taken into account. Livy does not mention either cannibalism or incest in that well known text but only general criminality and gross sexual indecency. See, for instance, Livy 39.13.10. That may be how early second century Roman readers, all of them familiar with that Livian text, understood *flagitia* in Pliny's Latin here. For further discussion, see below, 80–1.

42. See *Ep.* 10.96.4 for his comment on the *amentia* (madness) displayed by the Christians in preferring death to blaspheming Christ.

constituted a positive danger to the health of Roman society. How is this apparent contradiction to be explained? Only by fully appreciating Pliny's primary purpose in sending this communication to the emperor can this question be answered.

3.6. *The Primary Purpose of Pliny's Letter about the Christians*

Pliny's letter tends to be either described as a factual report[43] or seen as a typically abject request for advice from a notorious ditherer.[44] In fact, it is neither. Pliny, it is important to recall, was by profession an advocate who was renowned, both in his own day and by posterity, as an accomplished orator and a master of persuasion.[45] Those skills are to be observed not just in his *Panegyricus*, a speech still being used in Late Antiquity in the teaching of rhetoric,[46] and in the nine books of his carefully selected and edited personal letters,[47] but are very much on display in this carefully structured and highly rhetorical epistle,[48] the prime aim of which was to resolve a crisis largely of Pliny's own making.[49]

Roman provincial governors were not expected to search out Christians. Even when a formal charge had been laid against an individual of being a devotee of Christus a governor was not obliged to pursue the

43. See, for instance, Sherwin-White, *Letters of Pliny*, 692.

44. Stevenson/Frend, *New Eusebius*, 18 (citing Mackail); F. F. Bruce, *Jesus and Christian Origins Outside the New Testament* (London: Hodder & Stoughton, 1974), 24.

45. Woolf, 'Pliny's Province', 445.

46. On the reception of Pliny's *Panegyricus* in Late Antiquity, see now Rees, 'Afterwords of Praise', 175–88.

47. For a good, succinct discussion of their main rhetorical features, see *OCD³*, *s.v.* Pliny the Younger. On the enormous influence on Pliny of his former teacher of Latin rhetoric, the renowned Quintilian, see now Christopher Whitton, *The Arts of Imitation in Latin Prose: Pliny's Epistles/Quintilian in Brief* (Cambridge: Cambridge University Press, 2019).

48. On the formal, rhetorical structure of *Ep.* 10.96, see Cook, *Roman Attitudes*, 156–8. Woolf, 'Pliny's Province', 443 argues that the entire arrangement of Book 10 is 'shaped by rhetorical and panegyrical ends'.

49. On Pliny's actions against Christians in Pontus as a 'shoot-to-kill' policy gone wrong, see also James Corke-Webster, 'Trouble in Pontus: The Pliny-Trajan Correspondence on the Christians Reconsidered', *TAPA* 147, no. 2 (2017): 371–411. The case against Pliny presented here was developed independently. For an earlier version of it, see Margaret Williams, 'Pliny the Younger', in Keith et al., eds, *The Reception of Jesus*, 3:41–50.

case.[50] Pliny, however, had shown no restraint. By nature, conscientious to a fault, he had acted in this area, as he had previously in others, with an excess of zeal.[51] Not only had he applied the law rigorously against individuals against whom formal charges had been laid, summarily dispatching to their deaths provincials who had refused to deny that they were Christians,[52] but he had shown himself only too ready to search out individuals against whom mere allegations of association with the cult of Christus had been made either in or by dubious sources (i.e., in anonymous pamphlets and by informers).[53]

This zeal had not gone unnoticed by Pliny's notoriously factious subjects[54] who quickly perceived that they could exploit their governor's enthusiasm for hunting down Christians to settle old scores. As a result, accusations on the score of possessing Christian sympathies soon reached such a volume that Pliny found himself in danger of being overwhelmed. Particularly problematic for him were the many individuals now in custody who confessed that they had indeed once been Christians but

50. On the wide discretion that a provincial governor might exercise under the *cognitio extra ordinem* system, the judicial system under which trials of Christians were held, see G. E. M. de Ste Croix, 'Why Were the Early Christians Persecuted?', in Finley, ed., *Studies in Ancient Society*, 210–49 (218–21) and Ameling, 'Piety of a Persecutor', 295. In the case of Peregrinus (Chapter 7 below), we see a governor refusing to try him and so make a martyr of him (Lucian, *On the Death of Peregrinus* 14). For an earlier example of a governor refusing to take a case against the Christians, see Gallio at Acts 18:12-16.

51. For some earlier instances of Plinian over-conscientiousness, see *Ep.* 1.23; 9.13; 10.49 and 68.

52. Pliny's claim to know nothing of the law regarding Christians should be taken with a pinch of salt. So, correctly, Stevenson/Frend, *New Eusebius*, 19. Pliny's actions show that he was fully cognisant of the law, even if, as he insisted, he had never actually been present at the trials of Christians (*cognitionibus de Christianis*). Probably he had gained this knowledge at Rome. See Ameling, 'Piety of a Persecutor', 295. On the most likely reason for Pliny's plea of ignorance, see the previous chapter.

53. Pliny, *Ep.* 10.96.5-6. There is an interesting parallel here between Pliny and the consul, Postumius Albinus, in Livy's Bacchanalian narrative. He, too, had not scrupled to use informers to further his investigation, offering rewards for compromising information. See Livy, *Roman History* 39.17.1.

54. On the scourge of factional strife in the cities of Bithynia-Pontus, see David Magie, *Roman Rule in Asia Minor*, 2 vols (Princeton: Princeton University Press, 1950), 1:600–603. For the city of Prusa (modern Bursa) in particular, see C. P. Jones, *The Roman World of Dio Chrysostom* (Cambridge, MA: Harvard University Press, 1978), 100–103.

claimed that they no longer were so and, moreover, had provided proof of their apostasy.[55] Although Pliny's enquiries had established through the torture of two deaconesses (*ministrae*) of servile status (*ancillae*) that they were probably harmless, could he take the risk of pardoning them and letting them go free, a course of action that was certainly open to him?

Pliny had always shown himself to be risk-averse. That was why his career had so prospered under the tyrant, Domitian.[56] Unsurprisingly, therefore, we find him here acting true to form. Rather than incur any risk himself, he decided to let the responsibility lie with Trajan. Hence his lengthy letter of persuasion to the emperor, the goal of which was, as its clever construction makes clear, to secure authorization for what he wanted, but was afraid, to do – grant pardon for repentance.[57] Such an end, however, was unlikely to be attained unless the emperor could be convinced that these former devotees of Christus posed no threat to Roman society. Hence Pliny's emphasis in the central part of his discourse (the *argumentatio* or laying out of the case) on their harmlessness, loyalty to Rome and essential respectability. Hence, too, his favourable portrayal of the former object of their devotion, the god Christus.

That Trajan chose to be convinced is clear from his reply to Pliny (*Ep.* 10.97). Although he insisted that possession of the *nomen Christianum* should remain a capital offence, he agreed that pardon should be extended to those who repented of having once been Christ-worshippers, providing that they proved their renunciation of the latter's cult by an act of supplication towards the gods of Rome.

Given Pliny's position at the very heart of the Roman establishment, his determination to remain there and his utterly conventional views on everything, it would be only reasonable to expect that any portrayal by him of Christus and his followers would be thoroughly negative. That expectation, however, is not fulfilled. Although Pliny cannot shake off

55. On the custody of these prisoners being Pliny's main concern, see T. D. Barnes, 'Legislation against the Christians', *JRS* 58 (1968): 32–50 (36 n. 49) and (at greater length) *JRS* 61 (1971): 311–12 (review of the second, revised edition of R. Freudenberger, *Das Verhalten der römischen Behörden gegen die Christen im 2. Jahrhundert* [Munich: C. H. Beck'sche, 1969]).

56. See previous chapter.

57. That this was Pliny's principal aim was spotted long ago by E. G. Hardy. See his *Studies in Roman History* (London: Swan Sonnenschein, 1910), 85–6. The importance of the idea of pardon for repentance is shown, first, by Pliny's introduction of this idea in the opening section of his letter and, secondly, its reappearance at the climax of the *peroratio* (peroration) or summing up. The last words a reader would see/hear would be *paenitentiae locus* (an opportunity to repent).

entirely the prejudices of his class against this *superstitio externa* ('alien superstition'), we find that he does manage, though compelled to do so purely by a crisis largely of his own creation, to produce a picture that is substantially positive. By focusing in the central part of his communication to the emperor on what the devotees of Christus actually do (as opposed to what they refrain from doing, that is, acknowledging the gods of Rome and the emperor's divinity), he succeeds in depicting Christ-worship as a kind of hero cult to which few Romans can have found objection, and Christus as a god who, far from encouraging the performance of disgraceful, even criminal acts (*flagitia*), manifestly esteems moral values, such as *fides*, that are wholly Roman!

That Trajan likewise found it expedient to take a lenient view of the Christians is clear from his instructions to Pliny about how he was to deal with them in future: only if formal charges were laid against them was action to be taken; otherwise *conquirendi non sunt* – 'they are not to be sought out'. Trajan's reasons for taking this relatively relaxed view[58] about the followers of Christ are not hard to discern. His reign had seen nothing but an unbroken series of successes. A smooth accession to power after Nerva's death had been followed by a series of triumphs abroad, the most conspicuous of which was his recent, highly lucrative conquest of Dacia. Clearly the gods were not taking offence at the presence among his subjects of small groups of individuals who utterly repudiated their worship.

58. His letter makes it absolutely clear, however, that 'Christianity' still remained illegal. What is more, his reign is alleged (e.g., by Eusebius at *Hist. eccl.* 3.32) to have contained a number of martyrdoms. On the possible evidence for Trajan as a persecutor, see Julian Bennett, *Trajan: Optimus Princeps* (London: Routledge, 1997), 256 n. 37.

Chapter 4

TACITUS'S TESTIMONY FOR 'JESUS':
AUTHENTIC OR INTERPOLATED?

4.1. *Introduction*

The next classical reference to 'Jesus' (*Annals* 15.44.3) is to be found in
the last work to be undertaken by Pliny's close friend and slightly senior
senatorial colleague, the distinguished advocate, orator and historian,
Cornelius Tacitus.[1] Although a leading light of Roman society in his
own day, comparatively little is known about him now.[2] However, by
exploiting the little evidence that has survived,[3] it is possible to construct
at least a skeleton of his career. Unsurprisingly, this turns out to be very
similar to that of Pliny, for both were solid establishment figures from
almost identical social backgrounds. The first in their respective families
to attain the consulship,[4] these 'new men' (*novi homines*) made it their
business to ingratiate themselves with the emperor of the day, no matter
who the latter happened to be or how he behaved.

Politically, their careers were, in essentials at least, almost identical.
Like Pliny, Tacitus attained the consulship around the age of forty.[5] Like

1. On the relationship between the two, see Miriam T. Griffin, 'Pliny and Tacitus',
in Gibson and Whitton, eds, *Epistles of Pliny*, 355–77.

2. For a detailed but inevitably rather speculative discussion of the evidence
for his life and career, see A. R. Birley, 'The Life and Death of Cornelius Tacitus',
Zeitschrift für Altegeschichte 49, no. 2 (2000): 230–47.

3. For the most important pieces, see Appendix 1, B.

4. It is generally assumed that the early imperial equestrian procurator of Gaul
called Cornelius Tacitus, a man known personally to Pliny the Elder (*Nat.* 7.76), was
the father of the identically named senatorial historian. For discussion, see Birley,
'Life and Death', 233.

5. For Tacitus's consulship in 97 CE, see Pliny, *Ep.* 2.1.6 and Christopher Whitton,
ed., *Pliny the Younger: Epistles Book II* (Cambridge: Cambridge University Press,
2013), *comm. ad loc.*

Pliny, he enjoyed the distinction of membership of one of Rome's ancient priestly colleges – in his case, the Quindecimvirate, the fifteen-strong body of elite male Romans whose responsibilities included the oversight of foreign cults, the interpretation of prodigies and the consultation of the Sibylline Oracles at times of national emergency.[6] And his last known public appointment, like that of Pliny, was to a provincial governorship – in Tacitus's case that of Asia, the province 'next door' to Bithynia-Pontus.[7] Whether his tenure of that province coincided with Pliny's governorship of Bithynia-Pontus cannot be firmly established but it remains a possibility.[8] What admits of no doubt, however, is that Tacitus, like Pliny, would have included many Christians among his provincial subjects. By the first quarter of the second century CE, Asia was the home of many flourishing Christian communities (Rev. 1.4).

In literary terms too Tacitus's career was very similar to Pliny's. Having refrained from 'going into print' for as long as Domitian was in power, Tacitus determinedly made up for lost time once the latter had been overthrown. Just as Pliny celebrated the restoration of freedom under Nerva and Trajan by commencing on the 'publication' of his epistolary autobiography,[9] so within a year or so of Domitian's assassination we find Tacitus putting into the public domain, first, a biography of his late father-in-law, the 'conqueror' of the Caledonians, Gnaeus Julius Agricola,[10] and then (98 CE) an ethnographic work on the German

---

6. The unusually young age at which Tacitus received this honour from Domitian (he was only in his early thirties) illustrates the high favour that he must have enjoyed with that emperor. Born *ca.* 56/57 CE, he was already a Quindecimvir by 88 CE. See *Annals* 11.1.1. Most appointees to this priestly college were of consular status and, therefore, in their forties at the very least and often considerably older. See Birley, 'Life and Death', 234.

7. See *OGIS* 487, an honorific inscription from Mylasa, modern Milas in southwestern Turkey. For the Greek text of this inscription, see E. Mary Smallwood, *Documents Illustrating the Principates of Nerva, Trajan and Hadrian* (Cambridge: Cambridge University Press, 1966), no. 203. For a translation, Appendix 1, B, no. 2.

8. Dates suggested for Pliny's governorship are 109–11, 110–12 and 111–13 CE. See Birley, 'Pliny's Family, Pliny's Career', 65–6. Tacitus's proconsulship has to be dated to either 112–13 or 113–14 CE. See Syme, *Tacitus*, 2:664–5 (= Appendix 23).

9. Gibson and Morello, *Reading the Letters*, 26 – 'The clock of this book [*sc.* Book 1] starts ticking precisely at the moment of Domitian's death'. On the general problem of dating the letters, see Gibson and Morello, *Reading the Letters*, 19–20.

10. For early 98 CE as the 'publication' date of the *De vita Agricolae*, see A. J. Woodman, 'Tacitus and the Contemporary Scene', in *The Cambridge Companion to Tacitus*, ed. A. J. Woodman (Cambridge: Cambridge University Press, 2009), 31. The writing, however, was well underway in 97 CE. See Tacitus, *Agricola* 3.1.

tribes.[11] Switching subsequently to the most prestigious form of prose-composition of all, the genre of historiography, he went on to produce over the next twenty years or so the two great narrative histories upon which his posthumous reputation largely rests. These are the works now known by the titles given them by Renaissance scholars in the sixteenth century – the *Histories* and the *Annals*.[12] Between them, these works cover (or at least were planned to cover[13]) the history of Rome under its first two imperial dynasties, the Julio-Claudian and the Flavian. The earlier of these works, the *Histories*, written in the course of the first decade of the second century,[14] deals with the reigns of the three Flavian emperors and the civil wars that brought their family to power (68–96 CE). The later work, Tacitus's masterpiece, the *Annals*, goes back in time and focuses on the four Julio-Claudians who ruled from 14 CE (death of Augustus) down to 68 CE, the year when Nero, the last member of that dynasty, was overthrown. The composition of this work, although begun under Trajan, almost certainly continued into the early years of Hadrian's reign (117–138 CE). Around 120 CE seems a reasonable composition-date.[15] However, 'nothing forbids the assumption' that some of the work might have been written as late as 123 CE.[16] It is in the last book of this work to survive complete, *Annals* 15, that we find the sole surviving comments about Jesus (or rather Christus) in the entire Tacitean corpus.

11. For the 'publication' date of the *Germania*, see R. M. Ogilvie and Ian Richmond, eds, *Cornelii Taciti De Vita Agricolae* (Oxford: Clarendon, 1967), 10–11.

12. See *OCD³*, *s.v.* Tacitus (1) and, in more detail, A. J. Woodman (trans.), *Tacitus: The Annals* (Indianapolis: Hackett, 2004), xix.

13. Death may have prevented the completion of the *Annals*. The work as we have it goes only as far as 66 CE, at which point it breaks off in mid-sentence. Whether Tacitus actually finished it is unknown. The seemingly unrevised state of the last books to survive complete, Books 13-15, in addition to the fragmentary state of the final book (Book 16), have suggested that Tacitus, already a fair age (about fifty) when he embarked upon this work, may have died before finishing it. See Syme, *Tacitus*, 2:742–5 and 748.

14. For Tacitus's progress on this work during the first decade of the second century CE, see Pliny *Ep.* 6.16.1-3 and 7.33.1-3.

15. As suggested by, *inter alios*, John M. G. Barclay, 'Jews and Christians in the Eyes of Roman Authors c. 100 CE', in *Jews and Christians in the First and Second Centuries: How to Write Their History*, ed. P. J. Tomson and J. Schwartz (Leiden: Brill, 2014), 313–26 (318).

16. Syme, *Tacitus*, 2:473. The case, first made by Syme (*Tacitus*, 2:473 and 768–70) for a Hadrianic date for the later books of the *Annals* at least, is now widely accepted, at least by classicists. See, for instance, Ronald Martin at *OCD³*, *s.v.* Tacitus (1); Birley, 'Life and Death', 241–2; Herbert W. Benario, 'The Annals', in *A*

Seemingly intended merely to explain the term, 'Christian', Tacitus's only explicit reference to Christus (*Annals* 15.44.3) does no more than present some rather basic material about him – namely, that he had suffered the supreme penalty through the agency of a Roman official named Pontius Pilatus when Tiberius was emperor (*Tiberio imperitante per procuratorem Pontium Pilatum supplicio affectus erat*). If this treatment of the author (*auctor*) of the so-called Christian superstition (*superstitio*) seems disappointingly brief, it must be borne in mind that Tacitus's principal concern at this point in his narrative was not Jesus, a provincial nobody, but the last ruler of the Julio-Claudian dynasty, the increasingly despotic Nero. Focused on tracing the latter's seemingly unstoppable deterioration from model princeps to widely loathed tyrant, Tacitus identifies as the key factor in this decline Nero's spectacular mishandling of the crisis produced by the 'Great Fire of Rome' in 64 CE, the devastating conflagration that reduced the greater part of the imperial capital to ashes. In the view of Tacitus, it was the sadistic treatment of the local *Chrestiani* [*sic*], scapegoated by Nero for that catastrophe, which accelerated his unpopularity, not least with the common people of Rome, and so hastened both his own fall from power and thus the end of Julio-Claudian rule: 'pity for them (*sc.*, the *Chrestiani*) began to well up because it was felt that they were being exterminated not for the public good, but to gratify one man's cruelty'.[17]

Brief as the 'Jesus' sentence is,[18] it is important for its factual content. Pliny, as we saw in the previous chapter, supplies no personal information at all about Christus. He had done no more than imply that, although worshipped as a god, he had once been a human being. From the succinct

---

Companion to Tacitus, ed. Victoria Emma Pagán (Malden: Wiley-Blackwell, 2012), 101–22 (105); David S. Potter, 'Tacitus's Sources', in Pagán, ed., *Companion*, 125–40 (126). The Trajanic date (115 or 116 CE) given in virtually all Historical Jesus handbooks (e.g., Van Voorst, *Jesus*, 39; Eddy and Boyd, *Jesus Legend*, 179) is implausibly early – there would not have been time for a work thought to have been started by Tacitus only after he had returned from his governorship of the province of Asia (*ca.* 112/113 CE) to have been researched and written in such a short length of time.

17. *Annals* 15.44.5. For this translation, see J. C. Yardley (trans.), *Tacitus: The Annals* (Oxford: Oxford University Press, 2008), 360. On the structural significance of this episode in Tacitus's overall treatment of Nero's reign, see now van der Lans and Bremmer, 'Tacitus and the Persecution of the Christians', 304–9 = section 2.

18. Strictly, in the Latin it forms an epexegetical clause. Wellesley, uniquely among the editors of this text, neatly illustrates this by opting to enclose it in parentheses. See Kenneth Wellesley, *Cornelius Tacitus 1.2, Annales XI–XVI* (Leipzig: Teubner, 1986), 115. His aim was simply to facilitate comprehension. There is no suggestion on Wellesley's part that the bracketed material is an interpolation.

description of Christus in this *Annals* passage, however, quite a lot can be learned. In the first place, we are told that the latter had lived relatively recently: as a subject of the emperor Tiberius (*Tiberio imperitante*), he fell easily within the time-frame of the *Annals* itself (14–68 CE); secondly, we are informed that this petty provincial, Christus, had somehow got on the wrong side of the Roman authorities and consequently had been put to death by them (*supplicio affectus erat*) and, thirdly, we learn that the official who had sentenced him was none other than Pontius Pilatus, Tiberius's 'man' in Judaea.[19] Since Pilate's tenure of that office can be dated with unusual precision thanks to information supplied by Josephus,[20] Jesus can, for the first time in classical literature, be placed in a precise historical context.[21]

Clearly this material has to be taken very seriously. What we appear to have here is the first unambiguous, independent (i.e., non-Christian) evidence for the existence of Jesus. Although the testimony concerning Jesus of the Jewish historian, Flavius Josephus, was written some twenty or so years earlier, it has suffered so badly through subsequent Christian 'editing' that Josephus's original words (assuming that there is a genuine Josephan core to this evidence) can no longer be identified with confidence.[22] Hardly a surprise, then, that this passage of Tacitus has received so much attention over the years. While scholars keen to establish the historicity of Jesus regard this as the most important piece of independent evidence for Christ to have survived and so treat it with immense respect,[23] those with a diametrically opposed viewpoint not only challenge its reliability but dispute its very authenticity.

---

19. For the best modern study of the various ancient sources for Pilate, see Helen K. Bond, *Pontius Pilate in History and Interpretation* (Cambridge: Cambridge University Press, 1986). For a brief overview of the prefects and procurators who governed Judaea between 6 and 66 CE, Margaret H. Williams, 'Prefects and Procurators', in *Encyclopedia of the Dead Sea Scrolls*, 2 vols, ed. Lawrence H. Schiffman and James C. VanderKam (Oxford: Oxford University Press, 2000), 2:686–7.

20. His governorship ran from 26–36 CE (Josephus, *Ant.* 18.89).

21. For *ca.* 30 CE as the generally accepted date of Jesus' death, see Chapter 1 n. 19 above.

22. For van Henten's recent discussion of the whole controversy surrounding Josephus's main evidence for Jesus, the so-called *Testimonium Flavianum* (= *Ant.* 18.63-64), see Keith et al., eds, *The Reception of Jesus*, 1:365–9.

23. In addition to the discussions of Evans and Eddy and Boyd on this point (Chapter 1 nn. 76 and 77), see Harris, 'References to Jesus', 352 ('of special importance') and Van Voorst, *Jesus*, 52 ('strongest evidence outside the New Testament for the death of Jesus').

Among the latter, the most prominent, unsurprisingly, are the mythicists. To individuals convinced that Jesus never existed as a creature of flesh and blood, the matter-of-fact character of this material, with its firm anchoring in time and place, presents an existential challenge. Hence their vigorous efforts to discredit it either by casting doubt on Tacitus's competence as an historian[24] or by arguing that some or all of this section of Tacitus's work has suffered at the hands of Christian interpolators.[25]

By no means all of the critics of Tacitus's text, however, are mythicists. Classicists and ancient historians have expressed doubts too. While some are convinced that Tacitus has wrongly identified Nero's victims as Christians and so believe that the passage has nothing to do with Jesus,[26] others are not persuaded that the events narrated in *Annals* 15.44 ever took place. Rougé, for instance, argued on the basis of a parallelism (perceived by him) between Nero's burning of Rome and Galerius's torching of Nicomedia in 303 CE that the whole of *Annals* 15.44 was an interpolation.[27] More recently Shaw has attempted to revive the idea that the Neronian persecution of Christians is simply a myth.[28] And another sceptic about the authenticity of *Annals* 15.44 in general, and the Christus sentence in particular, is the Roman imperial historian, Anthony Barrett. The fact

24. This features as a constant element in the substantial output of Wells on the subject of the ahistoricity of Jesus. See, for instance, *Did Jesus Exist?*, 13–14 and *Historical Evidence for Jesus*, 16–17.

25. For the most recent example of this line of attack, see Carrier, 'The Prospect of Christian Interpolation in Tacitus'. For earlier advocates of interpolation, see Van Voorst, *Jesus*, 42–3 n. 60.

26. E. Koestermann, 'Ein folgenschwerer Irrtum des Tacitus?', *Historia* 16 (1967): 456–69. Convinced that the *Chrestiani* of *Annals* 15.44.2 were latter-day supporters of a Jewish rabble-rouser named Chrestus active in Claudian Rome (Suetonius, *Div. Claud.* 25.4), Koestermann argued that Tacitus had committed a terrible blunder in identifying them as Christians. Although never enjoying much scholarly support, this hypothesis recently has found a new champion in Carrier. See his 'Prospect of Christian Interpolation', 283. Among the scholars dismissive of Koestermann, however, see Peter Lampe, *From Paul to Valentinus: Christians at Rome in the First Two Centuries*, trans. Michael Steinhauser (London: T&T Clark International, 2003), 13 n. 4 and H. Dixon Slingerland, *Claudian Policymaking and the Early Imperial Repression of Judaism at Rome* (Atlanta: Scholars Press, 1997), 204 n. 5.

27. Jean Rougé, 'L'incendie de Rome en 64 et l'incendie de Nicomédie en 303', in *Mélanges d'histoire anciennes offerts à William Seston* (Paris: Boccard, 1974), 433–41.

28. B. D. Shaw, 'The Myth of the Neronian Persecution', *JRS* 105 (2015): 73–100 (74 – 'this event never happened'). For a sympathetic response to Shaw, see Corke-Webster, 'Trouble in Pontus', 383 n. 50. For powerful rebuttals of Shaw's thesis,

that sections 2 to 5 of that chapter can be excised without any noticeable interruption to the narrative flow suggests to him that we might perhaps be dealing with a post-Tacitean, Christian interpolation here.[29] Indeed, it cannot be denied that if, by way of experiment, the paragraph relating to the persecution of the Christians is momentarily set aside, the reader does pass smoothly from a description of Nero's costly efforts at rebuilding Rome and appeasing the gods to a discussion of the economic impact of those measures on the people of Italy.[30]

Given the fact, then, that challenges to Tacitus's testimony are not a matter of history but continue to be made up to the present day, clearly we need to establish first and foremost that he really is the author of the material now found in *Annals* 15.44. Otherwise there will be no point in our proceeding. To aid the discussion, I shall begin by setting out the Latin text of the relevant parts of that chapter. I then offer a translation, largely my own, of this text.[31] I have chosen to make this translation very literal. Although other versions are available that sound better to the modern ear,[32] these sometimes fail to register adequately those nuances of the Latin that are crucial to the discussion here.

4.2. *The Disputed Evidence: Text and Translation*

At *Annals* 15.44.2-5, Tacitus writes as follows:

> (2) Sed non ope humana, non largitionibus principis aut deum placamentis decedebat infamia, quin iussum incendium crederetur. Ergo abolendo rumori Nero subdidit reos et quaesitissimis poenis adfecit, quos per flagitia invisos vulgus Chrestianos appellabat. (3) Auctor nominis eius Christus Tiberio imperitante per procuratorem Pontium Pilatum supplicio affectus erat; repressaque in praesens exitiabilis superstitio rursum errumpebat, non modo per Iudaeam, originem eius mali, sed per urbem etiam, quo cuncta undique atrocia aut pudenda confluunt celebranturque. (4) igitur primum

however, see C. P. Jones, 'The Historicity of the Neronian Persecution: A Response to Brent Shaw', *NTS* 63 (2017): 146–52 and Van der Lans and Bremmer, 'Tacitus and the Persecution of the Christians' (Chapter 1 n. 36).

29. See Anthony A. Barrett, 'The Great Fire', in *The Emperor Nero: A Guide to the Ancient Sources*, ed. Anthony A. Barrett, Elaine Fantham and John C. Yardley (Princeton: Princeton University Press, 2016), 149–70 (164–5).

30. See Tacitus, *Annals* 15.42-45 (omitting most of 44).

31. Where use has been made of the translations of others, this is acknowledged in the footnotes.

32. Most notably, that of Michael Grant. See his *Tacitus: The Annals of Imperial Rome* (Harmondsworth: Penguin, 1956), 354.

correpti qui fatebantur, deinde indicio eorum multitudo ingens haud proinde in crimine incendii quam odio humani generis convicti sunt. et pereuntibus addita ludibria, ut ferarum tergis contecti laniatu canum interirent aut crucibus adfixi [aut flammandi atque],[33] ubi defecisset dies, in usu<m> nocturni luminis ururerentur. (5) hortos suos ei spectaculo Nero obtulerat et circense ludicrum edebat, habitu aurigae permixtus plebi vel curriculo insistens. unde quamquam adversus sontes et novissima exempla meritos miseratio oriebatur, tamquam non utilitate publica, sed in saevitiam unius absumerentur.[34]

(2) Despite human help, the generosity of the princeps and the measures taken to propitiate the gods,[35] the infamous report that the fire had been ordered continued to be believed. Therefore to quash the rumour Nero conjured up defendants[36] and he inflicted the most rarefied forms of punishment[37] upon those individuals, loathed for their abominable practices,[38] whom the common people (of Rome) dubbed *Chrestiani*.[39]

---

33. The text here is so corrupt that there is no consensus as to how it should be restored and read. Fortunately this problem has no bearing on our discussion and so can be ignored here.

34. For this version of Tacitus's text, see H. Heubner, ed., *P. Cornelii Taciti libri qui supersunt, I: Ab excessu divi Augusti* (Stuttgart: Teubner, 1994).

35. Both have been described in some detail in the preceding narrative. See *Annals* 15.39.2 for Nero's relief measures and 15.44.1 for the rituals prescribed by the Sibylline Books.

36. For this translation of the phrase *subdidit reos*, see Ash, *Annals XV*, 205, since it captures particularly well Tacitus's deliberate insinuation that Nero's action was fraudulent and the *Chrestiani* were, in consequence, the victims of a judicial stitch-up. For other examples in the *Annals* of this fairly common usage of the verb *subdere* (= to introduce fraudulently), see *OLD*, *s.v. subdo* 6a. For useful comments on this particular instance, see Jones, 'Historicity of the Neronian Persecution', 148.

37. The punishments tantalizingly alluded to here are treated in some detail later in the passage (*Annals* 15.44.4). For discussion, see nn. 44 and 45 below.

38. For the likely meaning of *flagitia* ('abominable practices') in this context, see above Chapter 3 n. 41 and below 80–1.

39. This is the original reading in the Second Medicean, our earliest (eleventh century CE) and most reliable manuscript. Although a marginal gloss 'corrects' it to *Christiani*, modern editors of Tacitus's *Annals* are virtually unanimous in preferring the original (and more difficult) reading. See E. Koestermann, *Cornelius Tacitus Annalen, Band 4. Buch 14-16* (Heidelberg: Winter, 1968); P. Wuilleumier, *Tacite – Annales Livres XIII–XVI* (Paris: Société d'édition 'Les Belles Lettres', 1978), and the editions of Wellesley and Heubner (see above nn. 18 and 34). For discussion, see Van Voorst, *Jesus*, 43–4. For an illustration of the manuscript page in question, see Harald Fuchs, 'Tacitus über die Christen', *VC* 4, no. 2 (1950): 65–93. Ash's substitution of

(3) Upon Christus, the author of that name, the death penalty had been inflicted during Tiberius's reign through the agency of the procurator Pontius Pilatus. Repressed for the time being, the deadly superstition[40] was breaking out again, not only throughout Judaea, the original source of that evil, but throughout the city (of Rome) too, where everything that is appalling and shameful everywhere else gathers and gains popularity.[41] (4) And so, first of all, those who confessed were arrested;[42] then, on their information, a vast number[43] was convicted, not so much on the charge of

Heubner's *Chrestiani* with *Christiani*, without offering any explanation, is inexcusable, given the controversy surrounding the reading of this word and her promise in her introduction (*Annals XV*, 28) to explain any significant deviations from Heubner's text that she has made.

40. On the harshness of Tacitus's language in respect of the Christian superstition, compared with that of Pliny at *Ep.* 10.96.8, and the disease connotations of the epithet *exitiabilis* (deadly), see Henry Furneaux, ed., *The Annals of Tacitus, Vol. II. Books XI-XVI*, rev. H. F. Pelham and C. D. Fisher (Oxford: Clarendon, 1907), note *ad loc.* On Tacitus's liking for metaphors drawn from disease and medicine, see A. J. Woodman, ed., *Tacitus. Agricola* (Cambridge: Cambridge University Press, 2014), 35. For Tacitus's use of the metaphor of contagion in respect of both the Christian superstition and its Jewish 'parent', see Peter Schäfer, *Judeophobia: Attitudes toward the Jews in the Ancient World* (Cambridge, MA: Harvard University Press, 1997), 190–1.

41. The translation offered here attempts to replicate Tacitus's use of alliteration in the closing phrase *confluunt celebranturque*. Meier, *A Marginal Jew*, 1:90, strives for the same effect with his 'converge...fervently cultivates'. Ideally the translation should reflect more accurately the idea of the flowing together of rivers. For Juvenal's comparable (but far cruder) riverine image of eastern immigration into Rome, see *Satire* 3.63: *iam pridem Syrus in Tiberim defluxit Orontes.* Peter Green (trans.), *Juvenal: The Sixteen Satires* (Harmondsworth: Penguin, 1967), 89 renders the line thus: 'For years now Syrian Orontes has poured its sewerage [*sic*] into our native Tiber'.

42. Whether they confessed to arson or to being Christians is hotly disputed. Most scholars believe that it was to the latter but the logic of the situation, as Heemstra cogently argues (*Fiscus Judaicus*, 88 n. 11), points to the former: 'If Nero wanted to put the blame for the fire on the Christians, he must have executed his victims on the basis of their being guilty of arson. This implies that some of them pleaded guilty to this crime'. Since Christians at that point in time still believed in the imminence of the Second Coming, an event to be preceded by a huge conflagration, some of them could indeed have convinced themselves that the End Time had now started and, in consequence, have been keen to help the fire along and to gain some credit (with God) for having advanced the Eschaton. For some exponents of this view, see Cook, *Roman Attitudes*, 46 n. 75.

43. The phrase *ingens multitudo*, is probably a deliberate allusion to Livy, *History of Rome* 39.13.14, where those accused of involvement in the Bacchanalian

arson as for their hatred of the human race. And as they died, mockeries were added,[44] so that, covered by the hides of wild animals, they perished by being ripped apart by dogs[45], or, fixed to crosses [and made flammable], when the daylight had gone, they were burned to provide nocturnal light. (5) Nero had made his gardens available for the spectacle and he put on a show (there) in his private racing arena.[46] Dressed like a charioteer, he (either) mingled (on foot) with the common people or stood up in his racing chariot. Whence, although (action was being taken) against guilty individuals deserving the ultimate in punishment, pity arose because it was felt that they were being annihilated not for the public good but to satisfy the savagery of one man.

4.3. *Tacitus's Handling of this Evidence Unprofessional?*

So much, then, for the evidence. How far is it to be trusted? Among mythicists unwilling to go as far as claiming that the 'Jesus' material in *Annals* 15.44 is inauthentic, a favourite tactic for attacking its credibility is to question Tacitus's professional competence. Targeting the weakest part of his testimony – namely, his apparent error in respect of Pilate's

'conspiracy' are likewise described as constituting a 'huge multitude' (*multitudinem ingentem*). On the rhetorical exaggeration likely in both these texts, see, for Livy, Gibbon, *Decline and Fall*, 2:61; for Tacitus, Furneaux, *Annals, comm. ad loc.* and Larry W. Hurtado, *Lord Jesus Christ: Devotion to Jesus in Earliest Christianity* (Grand Rapids: Eerdmans, 2003), 619 n. 171 – 'But given that the church of Nero's day could not have had "vast numbers" of adherents, this is either a rhetorical exaggeration or many others beyond the Christians were included'.

44. I.e., their deaths were made a subject for derision. What follows is an amplification of the phrase, 'the most rarefied forms of punishment' (*quaesistissimae poenae*), occurring earlier in the passage. These are now thought to have been 'executions staged as mythological enactments', a form of popular entertainment certainly promoted, and quite possibly pioneered, by Nero. On these grotesque punishments, see K. M. Coleman, 'Fatal Charades: Roman Executions Staged as Mythological Enactments', *JRS* 80 (1990): 44–73, especially 64 and 70; Edward Champlin, *Nero* (Cambridge: Belknap, 2003), 121–6 and Tassilo Schmitt, 'Des Kaisers Inszenierung: Mythologie und neronische Christenverfolgung', *ZAC* 16 (2013): 487–515.

45. That this was a re-enactment of the myth of Actaeon is argued by both Champlin (*Nero*, 123) and Schmitt ('Des Kaisers Inszenierung', 505–7). For his impiety in gazing upon the goddess Diana while she bathed, Actaeon had been transformed into a stag and then torn to pieces by hunting dogs.

46. For this private race-track, constructed by the emperor Gaius (Caligula) in the imperial gardens on the Vatican Hill, see Pliny, *Nat.* 36.74. For its previous use by Nero for chariot-racing, see *Annals* 14.14.2.

official title,[47] they conclude, first, that Tacitus clearly has made a mistake and, secondly, that the mistake itself, just one of the several deficiencies perceived by them in his handling of the evidence, is so serious that the totality of his testimony in regard to Christ is fatally compromised.[48]

What are we to make of this particular objection? Rightly have most scholars questioned whether it is justifiable to dismiss Tacitus's testimony so comprehensively on the basis of so slight an error, if indeed it is an error at all. Harris, for one, has suggested that, rather than see Tacitus's use of the term procurator as a mistake, we should view it as a reflection of 'a certain fluidity of terminology regarding the titles of the governor of Judaea, *at least in popular usage*, during the period A. D. 6–66'.[49] Others believe that Tacitus was being intentionally anachronistic, using 'for the sake of clarity' a title with which his audience would be more familiar.[50] Whether or not these explanations pass muster is a matter to be considered in the next chapter. Here it will be sufficient to note that they clearly demonstrate that an elementary error on Tacitus's part cannot simply be assumed.

But it is not just for (allegedly) getting a single term wrong that Tacitus is criticized as an unreliable authority. He also stands accused by his most severe critics of engaging in poor working practices – namely, not consulting the archives, failing to provide any documentation for the information he supplies about 'Jesus' and, worst of all, apparently being content to make use of oral testimony. Had he conducted himself in a more professional manner, so the case against him goes, he would have discovered that the actual name of the author of 'Christianity' was Jesus. By calling him Christus, which is not a name at all but a title meaning messiah, Tacitus reveals not only his ignorance and lack of scholarly rigour but even the dubious source of his information. That can only have

47. Whereas Tacitus refers to Pilate as a procurator, a public inscription from Caesarea Maritima, the administrative capital of early Roman Judaea, reveals that his official title actually was *praefectus Iudaeae* (prefect of Judaea). For this badly damaged Latin text referring to the restoration of a structure bearing the unique name, Tiberieum, see now *CIIP* II no. 1277.

48. See, for instance, Wells, *Did Jesus Exist?*, 14 and R. T. France, *The Evidence for Jesus* (London: Hodder & Stoughton, 1986), 22–3. Barrett ('Great Fire', 165) also takes a dim view of this 'serious and elementary historical anachronism' on Tacitus's part.

49. See his 'References to Jesus', 350 (my italics). This popular explanation has been followed by, *inter alios*, Meier, *A Marginal Jew*, 1:100 n. 8 and Evans, 'Jesus in Non-Christian Sources', 466.

50. See, for instance, Eddy and Boyd, *Jesus Legend*, 181.

been hearsay and – what is infinitely worse – hearsay of Christian origin! Consultation of the trial records would have revealed Jesus's correct name.[51]

Plausible as the objections may appear to a modern reader lacking training in the classics, they actually have no validity, since they rest on a complete misunderstanding of the nature of ancient (i.e., Graeco-Roman) historiography.

Take archival research which these critics clearly believe is essential for the production of intellectually respectable history. Such an activity was not regarded in the ancient world as a prerequisite for the production of serious historiography.[52] Most writers of history did no more (and were expected to do no more) than read and re-vamp the works of their predecessors. The testimony of Pliny the Younger is crucial here: encouraged by his friends to turn his hand to the writing of history, he not only declines to do so but he sets out the reasons for his decision (*Ep.* 5.8.). For him, historiography amounted to no more than collating the versions of other writers prior to producing a more compelling – i.e., a rhetorically more accomplished version.[53] Since this operation (i.e., collation) could not be anything but burdensome (*onerosa*), Pliny concluded that his time would be spent more profitably revising for publication the various speeches he had delivered.[54]

The fact that Pliny himself viewed historiography as no more than making a fresh compilation out of pre-existing works does not mean, however, that ancient historians in general never did any original research and never made use of archival material. Tacitus, for one, did just that. His exploitation of such material, however, appears to have been rather uneven[55] and the range of documentary sources that he thought worth taking into consideration was extremely narrow. In Tacitus's opinion, the

---

51. Wells, *Did Jesus Exist?*, 14 and *Historical Evidence for Jesus*, 16–17.

52. A. D. Momigliano, *Studies in Historiography* (London: Weidenfeld & Nicolson, 1966), 211–20.

53. For the highly rhetorical character of ancient historiography, see below n. 68 and 77–8.

54. This view of historiography as a time-consuming, tedious exercise is not confined to Pliny. His great idol, Marcus Tullius Cicero, had once justified his refusal to write a history of his own times in very similar terms (*Laws* 1.5-8). On the relationship between Pliny, *Ep.* 5.8 and Cicero, *Laws* 1.5-8, see now Gibson and Morello, *Reading the Letters*, 115–16.

55. Syme detects a far heavier use of archival material in the earlier (Tiberian) books of the *Annals* than in the later (Neronian) ones. See his *Tacitus*, 1:281–2 and 296.

contents of the *Acta Diurna* (Daily Record), the nearest thing that the Romans had to a popular daily gazette,[56] deserved no place in a respectable work of history like his own, as his sniffy comments about that publication at *Annals* 13.31.1 make clear. Epigraphic evidence he never uses.[57] And as for sifting through documentation produced by petty officialdom in far-off provinces, something that the mythicists and many biblical/NT scholars clearly thought he ought to have done in the case of Jesus's trial and sentencing, that would have been unthinkable for a literary craftsman such as him, even on the unlikely supposition that documentation of that kind was available for a Rome-based scholar to consult.[58]

As far as can be seen, the only documentary source that Tacitus really set any store by was the *Acta Senatus*, the official record of proceedings (mostly debates) in the Senate, the Roman equivalent of Hansard, the official report of the UK Parliament.[59] Even here, the degree to which he made use of that source is hotly disputed. While Syme has argued powerfully for extensive, *direct* consultation,[60] Tacitus actually refers to his own consultation of the *Acta Senatus* just once (*Annals* 15.74.3)! Although

56. For the non-elite character of the readership of this official publication, see Brian J. Wright, 'Ancient Rome's Daily News Publication with Some Likely Implications for Early Christian Studies', *TynBul* 67, no. 1 (2016): 145–60.

57. Unlike writers of a more antiquarian bent such as Pliny the Elder and Suetonius. See, for instance, Suetonius, *Div. Aug.* 7.1; *Gaius* 8.1 (citing epigraphic evidence produced by Pliny the Elder and disputing his interpretation of it) and *Vespasian* 1.2.

58. That records of trials held by provincial governors originally existed is certain: Roman legal procedure required that a charge be submitted in writing and, if a hearing took place, the ensuing judgement (*sententia*) be recorded. Prof. Jill Harries – personal communication. How long these provincial trial-records were kept and whether copies were made for archiving in Rome is unknown. On the absence of guidelines for archiving administrative documents and the small proportion of documents deposited in the archives of provincial governors prior to the second century, see Werner Eck, 'Provincial Administration and Finance', in *The Cambridge Ancient History, vol. XI: The High Empire, AD 70–192*, ed. Alan K. Bowman, Peter Garnsey and Dominic Rathbone (Cambridge: Cambridge University Press, 2000), 290–1. Ehrman's contention (*Did Jesus Exist?*, 44 and 56) that the Romans did not keep detailed records is simply wrong.

59. For Hansard, see https://hansard.parliament/uk. There is no way (contra Eddy and Boyd, *Jesus Legend*, 184) that the *Acta Senatus* would have contained any reference to the trial and punishment of Jesus, who was far too unimportant a figure ever to feature in a senatorial debate. These focused on larger state issues, both foreign and domestic.

60. *Tacitus*, 1:186–8, 278–85, 295–6. For additional bibliography on this point, see Woodman, *Tacitus – The Annals*, xv n. 17.

wider use by him of this resource is not to be doubted,[61] the fact remains that for him, as indeed for historians right down to the nineteenth century when use of documentary evidence first began to be considered essential,[62] written (i.e., literary) sources remained the bedrock of their craft.[63] Indeed, some ancient historians (e.g., Cassius Dio) consulted no other type of material.[64]

Just as historians were not expected to conduct original research in the archives, so they were not expected to cite their sources. Provision of an *apparatus criticus* (i.e., footnotes) played no part in ancient historiography, for the simple reason that the purpose of history was differently understood and, as a consequence of that, the way in which it entered the public domain was different too. The Romans in particular viewed history as much as a vehicle for moral improvement as a way of imparting information about the past.[65] For them, 'publication' effectively meant the reading aloud of sections of their latest work before an invited audience consisting of their friends and colleagues.[66] To us, for whom the serious study of history invariably is a silent, solitary activity, the live-performance

61. Tacitus's own, improved version of Claudius's speech to the Senate about the admission to that body of tribal leaders from Gaul, for instance, could not have been written without prior reading and study of the original text, which he presumably found in the *Acta Senatus*. As Woodman, *Annals*, xvi notes, '...we may be certain that he had in front of him a copy of Claudius' original: half a dozen main points are common both to the original and to Tacitus' version'.

62. On the document-based 'scientific history' then championed by Leopold von Ranke (1795–1886), see C. W. Fornara, *The Nature of History in Ancient Greece and Rome* (Berkeley: University of California Press, 1983), 196–7.

63. Edward Gibbon was rather unusual in making at least some use of numismatic and inscriptional evidence. However, out of the 8000 or so references contained in the *Decline and Fall*, only 120 (approx.) are concerned with epigraphic material. Roy Porter, *Gibbon: Making History* (London: Phoenix, 1995), 72–3.

64. On the restricted nature of the sources used by Dio, see Fergus Millar, *A Study of Cassius Dio* (Oxford: Clarendon, 1964), 34–8.

65. Thus we find Tacitus at *Annals* 3.65.1 declaring 'I am of the opinion that the principal duty of history (*praecipuum munus annalium*) is that virtues should not be left unrecorded and also that fear of disgrace in posterity should attend crooked words and actions'.

66. For a contemporary example of such a 'recitation' from a 'work in progress', see Pliny, *Ep.* 9.27. For the suggestion that the performer on this occasion was Tacitus himself and the recited material an extract from his *Histories*, see Philippe Fabia, 'Les ouvrages de Tacite réussirent-ils auprès des contemporains?', *Rev.Phil.* 19 (1895): 1–10 (8–9), followed by, *inter alios*, Christopher Whitton, '"Let us tread our path together": Tacitus and the Younger Pliny', in Pagán, ed., *Companion*, 345–68 (363–4).

and declamatory character of ancient historiography inevitably must seem strange.[67] Once, however, it is realized that the Romans regarded history as an activity closely akin to oratory,[68] then the absence of a critical apparatus becomes entirely understandable. In such an elevated form of discourse, the principal aim of which was to edify by providing examples (*exempla*) of good and bad behaviour,[69] the presence of a critical apparatus would have been decidedly out of place.

That does not mean, of course, that ancient historiographical texts are totally devoid of references to the sources on which they are based, whether literary or documentary. Tacitus's citation of the *Acta Senatus* at *Annals* 15.74.3 has already been mentioned. In addition to that, we find about half a dozen specific references, also in the *Annals*, to individuals whose writings he had used – namely, the historians, Pliny the Elder,[70] Cluvius Rufus and Fabius Rusticus,[71] Nero's mother, the Younger Agrippina, whose memoirs he consulted at least once,[72] and the great general, Gnaeus Domitius Corbulo, whose account of his campaigns in Armenia formed the basis of Tacitus's own narrative in books 12 to 15 about Nero's Armenian wars.[73]

That these references cluster in the final (Neronian) books of the *Annals* is interesting – and almost certainly significant. Those books, as mentioned earlier,[74] are thought to have been unrevised. Syme, for one,

---

67. Such declamation continued to be the case throughout the whole of antiquity and is attested for the Middle Ages as well. See Roberto Nicolai, 'The Place of History in the Ancient World', in *A Companion to Greek and Roman Historiography*, ed. John Marincola (Malden: Wiley-Blackwell, 2011), 13–26 (23).

68. For this view of ancient historiography, see A. J. Woodman, *Rhetoric in Classical Historiography* (London: Croom Helm, 1988) and *Annals*, xviii (a brief discussion of the main ancient testimonia).

69. On the elevated nature of historical writing, a genre associated with power (*potestas*), dignity (*dignitas*), majesty (*maiestas*) and even inspired religious authority (*numen*), see, in particular, Pliny, *Ep.* 9.27.1. On its provision of morally improving *exempla*, see Livy, *History of Rome*, Praef. 10 – 'For in history…you can find for yourself and for your country both examples and warnings: fine things to take as models, base things, rotten through and through, to avoid'. See Aubrey de Sélincourt (trans.), Livy, *The Early History of Rome* (Harmondsworth: Penguin, 1960), 18.

70. For his consultation of Pliny's two historical works, both his study of Rome's German wars and his annalistic history of the later Julio-Claudian period, see *Annals* 1.69.2; 13.20.2 and 15.53.3.

71. These are mentioned together at *Annals* 13.20.2 and 14.2.1-2.

72. *Annals* 4.53.2.

73. See *Annals* 15.16.1 with *OCD³*, *s.v.* Domitius Corbulo, Gnaeus.

74. Above, n. 13.

was of the opinion that had a final elaboration taken place, then those references probably would have been 'expunged for artistic reasons'.[75] The ancients' view of the citation of source material was diametrically opposed to our own. Whereas we academics regard the inclusion of source-references as essential for underscoring the authority of what we have written (hence their super-abundance in this work), they saw them as infelicitous intrusions – material that marred the *Kunstprosa* which any historian worth his salt was expected to produce. Consequently, where such references occur, they are generally taken as evidence that the text, as we have it, is not the final, fair copy but simply 'work in progress'.

To berate Tacitus, then, for failing either to consult the court records relating to the trial of Jesus or to provide any documentation in support of the few facts he supplies about him is wholly unjustified. It simply would not have occurred either to those who wrote historical works or to the elite Romans who came to listen to them that procedures of that nature were necessary for the creation of respectable history.

No less unreasonable is the condemnation of Tacitus for his likely use of hearsay evidence (i.e., oral testimony). Here too, it needs to be realized, ancient and modern historiographical practices are strikingly different.[76] To Tacitus and his contemporaries, availing themselves of such testimony would not have seemed as in any way reprehensible. Theirs was still a predominantly oral culture.[77] Consequently, using personal reminiscences as evidence would have been regarded as a perfectly reasonable thing to do; indeed, it would have been the only viable method of acquiring information about a subject if it had not yet been accorded literary treatment. Both Herodotus and Thucydides, the two 'greats' of ancient historiography, had operated in accordance with this principle. Such was their continuing authority throughout antiquity that it would not have occurred to historiographers writing in the centuries after their deaths to abandon that principle, even had that been practical.[78]

---

75. Syme, *Tacitus*, 2:742.

76. By 'modern historiography', what I have in mind is formal, academic history. Those working on oral history projects, in which the resources of modern technology are employed to save for posterity the reminiscences of 'ordinary' people, have much in common with the practices of ancient historians.

77. On the enduring orality of ancient culture, *even at its highest levels*, see E. J. Kenney, 'Small Writing and Less Reading', *CR* 41, no. 1 (1991): 168–9 – a review of William V. Harris, *Ancient Literacy* (Cambridge, MA: Harvard University Press, 1989), in which ancient literacy rates are put at somewhere between 5 and 10%.

78. On the paramount status of oral tradition among Greek and Roman writers of history, see Momigliano, *Studies in Historiography*, 214–17.

In his detailed discussions of Tacitus's likely sources, Syme stresses the extent to which the latter will have relied upon oral information gathered from his peers.[79] This would have been especially so in the case of the *Histories*, a work covering a period so recent and so dangerous to write about that very little will have been put on record.[80] Among the peers consulted for that period was Pliny the Younger. Around 107 CE Tacitus asked him to provide a description of the death of his uncle, Pliny the Elder, in the famous eruption of Vesuvius in 79 CE, so that he could 'transmit a more truthful account of it for posterity'.[81] True, Pliny's recollections would by then have become rather dated. Further, his account would in large parts necessarily have been second-hand, since he was, on his own admission (*Ep.* 6.16.7), nowhere in the vicinity of his uncle when the latter perished. However, for Tacitus, Pliny was an inherently reliable witness. How could he not be, seeing that he was a co-member of the Roman establishment, a senior senator, a state priest and a distinguished member of the legal profession? Being such an upstanding member of society, it followed that his testimony automatically deserved credence.

In assessing the quality of Tacitus's testimony for Jesus, judgement must be made in accordance with contemporary ideas about what constituted good historical practice, not those of the modern age. No ancient historian would have regarded as anything other than admirable Thucydides' description of how he went about collecting material for the history he was planning to write: 'With regard to my factual reporting of the events of the war I have made it a principle not to write down the first story that came my way, and not even to be guided by my own general impressions; either I was present myself at the events which I have described *or else I heard of them from eye-witnesses whose reports I have checked with as much thoroughness as possible*.[82] To insist that evidence somehow is lacking in validity unless it comes from a written, ideally documentary, source is profoundly anachronistic.

---

79. Syme, *Tacitus*, 1:176–7 and 299–303.

80. At *Agricola* 2.1 Tacitus recalls the savage treatment meted out to those who had produced works that had offended Domitian: they had been put to death and their works consigned publicly to the flames.

81. Pliny, *Ep.* 6.16.1.

82. Thucydides, *History of the Peloponnesian War* 1.22.2 (trans. Rex Warner; italics mine).

4.4. *Tacitus's Testimony Partially Inauthentic?*

Tacitus's testimony about Jesus has been impugned, however, not only on account of his alleged inadequacies as an historian. It has also been accused of being either partially or completely inauthentic. Prominent among the advocates of the former is Richard Carrier, current doyen of the mythicists.[83] Arguing that Tacitus's brief comments about Christus originated as a Christian marginal gloss which somehow or other had become incorporated in the main text of Tacitus,[84] he seeks to dispose of this highly inconvenient piece of evidence without resorting to the ill-grounded, easily countered accusations of authorial incompetence discussed above. Further, by reviving Koestermann's thesis (n. 26 above) that the *Chrestiani*, mentioned slightly earlier in the passage, are not Christians at all but members of an unruly Jewish faction 'suppressed under Claudius,'[85] he attempts to deprive *Annals* 15.44 of any relevance to the early Jesus movement whatsoever.

How plausible are these two hypotheses? With regard to the proposition that the Christus sentence should be seen as a late intrusion of Christian origin,[86] there are solid literary and linguistic reasons for seeing it as an integral part of *Annals* 15.44 *from the moment of its composition*. Harris, for instance, has drawn attention to the skilful way in which Tacitus connects the fate of Christ (mentioned in the clause) with that of his followers (described in the wider passage). By applying the same verb to both (*afficere*, meaning 'inflict'), Tacitus neatly underlines their common victimhood at the hands of the Roman judicial authorities.[87]

A further illustration of the tight connection between the main text and the Christus clause is to be seen in the careful collocation of *Chrestianos* and *Christus*. Although some scholars have emended the text so that it reads *Christianos/Christus*[88] or suggested that the original wording is likely to have been *Chrestianos/Chrestus*,[89] Fuchs was surely right

83. Less politely, the late Larry Hurtado once dubbed him 'the scholarly poster-boy for mythicists'. See https://larryhurtado.wordpress.com/2017/11/30/the-mythic-jesus-last-hurrah/ (accessed 24/09/2018).

84. 'Prospect of Christian Interpolation', 274.

85. 'Prospect of Christian Interpolation', 283.

86. More recently, Barrett ('Great Fire', 165) has also come out in support of this view.

87. Harris, 'References to Jesus', 349.

88. For example, Furneaux, *Annals* and now Ash, *Annals Book XV.*

89. Robert Renahan, 'Christus or Chrestus in Tacitus?', *La Parola del Passato* 23 (1968): 368–70.

to defend the text printed in all modern editions of the *Annals*, that is, *Chrestianos/Christus*: with elegant economy, Tacitus not only provides his readers with a short and correct definition of the former word but he deftly mocks the ignorance and illogicality of the common people of Rome (*vulgus*).[90] Although they hate the Christians for their *flagitia* ('abominable practices'), yet they call them by a name reflective of virtuous behaviour, *Chrestiani* being a derivative of *chrestos*, a Greek epithet meaning 'good', 'honest' and 'worthy'.[91] This jibe about pagan ignorance and illogicality, first seen here in a classical text, was to be made again and again by later Christian apologists.[92]

As for Carrier's revival of Koestermann's thesis that the *Chrestiani* of the passage are not Christians at all but a band of belligerent Jews,[93] rightly has this idea been dismissed by Lampe as 'a superfluous complication' and by Slingerland as an 'interesting but groundless thesis'.[94] There is no evidence that a group of Jewish agitators called *Chrestiani* ever existed either at Rome or anywhere else.[95]

4.5. Annals *15.44: The Entire Chapter a Christian Interpolation?*

But if the hypothesis of partial interpolation fails to persuade, what about the claim that the whole of *Annals* 15.44 is bogus? This idea has a long history. First articulated by Volney in the 1790s,[96] it has never been without powerful advocates. Indeed, so seriously did the arch-sceptic, Polydore Hochart, take this idea that he devoted an entire monograph to

90. Fuchs, 'Tacitus über die Christen', 69–74.

91. LSJ, *s.v.* χρηστός. On Tacitus's 'oppositional word play here' here, see Cook, *Roman Attitudes*, 49.

92. For example Tertullian, *Apol.* 3 and *Ad Nat.* 1.3; Lactantius, *Inst. Div.* 4.7. However, instances of the vulgar form *Chrestiani* are to be found even in reputable Christian texts. The original hand of the (fourth-century) Codex Sinaiticus (ℵ), for example, spells 'Christian' with an *eta* in all three New Testament occurrences of the word (Acts 11:26; 26:28; 1 Pet. 2:3). For a useful discussion of the terms *Christiani/Chrestiani* and the reasons, linguistic and onomastic, for the prevalence in Graeco-Roman society of the vulgar form, see Van Voorst, *Jesus*, 34–6. On the social significance of the label *Christianus*, see now David G. Horrell, 'The Label Χριστιανός: 1 Peter 4:16 and the Formation of Christian Identity', *JBL* 126 (2007): 361–81.

93. 'Prospect of Christian Interpolation', 281.

94. For the sources of these quotations, see n. 26 above.

95. For full discussion of the text that underlies the hypothesis of Koestermann and Carrier, namely, Suetonius, *Div. Claud.* 25.4, see Chapter 6 below.

96. See Drews, *Christ Myth*, 233 (in unnumbered note).

proving that the Neronian persecution of the Christians in 64 CE was no more than a pious fraud.[97] And since his time, there have been several more proponents of the view that this section of Tacitus's text is nothing more than a Christian interpolation.[98]

It is easy to understand why such a hypothesis can be so confidently advanced. Tacitus is unique in associating the persecution of the Christians with the 'Great Fire of Rome' in 64 CE. None of the other classical authors who refer to that catastrophe makes any such connection. Christians are conspicuous by their absence in both Pliny the Elder's brief treatment of 'the emperor Nero's conflagration' (*Neronis principis incendia*) and Cassius Dio's fuller account of the fire.[99] Although Suetonius mentions both Nero's punishment of the Christians of Rome and his culpability for the fire, he presents them as unconnected topics, the first as a meritorious act,[100] and the second as the supreme example of the emperor's propensity for cruelty.[101]

Early Christian apologists also are silent about any general persecution of Christians by Nero at the time of the 'Great Fire of Rome', even though its propaganda value to them would appear to be obvious.[102] Neither the late second/early third-century Christian apologist, Tertullian, nor the early fourth-century Christian authors, Eusebius and Lactantius, so much as hint at any such occurrence even though all three know of Nero as persecutor of Christians (more precisely as the ruler who martyred Peter

97. Polydore Hochart, *Études au sujet de la persécution des Chrétians sous Néro* (Paris: Ernest Leroux, 1885). Praised by Drews (*Christ Myth*, 231) for being a 'splendid and exhaustive enquiry', Hochart's study did not impress the Tacitean commentator, Furneaux, at all. At *Annals of Tacitus 2*, 416 n. 6 he demonstrates that Hochart's linguistic arguments lack all credibility.

98. For older examples, see Van Voorst, *Jesus*, 42–3; for more recent bibliography on this subject, see Carrier, 'Prospect of Christian Interpolation', 264 n. 1.

99. Pliny the Elder, *Nat.* 17.5; Dio, *Roman History* 62.16. On the mystery of Dio's total silence about the Christians, see Millar, *Cassius Dio*, 179.

100. Suetonius, *Nero* 16.2. Here the Christians of Rome are presented as low-status troublemakers justifiably disciplined by that emperor.

101. Suetonius, *Nero* 38.1. Although Suetonius does not connect the punishment of the Christians with the fire, it cannot be ruled out that that was indeed the occasion for it. For Suetonius's habit of using the same pieces of evidence to make different, sometimes even contradictory, points, see Wallace-Hadrill, *Suetonius*, 13.

102. E. Mary Smallwood, *The Jews under Roman Rule from Pompey to Diocletian*, SJLA 20 (Leiden: Brill, 1976), 218 – 'Apologists tended to wax eloquent on the false accusations brought against the Church'. Whether the accusations were entirely false, however, as Christian commentators (e.g., Harris, 'References to Jesus', 348) tend to assume, is a moot point. See n. 42 above.

and Paul).[103] Indeed, it is only with Sulpicius Severus at the very beginning of the fifth century (403 CE)[104] that we meet with the first *certain* reference among Christian authors to the material now found in *Annals* 15.44. At *Chronicle* 2.29.1, he makes generous use of this material, prompting the suggestion that the story of Nero's persecution of the Christians at the time of the 'Great Fire' was actually invented at some point during the second half of the fourth century and subsequently interpolated into Tacitus's text.[105]

4.6. *Silence of the Pagan Sources*

Plausible as these objections may appear, none is decisive in proving inauthenticity. Take the three classical sources just mentioned. The silence of Pliny the Elder is wholly understandable. His account of the fire, an event so devastating in its impact upon Rome that it must have received wide coverage in his history of the later Julio-Claudian period,[106] has not survived. His sole reference to the conflagration, the responsibility for which he lays firmly at Nero's door, occurs in a brief discussion about some ancient, highly prized nettle trees which had perished in the inferno.[107] Given such a context, there was no need to discuss the fire more widely, let alone mention any Christian involvement in it.

Although Dio's narrative of 'Nero's fire' has survived, it contains none of the circumstantial detail that is such a conspicuous feature of Tacitus's account of the event.[108] Indeed, Dio's treatment of the fire is so rhetorical and so generalized that he could almost be describing the burning down of any city at any time.[109] His aim here, as in his descriptions of other catastrophic events, is not to produce a factual account but to stir the emotions of his audience by dwelling upon the sufferings

103. See, for instance, Tertullian, *Scorp.* 15.3; Eusebius, *Hist. eccl.* 2.25.5; Lactantius, *Death of the Persecutors* 3.

104. For the date, see Cook, *Roman Attitudes*, 69.

105. For another (late fourth century?) reference to a connection between Christians and the 'Great Fire of Rome' but derived from a source other than Tacitus, namely, the apocryphal correspondence between Seneca and Paul, see Ep. Paul Sen. 12 (M. R. James, *The Apocryphal New Testament* [Oxford: Clarendon, 1953], 483–4).

106. Van der Lans in Van der Lans and Bremmer, 'Tacitus and the Persecution of the Christians', 301 n. 9.

107. Pliny the Elder, *Nat.* 17.1.5-6.

108. Cassius Dio, *Roman History* 62.16-18 (epitome of Xiphilinus).

109. Apart from the burning of the Palatine and the theatre of Taurus in the Campus Martius (*Roman History* 62.18.2), he supplies no details.

of those involved.[110] Since he is determined to ascribe responsibility for the conflagration of 64 CE wholly to Nero (*Roman History* 62.16.1-2), it would make no sense for him to entertain the notion of scapegoating. In his version of that event, Nero proudly takes full responsibility for engineering a conflagration on a par with the burning of Troy.[111]

As for Suetonius's failure to mention any Christian involvement in his brief account of the fire of 64 CE at *Nero* 38, that too is easily explicable. Suetonius took it for granted that his readership/audience was well informed about the history of the principate.[112] Consequently, he hardly ever bothers either to contextualize or to supply narrative details about the events which he mentions in his Lives of the Caesars. For him, events are of interest only to the extent that they can be used to illustrate a particular topic, more often than not an imperial virtue or vice.[113] At this point in his biography of Nero (*Nero* 36-38), his concern is with the latter's *saevitia* (savagery), a vice which reached its apogee in his decision to burn down his own capital so that he could re-build it to his own greater glory, re-naming it Neropolis.[114] That being his view of the matter, there was no need for him, any more than for Dio, to entertain the possibility of Nero scapegoating anyone. The latter rejoiced in what he had achieved,[115] even if it had meant destroying the livelihoods of thousands of the inhabitants of Rome.

4.7. *Silence of Christian Sources*

What, finally, about the silence of Christian writers – a key element in the case for Christian interpolation of Tacitus's text since the Enlightenment? Recent scholarship has shown that the silence of early Christian sources may not be quite as deafening as has generally been assumed.[116] Bremmer has now compiled a whole dossier of early Christian texts of both eastern

---

110. On Dio's generalizing rhetorical technique, see Millar, *Cassius Dio*, 42–4.

111. For his serenading of the fire from the roof of the palace, see Dio, *Roman History* 62.18.1.

112. Wallace-Hadrill, *Suetonius*, 13.

113. For Suetonius's composition by topic/category (*per species*), see *Div. Aug.* 9 and Appendix 3; for his treatment of imperial virtues and vices, see Wallace-Hadrill, *Suetonius*, 142–74.

114. Suetonius, *Nero* 55.

115. For his serenading of the fire from the Tower of Maecenas, see Suetonius, *Nero* 38.2.

116. See Bremmer in Van der Lans and Bremmer, 'Tacitus and the Persecution of the Christians', 310–15, to whom the following discussion is heavily indebted.

and western origin to demonstrate that the tradition of Nero as a persecutor of Christians started very much earlier than is usually assumed.[117] The key document for us is the anonymous pastoral epistle conventionally known as 1 Clement after its presumed author, Clement I, an early 'bishop' of Rome (*ca.* 88–97 CE). Composed probably in the late 90s CE,[118] this text refers not only to 'a series of recent calamities that have befallen us' (i.e., the Christian community in Rome)[119] but also a substantial persecution of Christians in the imperial capital within the lifetime of the writer.[120]

From the torments mentioned in connection with the latter event, namely, Christian women dying in droves[121] through forced participation in re-enactments of grisly myths,[122] scholars have been strongly reminded of the *ludibria* (mockeries) to which Tacitus alludes at *Annals* 15.44.4. Consequently, there is now a growing conviction that both texts refer to the same thing – i.e., the 'fatal charades' in which Christians had been forced to participate during the Neronian persecution.[123]

To be sure, the author of 1 Clement does not mention the 'Great Fire' of 64 CE as the occasion for the mythical enactments to which he refers. But there was no need for him to do so. His concerns in this letter to the Christian community of Corinth are entirely pastoral – to try and heal the divisions that were tearing their community apart. This factionalism, so he

117. For the belief that the earliest evidence for this tradition dated from the second half of the second century, see Jones, 'Historicity of the Neronian Persecution', 147, citing Melito of Sardis, as quoted by Eusebius at *Hist. eccl.* 4.26.9, and Tertullian, *Ad nat.* 1.7.8.

118. This remains the customary view despite attempts to date the text both earlier and later. For a date c. 96 CE, see *Encyclopedia of Early Christianity*, ed. Everett Ferguson, 2nd edn (New York: Garland, 1998), *s.v.* Clement of Rome and F. L. Cross, ed., *The Oxford Dictionary of Christian Church*, rev. E. A. Livingstone, 3rd edn (Oxford: Oxford University Press, 2005), *s.v.* Clement of Rome, St. For a date between 80 and 140, see Laurence L. Welborn, *ABD*, 1:1060, *s.v.* Clement, First Epistle of.

119. *1 Clem.* 1.1. Generally thought to be a reference to Domitian's recent hounding of the Christians.

120. *1 Clem.* 5.1 – τῆς γενεᾶς ἡμῶν ('our own generation').

121. *1 Clem.* 6.1 – πολὺ πλῆθος ('a great multitude'). Cf. Tacitus's *multitudo ingens* at *Annals* 15.44.4.

122. *1 Clem.* 6.2 – 'Through jealousy women were persecuted as Danaids and Dircae, suffering terrible and unholy indignities'.

123. For detailed analysis of the allusions to the Danaids and Dircae in 1 Clement and to the myths of Actaeon and Herakles at *Annals* 15.44.4, see Schmitt, 'Des Kaisers Inszenierung'. For a briefer analysis along the same lines, see Champlin, *Nero,* 121–6.

warns them, would be as ruinous for their community as similar divisions recently had been for the Christian community in Rome.

Clement's suggestion that the woes suffered by Christian martyrs in Rome in his time ('within our generation') were in part self-inflicted also chimes with Tacitus's text at *Annals* 15.44.4. It will be recalled that it was information disclosed by the first group of Christians to be arrested (the *confessi* – i.e., the self-confessed) that led to the implication and punishment of the much larger second group.

Admittedly, the evidence provided by 1 Clement is not absolutely decisive. Fortunately, however, we are not forced to depend to any great degree on 1 Clement in establishing the likely authenticity of Tacitus's testimony. There are far more compelling reasons for believing that the text as we have it is a product of his pen and no other's.

4.8. *Clinching Arguments for Authenticity*

First of all, there is the character of the writing, an issue largely ignored by those seeking to impugn Tacitus's testimony. If the Latin of *Annals* 15.44.2-5 could be shown to be at odds with Tacitus's very distinctive usage of that language, then the probability of interpolation would increase enormously. However, the three expert Latinists recently consulted by Shaw in the hope that they would judge this passage to be fraudulent, were unanimous in asserting its Tacitean character.[124] In fact, I know of no serious Tacitean scholar who considers for a moment that this passage is an interpolation.

But the clincher surely for authenticity is the extraordinarily negative language of the passage particularly in regard to 'Christianity'.[125] Is it credible that a pious Christian interpolator would designate 'Christianity' as a deadly superstition (*exitiabilis superstitio*) and an evil (*malum*), to depict its founder as a common criminal and to imply that his followers were not only inherently pre-disposed to shameless behaviour (*flagitia*) but actually little better than sewage? That is the clear implication of the final words in the passage quoted above in which the Christian superstition is included among all the 'atrocious and shameful things' (*atrocia aut pudenda*) that flow like a river into Rome.[126] Just how offensive Tacitus's language was to the Christian ear is shown by Sulpicius Severus's

124. Shaw, 'Myth of the Neronian Persecution', 80 n. 37.

125. On this, see Harris, 'References to Jesus', 348–9; Meier, *A Marginal Jew* 1:90; Van Voorst, *Jesus*, 43; Eddy and Boyd, *Jesus Legend*, 180.

126. For another, even more colourful expression of this sentiment, see the contemporary poem by Juvenal, *Satire* 3.62.

re-working of the fire-and-persecution narrative found in *Annals* 15. All the Tacitean slurs are done away with and the focus directed on Nero's sadism and the unquestionable innocence of his Christian victims.[127]

Compared with the virulence of Tacitus's language about 'Christianity' and his unsympathetic comments about the Christians (whatever they had or had not done, they deserved to die[128]), the terms in which he describes Christus have struck scholars as rather mild. Van Voorst, for instance, concludes that 'what he [Tacitus] explicitly says about Christ is neutral'.[129] Earlier he has characterized the comments about Jesus as 'merely descriptive'.[130] But are Tacitus's comments really so very anodyne? It is to this question that we must now turn our attention.

127. Sulpicius Severus, *Chronicle* 2.29.1.
128. *Annals* 15.44.5 – *novissima exempla meritos* ('deserving the ultimate in punishment').
129. Van Voorst, *Jesus*, 48.
130. Van Voorst, *Jesus*, 43.

Chapter 5

TACITUS ON CHRISTUS:
A MASTER RHETORICIAN AT WORK

5.1. *Introduction*

Tacitus's only explicit remarks about Christ, in contrast to what he writes about the Christians and 'Christianity', are, on the face of it, rather basic.[1] All we find is this short sentence: *auctor nominis eius Christus Tiberio imperitante per procuratorem Pontium Pilatum supplicio affectus erat.*[2] Translated literally, we end up with this: 'The author of that name (*sc.* Christian), Christus, during the reign of the emperor Tiberius, had been put to death through the agency of the procurator Pontius Pilatus'. But is this sentence as 'basic' as it is usually taken to be – i.e., a brief, anodyne explanation for an assumed ignorant readership of the term *Chrestiani*, a word that occurs in Tacitus's text directly before his comments on Christus?

In my earlier study of this sentence, that is what I took it to be – 'All that Tacitus was seeking to accomplish in his *Christus* sentence…was to provide a short explanation of the term *Chrestiani*'.[3] Further reflection and study have convinced me, however, that on a number of counts this interpretation of the passage is unsatisfactory. In the first place, it seems to me most unlikely that Tacitus's original audience, men very much like himself (i.e., highly educated members of Rome's governing elite),[4] were so ignorant that they needed to have spelt out for them what the term Christian signified and who Christus was. By the time that this section of

---

1. So described by Bond, *The Historical Jesus*, 38.

2. *Annals* 15.44.3.

3. See Margaret Williams, 'Tacitus', in Keith et al., eds, *The Reception of Jesus*, 3:61–70 (70).

4. Deducible from Pliny's descriptions of the kind of people who attended *recitationes* (public readings of work-in-progress) as well as from the complexity of the Latin of *Annals* and its large number of subtle and sophisticated literary allusions.

the *Annals* was written, probably the early years of Hadrian's reign (*ca.* 120 CE),[5] considerable numbers of Tacitus's peers must have come across Christians and the cult of Christ primarily through their governorship of Rome's eastern provinces. Take, for instance, the province of Asia, an area containing quite a few well-established Christian communities by Tacitus's day (Rev. 1.4, 11). The governorship (proconsulship) of that province, a highly coveted position filled annually by lot, was held by the successful candidate for one year only. That means that by the early 120s CE, there will have been a very large number of senators in Rome who had crowned their career through the tenure of that post. Indeed, from the period 103/4 to 120/21 CE alone, no fewer than seventeen such individuals can be identified.[6] That at least some of those governors had had dealings with Christians is surely a safe assumption to make, given that in the course of fulfilling their judicial duties they will have visited places containing substantial Christian communities. Obvious examples are the assize cities of Ephesus, Smyrna and Pergamum. *Mutatis mutandis* the same situation will have prevailed in all the other eastern provinces of the empire which had Christian inhabitants. Annaeus Gallio (governor of Achaea in the early 50s CE) and Pliny in Bithynia-Pontus (*ca.* 110 CE) cannot have been the only provincial governors in the course of some seven or eight decades who had been required to deal with Christian issues, even if they are virtually the only ones to be attested in our sources.[7]

Nor will the Roman elite's knowledge about the Christians have been derived solely from their governance of provinces containing sizeable Christian communities. In the imperial capital itself the formal duties of senior senators appointed to the office of *praefectus urbi* (Prefect of the City)[8] will have increased the number of elite Romans who must have had some knowledge, even if slender, about the cult of Christ. As the official responsible for the maintenance of law and order in the city, it was the *praefectus urbi* who almost certainly presided over the trials of Christians that we know took place there from the time of Nero onwards.[9] Nor did he conduct those trials solo. Other members of the elite regularly were in attendance whether as advocates or assessors.[10]

5. For the likely date of the *Annals*, see above 52.

6. For the list of their names, see Syme, *Tacitus*, 2:664–5 (Appendix 23).

7. Acts 18:12-16 and Pliny, *Ep.* 10.96-97.

8. Generally, they were men of consular rank. See *OCD³*, *s.v. praefectus urbi* (2).

9. On Rome as the likely location of the *cognitiones* (trials) of Christians mentioned by Pliny at *Ep.* 10.96.1, see Sherwin-White, *Letters*, 694–5.

10. Pliny himself is known to have served in the latter capacity (*Ep.* 6.11.1) but not, it so happens, when the trials were of Christians (*Ep.* 10.96.1).

Finally, we might note that Pliny's celebrated despatch to Trajan about the Christians (*Ep.* 10.96) presupposes that the term *Christianus* was well known. He felt no need to supply the emperor with an explanation of it.[11]

But a likely collective knowledge on the part of Rome's governing elite about the cult of Christ is not the only reason for finding the standard interpretation of Tacitus's comments on Christus unsatisfactory. A major failing of previous treatments of this evidence (including my own) is the lack of attention paid to Tacitus's arrangement of the material he presents about 'Jesus' and the language in which he chooses to couch it. Discussions tend to focus firmly on the factual, above all on Tacitus's name for the author of 'Christianity' (i.e., Christus, not Jesus) and the allegedly erroneous titled applied to Pontius Pilatus (i.e., procurator, not prefect). But this focus now seems to me to be thoroughly inadequate and for these reasons. The first is the character of ancient, as opposed to modern, historiography. This was viewed by the Romans as a 'singularly rhetorical' art-form,[12] oratory and history having, to quote Pliny, 'a great many things in common' (*habet quidem oratio et historia multa communia*).[13] Also requiring to be taken into account is Tacitus's renown as an unusually accomplished rhetorician, both in his own day[14] and subsequently. Goodyear, for instance, a significant modern authority on Tacitus, is of the opinion that he possessed 'the surest and most subtle command of rhetoric of all writers of the Silver Age'.[15] No surprise, then, to see throughout the *Annals*, Tacitus's final work and his universally acknowledged masterpiece, a sustained demonstration of that expertise. To this work he brought not only decades of experience as a pleader in the courts and as a public orator,[16] but a well-honed historiographical technique too. His earlier historical work, the *Histories*, a work of considerable sophistication as the surviving books show quite clearly,[17] had taken him almost a decade of diligent application.[18]

11. On the familiarity of the term by the early second century at least, see Ash, *Annals XV*, 205.

12. Cicero, *Laws* 1.5 – *opus...oratorium maxime* ('a singularly oratorical task').

13. See Pliny, *Ep.* 5.8.9, where many examples of their shared characteristics are set out. On historiography's thoroughgoing dependence upon rhetorical invention (*inventio*), see Woodman, *Rhetoric in Classical Historiography*, in general and especially 98–101.

14. Pliny, *Ep.* 4.13.10 and especially *Ep.* 9.23.3 with Sherwin-White's note *ad loc.*

15. F. R. D. Goodyear, *The Annals of Tacitus: Books 1-6*, 2 vols (Cambridge: Cambridge University Press, 1972 and 1981), 1:46.

16. Pliny, *Ep.* 2.1.6; 2.11.17 and 4.13.10.

17. Rhiannon Ash, *Tacitus* (London: Bristol Classical Press, 2006), 71–7.

18. Pliny, *Ep.* 6.16.1-3 and 7.33.1-3 for Tacitus's progress on this work.

To be an effective rhetorician in any culture requires an ability to select the right words for the occasion and to position them where they will exert the maximum persuasive power. No surprise, then, to find Tacitus excelling in both these areas. Experts on Tacitus are unanimous in their praise for the meticulous, almost obsessive, attention that he pays to the all-important matter of the selection of vocabulary (*delectus verborum*).[19] No less skilful is his placement of his chosen words. Knowing the importance of setting the agenda, Tacitus always exercises particular care with his choice of opening words. Notoriously, his narrative of the reign of Tiberius opens with the phrase 'the first crime of the new principate' (*primum facinus novi principatus*),[20] words that leave us in no doubt as to how he intended his original audience to view that emperor's reign.[21] No less care is taken with endings, the final words being 'what he wanted his readers to remember'.[22] Thus his narrative of the 'Great Fire of Rome' ends with emphasis being placed squarely on Nero's *saevitia* (savagery/cruelty), that quality being, for Tacitus, a major factor in the latter's loss of popularity and ultimately in his fall from power – 'Pity for them (*sc.*, the *Chrestiani*) began to well up because it was felt that they were being exterminated not for the public good, but to gratify one man's cruelty (*saevitia*)'.[23]

But arresting as Tacitus's beginnings and endings invariably are, it is not in them alone that his masterly manipulation of language is to be observed. One gets the impression when reading Tacitus of every single word having been weighed. Since his chief priority is to ensure that it is *his* interpretation of individuals and events that prevails, he does not shy away from using every device available in the rhetorician's box of tricks to achieve that end. Hence his deliberate employment of loaded, not always strictly accurate, vocabulary.[24] Hence also his practice of attrib-

19. See, for instance, F. R. D. Goodyear, *Tacitus*, New Surveys in the Classics 4 (Oxford: Clarendon, 1970), 36 – 'He chooses his words with immense care and fine sense for their quality'.

20. *Annals* 1.6.1.

21. His narrative of Nero's reign starts similarly at *Annals* 13.1.1 with the words *prima novo principatu mors* ('the first death of the new principate'). On Tacitus's use of this tactic 'to impose an interpretation of events and individuals', see Martin and Woodman, *Annals IV*, 77.

22. Erich S. Gruen, *Rethinking the Other in Antiquity* (Princeton: Princeton University Press, 2012), 190. On Tacitus's frequent use of 'the later and more emphatic position', see also Goodyear, *Annals of Tacitus*, 1:111 (note on 1.3.3).

23. *Annals* 15.44.5 (trans. Yardley).

24. C. S. Kraus and A. J. Woodman, *Latin Historians*, New Surveys in the Classics 27 (Oxford: Oxford University Press for the Classical Association, 1997), 111 and 118 n. 117.

uting to anonymous bystanders wholly unverifiable thoughts generally of a negative character.[25] Although this tactic is condemned by Goodyear as 'insidious and reprehensible',[26] there can be no doubt about its efficacy. The negative view generally taken of Tiberius, for instance, is largely a product of Tacitus's heavy use of this deeply unfair tactic.[27]

Given these common, indisputable characteristics of Tacitus's modus operandi, it would seem most unlikely that his comments about Christus can be anything other than calculated. The heavy use of alliteration in the Christus sentence (*Tiberio imperitante per procuratorem Pontium Pilatum*) is a clear indication that careful consideration has gone into its composition. Might not that consideration have extended further and influenced also Tacitus's choice of facts about 'Jesus' and the order and manner in which they are presented?

In what follows I shall be arguing that Tacitus's comments on Christus are not 'merely descriptive'.[28] Nor is the Christus sentence the sole neutral element in an otherwise hostile passage.[29] Tacitus, as Gruen has observed, 'almost never did anything inadvertently'.[30] The case to be presented here is that in this thumbnail sketch of Christus we have a calculated attempt to cast Jesus in an extremely unfavourable light, each element of the sentence being designed to portray him (and, by implication, his cult) as worthless and contemptible.

5.2. *Tacitus's Opening Words on Christus*

We have already seen through our discussion of the closely positioned words, *Chrestiani* and *Christus*, that Tacitus's introduction of Christ into his narrative (*auctor nominis eius Christus*) is not quite as straightforward as it appears at first sight.[31] Most likely Tacitus is engaging in clever wordplay here, the purpose being to poke fun at the ignorance of the common people of Rome.[32] But was mockery of the *vulgus* his only aim in the opening words of his sentence about Christ?

25. For discussion and examples, see Syme, *Tacitus*, 1:314–15.

26. Goodyear, *Annals of Tacitus*, 1:35.

27. For some examples, see B. Walker, *The Annals of Tacitus* (Manchester: Manchester University Press, 1952), 48–9.

28. Van Voorst, *Jesus*, 43.

29. Van Voorst, *Jesus*, 48.

30. Gruen, *Rethinking the Other*, 180.

31. See above, 67–8.

32. On Tacitus's contempt for the latter, see *Histories* 1.4.3 (*plebs sordida*); *Annals* 15.46.1 and 64.2 and Syme, *Tacitus*, 2:531–2.

Immediately before his direct comments about Christ, Tacitus claims that the latter's adherents, the *Chrestiani* [*sic*] were a thoroughly disreputable bunch. Without offering a shred of supporting evidence, he baldly states that they were popularly 'loathed on account of their shameful/abominable practices' (*per flagitia invisos*).[33] Given that a clear link is being made here between the Christians, on the one hand, and their author, Christus, on the other, the implication could not be clearer that his behaviour was likely to have been no less shameful than theirs. As Meier observes, 'By implication, the same hateful vices of the movement that caused their execution under Nero caused the execution of Christ under Tiberius'.[34]

Precisely how Christian behaviour was shameful, Tacitus typically does not spell out. *Flagitium* itself does not signify a specific offence but is a general term for 'a shameful act, an offence against decent feeling, an outrage, enormity, sin'.[35] Lest, however, his audience/readers should *not* be inclined to put the worst possible construction upon the word, Tacitus helpfully steers them in that direction. Through unmistakable allusions to Livy's lurid account of the clandestine activities of the devotees of Bacchus suppressed by the senate in 186 BCE,[36] he indicates very clearly the lines along which their thoughts should run. That text will have been thoroughly familiar to the members of Tacitus's audience, given the importance placed by Roman educators on Livy's patriotic history of Rome.[37]

So what was the construction that Tacitus's readers were being encouraged to place upon his reference at *Annals* 15.44.2 to *flagitia*? Generally scholars see this as a covert allusion to incest and cannibalism,[38] crimes for

33. *Annals* 15.44.2. Tacitus, of course, cannot have known what the common people of Rome in Nero's day (the *vulgus*/mob) thought about the Christians. The view that he attributes to them is probably no more than a reflection of what he himself and his social peers thought about Christians. On this and other signs of early second-century ideology at *Annals* 15.44, see Shaw, 'Myth of the Neronian Persecution', 86–7.

34. Meier, *A Marginal Jew*, 1:91.

35. *OLD*, *s.v. flagitium* 4a.

36. Livy, *History of Rome* 39.8-19. Tacitus's referencing of Livy was noticed long ago by Gibbon. See *Decline and Fall*, 2:61 nn. 168 and 169.

37. Quintilian, *Inst. Or.* 4. 5.18. On Livy as a repository of *exempla virtutis* (models of virtue), see Gibson and Morello, *Reading the Letters*, 115 n. 40. Presumably that was why the Elder Pliny prescribed as a 'homework exercise' for the teenage Pliny the taking of extracts from that work (Pliny, *Ep.* 6.16.7) and Pliny's own emphasis on his dutiful performance of that task (*Ep.* 6.20.5). He persevered with it, notwithstanding the ongoing spectacular eruption of Vesuvius!

38. E.g., Furneaux and Ash in their respective commentaries on this passage. Historical Jesus specialists usually refrain from making any comment on these alleged Christian *flagitia*.

which Christians were increasingly accused from the middle of the second century onwards.[39] However, in Livy's narrative, the text to which Tacitus clearly is directing the thoughts of his readers, neither of those offences features among the *flagitia* allegedly committed by the votaries of Bacchus. Mostly Livy contents himself with vague 'and perhaps exaggerated'[40] references to general criminality and debauchery, the latter especially. Fairly typical of his comments is the following: 'With men mingling with women and additionally with the permissiveness of darkness, no crime (*facinus*), no outrage (*flagitium*) had been left uncommitted there. There were more obscenities (*stuprum*) practised between men than between men and women'.[41] This lack of specificity on Livy's part suggests that the traditional interpretation of *flagitia* of *Annals* 15.44 is probably anachronistic.[42] Very likely Tacitus is doing no more in this passage than using dog-whistle tactics to stir up prejudice against the Christians and their founder, Christ, knowing full well that the elite Romans in his audience had been conditioned through their study of Livy during their schooldays to believe that any adherent of an *externa superstitio* (foreign superstition), and especially one whose cult-meetings were clandestine, was likely to be *flagitiosus* (i.e., given to outrageous/shameful practices).

5.3. *The Final Segment of Tacitus' 'Christus' Sentence*

While Tacitus's opening words do no more than hint at the despicable character of 'Christianity's' founder, his final comment, placed for maximum impact at the very end of the Christus sentence, is unambiguously negative. As a man who had suffered the supreme penalty at the hands of the Roman authorities (*supplicio affectus erat*),[43] Christus can have been no more than a common criminal.

To biblical scholars it tends to come as a bit of a surprise that Tacitus makes no mention in this sentence of either the manner of Christ's

---

39. For a brief discussion of the ancient evidence, all of it Christian and apologetic, see Wilken, *Christians as the Romans Saw Them*, 17–21 and, at far greater length, Wagemakers, 'Incest, Infanticide, and Cannibalism', 337–54.

40. Gibbon, *Decline and Fall*, 2:61 n. 169.

41. Livy, *History of Rome* 39.13.10.

42. For Cook's entirely justifiable warnings about over-interpreting this passage, see his *Roman Attitudes*, 47 and 57. Interestingly, at *Annals* 15.37.4, the previous occasion on which Tacitus uses the word *flagitium* (this time of Nero), it clearly signifies gross sexual practices, but not incest.

43. On this common euphemistic expression for capital punishment, see Keith R. Bradley, 'Suetonius, *Nero* 16.2: "afflicti suppliciis Christiani"', *CR* 22 (1972): 9–10.

death (i.e., crucifixion)[44] or his resurrection. Cook, for instance, finds it 'intriguing that there is not a shred of a mention of the claim that Christ was raised from the dead'.[45] There are, however, good reasons for Tacitus's silence here. To mention Christ's resurrection (assuming, of course, that Tacitus knew about this tenet of the Christian faith[46]) would imply that there was something rather special about him, a concession that Tacitus (unlike Pliny) was not prepared to make. And the spelling out of the precise nature of Christ's end was not only unnecessary (it was sufficient for Tacitus's purpose that the Roman authorities had regarded him as a common criminal) but it would have offended against good taste. The genre of historiography required the avoidance of anything coarse and commonplace.[47] What could be coarser and more commonplace than crucifixion – a thoroughly degrading form of execution reserved largely for slaves?[48]

Sandwiched between this emphatically negative closure to the Christus sentence and the opening insinuation about Christ's shamelessness are two seemingly neutral pieces of information: first, the Tiberian date of his execution (*Tiberio imperitante*), and, second, the authorization of that act by the procurator, Pontius Pilatus (*per procuratorem Pontium Pilatum*). But are these comments about 'Jesus' as neutral as is generally assumed?

5.4. *The Tiberian Date of the Execution of Christus*

In almost all the discussions of this passage that I have read, the phrase, *Tiberio imperitante* ('while Tiberius was imperator/emperor'), is passed over in silence, presumably because of its apparently uncontroversial

---

44. Meier, *A Marginal Jew*, 1:90 and Van Voorst, *Jesus*, 47 both draw attention to this omission.

45. Cook, *Roman Attitudes*, 50.

46. The first surviving classical writer to do so is Celsus. See Origen, *Contra Celsum* 2.54-55.

47. See Goodyear, *Tacitus*, 27–8, where he contrasts the different ways in which Suetonius and Tacitus, both using a common source, treat the last hours and death of the emperor Vitellius. While the narrative of Suetonius in his biography of that emperor (*Vitellius*, 16–17) is 'circumstantial and sordid', Tacitus, with his 'greater sense of the dignity of history' not only strips out the sordid but 'verges on the poetical' and is 'calculated(ly) vague'.

48. On the reluctance of elite Roman writers, 'the cultured literary world', to make any mention of this common punishment, see Martin Hengel, *Crucifixion*, trans. John Bowden (London: SCM, 1977), 38.

character.[49] The general scholarly consensus, arrived at after centuries of meticulous research, is that Jesus was crucified *ca.* 30 CE,[50] a date which places him squarely within Tiberius's reign (14–37 CE). But familiar as the Tiberian date of the crucifixion is *to us*, that may well not have been the case with elite Romans in the early second century CE. Although the Christian 'superstition' itself certainly was causing disquiet in elite Roman circles at that time, there is nothing to suggest that that disquiet had led to much interest in the actual origins of the cult. Pliny, for instance, seems to have been interested only in what present-day Christians were getting up to, not the history of their movement. Suetonius likewise is concerned only with Christian behaviour (*Nero* 16.2), not with their origins. That situation prompts an obvious question: why did Tacitus regard it as desirable to draw attention to the Tiberian date of 'Christianity'?[51]

Tacitus, as was pointed out earlier, 'almost never did anything inadvertently'.[52] Not only is the scrupulousness with which he chooses his words universally acknowledged;[53] the care and sophistication with which he could handle chronological matters draws widespread admiration too.[54] When it comes to indicating when individual events took place, Tacitus clearly is not content to use only the dating system by consuls traditional with writers of annalistic history.[55] Rather, he uses a variety of ways to

---

49. The only scholar known to me who attempts to get any mileage out of it is the arch-sceptic, Hochart. Observing at *Persécution des Chrétiens sous Néron*, 76–7 that the expression is unusual for Tacitus ('étrangère au style de Tacite'), he tries to use this as proof of the inauthenticity of *Annals* 15.44. For pertinent criticism of Hochart on this point, see Furneaux, *comm. ad loc.*, who points out that the expression, although very rare in Tacitus, is not confined to *Annals* 15.44.

50. See, for instance, Meier, *A Marginal Jew*, 1:89.

51. For Tacitus's knowledge of the history of early Roman Judaea (6–66 CE), see *Histories* 5.9.2–10.1 and *Annals* 12.54. That one of the missing Tiberian books of the *Annals* could well have contained some mention of Pilate's ten-year governorship of Judaea is hypothesized by Syme at *Tacitus*, 1:449 n. 7, Judaea being such a crucial element in the overall structure of the *Annals*. It was the revolt there in 66 CE that played a significant part in the downfall of Nero and the replacement of the Julio-Claudian dynasty with the Flavian.

52. Gruen, *Rethinking the Other*, 180.

53. See n. 19 above.

54. Martin and Woodman, *Annals IV*, 14 and 78.

55. That involved opening each year's narrative with the names of the two consuls who had taken up office on 1 January (as in the examples in nn. 60 and 61 below) and then compiling an otherwise undated list of the noteworthy events, foreign and domestic, that had occurred during their tenure.

indicate when things happened, his choice dependent upon the precise point he wants to make.

Calendrical dating, for instance, a method favoured by compilers of archives, he largely avoids since it was considered to lack the elegance required for historical writing.[56] Used only once in the *Annals*, it clearly was chosen to underline a moment of high drama – Nero's first public appearance as emperor in the wake of Claudius's death (or murder): *Tunc medio diei tertium ante Idus Octobris, foribus palatii repente diductis... Nero egreditur* ('Then, at mid-day, on the third before the Ides of October (13 October), the doors of the palace suddenly were flung open and Nero stepped forth').[57]

Dating by regnal (i.e., imperial) years likewise is almost entirely eschewed. Here, however, the avoidance is for ideological rather than literary reasons: using imperial years to date events would imply recognition, even approval, of a system which had put an end to political freedom (*libertas*) at Rome and that was something that the conservative Tacitus was most reluctant to do.[58] On the sole occasion when he does make reference to a regnal year, at the start of his narrative for 23 CE (*Annals* 4.1.1), it is to draw attention to its watershed character. It was Tacitus's firm belief that it was in that year, 'Tiberius's ninth' (*nonus Tiberio annus*), that the latter's rule took a definite and irreversible turn for the worse.[59]

And even when Tacitus does use the consular dating system conventional in annalistic history, he modifies it in a highly suggestive manner. By altering syntactically the way in which the names of those two officials are presented – i.e., by shunting their names into an ablative absolute rather than presenting them in the nominative,[60] he neatly demonstrates the marginalization under the Principate of that once quasi-royal pair, the two magistrates who under the Republic had effectively ruled the state during their year in office and given that year its name in perpetuity.[61]

---

56. On this literary convention, see Millar, *Cassius Dio*, 44.

57. *Annals* 12.69. On the build-up to this dramatic event, see *Annals* 12.66-68.

58. Syme, *Tacitus*, 1:390 – 'the Roman senator could not bear to use the regnal years of emperors'.

59. For discussion of the multiple dating systems used by Tacitus to mark this crucial year, see Martin and Woodman, *Annals IV*, commentary on *Annals* 4.1.1.

60. As at *Annals* 1.55.1 (15 CE); 2.1.1 (16 CE); 2.41.2 (17 CE); 2.59.1 (19 CE).

61. On the different ways in which Livy and Tacitus introduce the names of the annual consuls and the significance of this, see Martin and Woodman, *Annals IV*, commentary on *Annals* 4.1.1. Only when the emperor is one of the consuls who

Given this close attention to presentation in matters of dating, it seems only reasonable to assume that Tacitus's statement that the reign of Tiberius was the time when Jesus was executed can only be deliberate. This, after all, was not information that, on the face of it, he needs to provide.

So what is the point that Tacitus is intent on making here? From the perspective of Tacitus and his elite audience, the reign of Tiberius was not a distant era. Men were still alive and active who had been born under that emperor – e.g., the imperial councillors (*amici*) Vestricius Spurinna (born *ca.* 23 CE) and Arrius Antoninus, the grandfather of the future emperor, Antoninus Pius (born in 30 CE).[62] For men such as these and, of course, for Tacitus himself, the Christian superstition was not some venerable old cult, its origins lost in the mists of time, but a relatively new phenomenon, 'a recent invention'.[63]

But why was that worth emphasizing? For Tacitus, as for most members of the Roman elite, novelty (*novitas*) was something of which to be deeply suspicious – the expression, *res novae* (new things), did, after all, signify political revolution or engagement in subversive or seditious activities.[64] Antiquity, by contrast, was a quality to be revered. We have already had occasion to remark upon Tacitus's nostalgia for the Republic, a system of government he believed to be superior to the Principate. This was far from being the only area, however, where his reverence for the past is on display. It is also to be seen in the sphere of religion. Tacitus is on record for his belief that what really counted in matters of cult was their age: much as he disapproved of Judaism, for instance, he refused to condemn it utterly, since its rites were 'defended by their antiquity' (*hi ritus...antiquitate defenduntur*).[65] His whole treatment of cultic issues in the *Annals* reveals an individual for whom what was ancient exercised the greatest attraction. This can be observed in, firstly, his detailed coverage at *Annals* 6.12 of an arcane matter relating to the college of the *Quindecimviri Sacris Faciundis* (the Fifteen

opens the year, as in 18 and 21 CE (*Annals* 2.53.1 and 3.31.1), is the ablative absolute abandoned in favour of a nominative construction, since the emperor clearly is not a marginal figure.

62. For Pliny's letters to these men, see *Ep.* 3.10 and 5.17 (Spurinna) and *Ep.* 4.3; 4.18 and 5.15 (Arrius Antoninus). For the long and distinguished careers of both, see Crook, *Consilium Principis*, 151 (no. 32) and 188 (no. 339).

63. Meier, *A Marginal Jew*, 1:90.

64. *OLD, s.v. novus* 10a and 10b.

65. *Histories* 5.1.1.

Men for the Performance of Sacred Rituals), the ancient and prestigious priestly order of which he was such a proud member;[66] secondly, in the special treatment he accords the ancient temples destroyed in Nero's fire: only those of the regal period and the even earlier mythical period are identified by name (*Annals* 15.41.1) and, thirdly, in his veneration for the Sibylline Books, a collection of ancient oracles regarded as so special that consultation of them took place only on those (fortunately rare) occasions when Rome itself was in existential danger. Tacitus, as a member of the Quindecimviral college, was one of custodians of those sacred texts. The high regard in which he held them can be deduced from his detailed description of the rituals prescribed by them in the aftermath of the 'Great Fire' of 64 CE (*Annals* 15.44.1) – information, significantly, supplied by no other source for that catastrophe.

The flip-side of this veneration for the antique was, of course, contempt for the new. It is this value system, I suggest, that induces Tacitus to give such prominence to the Tiberian date of the life and death of Christ.

In holding such views, Tacitus was far from alone. His contemporary, Suetonius, also a traditionalist in matters of religion,[67] is on record as approving of Nero's punishment of the Christians on the grounds that theirs was 'a new and evil superstition' (*superstitio nova ac malefica*).[68] Nor is this view confined to the period of Tacitus and Suetonius. In the writings of later pagan critics of the cult of Christ, among the reasons regularly put forward for not taking it seriously, indeed for condemning it, is its recent origin. Celsus brings this charge against 'Christianity' again and again,[69] comparing it unfavourably with ancestral cults so old that their origins are lost in the mists of time. The idea surfaces yet again in the works of Libanius and the emperor Julian (fourth century CE). Even though by that stage 'Christianity' was several centuries old, Christ was still viewed as 'a recent intruder'[70] who could be summarily dismissed as 'that newfangled Galilaean god'.[71]

---

66. One of Tacitus's few autobiographical comments relates to his membership of that ancient college. See *Annals* 11.11.1.

67. Wallace-Hadrill, *Suetonius*, 131–2.

68. Suetonius, *Nero* 16.2.

69. See Origen, *Contra Celsum*, 1.26; 2.4; 6.10; 8.12 (each passage containing a quotation from Celsus's work).

70. Libanius, *Or.* 13.12.

71. Julian, *Ep.* 55, where he also writes of the 'divinity falsely ascribed to him'.

5.5. Death through the Agency of the Procurator, Pontius Pilatus

And what of the one outstanding element of Tacitus's Christus sentence to require consideration – namely, his reference to the snuffing out of Christ *per procuratorem Pontium Pilatum*? Is this as negative as the remainder of the sentence has been argued here to be? The possibility that Tacitus's language in this phrase may be deliberately demeaning rarely gets an airing in the extensive literature on this passage.[72] The scholarly consensus rather is that this is simply a neutral, rather basic statement, whose only defect is Tacitus's apparent mistake over Pilate's title. Routinely we find it averred that the dedicatory inscription from Caesarea Maritima put up by Pilate in his official capacity as *praefectus Iudaeae* (i.e., governor of Judaea[73]) 'prove[s] beyond any doubt' that Tacitus must be in error here.[74] To date, I have come across only one scholar – namely, Stauffer – who refuses to believe that Tacitus was capable of making such a mistake.[75]

For the alleged error itself three explanations are commonly put forward. Some attribute Tacitus's apparent slip to 'a certain fluidity of terminology regarding the titles of the governor of Judaea, *at least in popular usage*, during the period AD 6–66'.[76] Others think 'procurator' is an inadvertent anachronism, Tacitus casually applying to Pilate a term current in his own day but not actually used in Judaea until the time of Claudius (41–54 CE).[77] A third group of scholars, while conceding that the application to Pilate of the term procurator is anachronistic, believes that

72. For an exception, see the present writer in Keith et al., eds, *The Reception of Jesus*, 3:66–7. The hypothesis to be advanced here represents both a modification and an amplification of the position taken in that essay.

73. For this text, see now *CIIP* II no. 1277.

74. Theissen and Mertz, *Historical Jesus*, 83 n. 59. For similar assessments of the evidence, see the works listed by Louis H. Feldman in *Josephus and Modern Scholarship (1937–1980)* (Berlin: de Gruyter, 1984), Section 15.10.

75. See Ethelbert Stauffer, *Die Pilatusinschrift von Caesarea.* Erlanger Universitätsreden, N.F.12 (Erlangen, 1966), as summarized by Feldman at *Josephus and Modern Scholarship*, 319 – 'Stauffer finds it difficult to believe that Tacitus was guilty of an anachronism, assumes that he had good grounds for calling him a procurator, and predicts that some day Tacitus may be proven right'.

76. Harris, 'References to Jesus', 349–50 (my italics). This explanation is also to be found at Meier, *A Marginal Jew*, 1:100 n. 8 – 'it is not impossible that...*people spoke loosely* (my italics) of either "the prefect" or "the procurator"'.

77. Evans, 'Jesus in non-Christian Sources', 465 and Ash, *Annals XV*, 205. For Barrett ('Great Fire', 165), so serious is this 'elementary historical anachronism' that he regards it as *prima facie* evidence for the Christus sentence being a Christian

this anachronism was deliberate: in the interests of easy comprehension Tacitus had opted to use a term with which his audience/readership would have been more familiar and so more comfortable.[78]

But plausible as each of these explanations sounds, all are fatally undermined by their failure to take any account of the ways in which Tacitus, a meticulous literary craftsman and serious researcher, operates. Take the accusations of looseness in the use of language and carelessness with factual detail. That flies in the face of the general consensus among Taciteans that, by ancient standards, Tacitus is the most exacting and precise of writers[79] and 'the most accurate of all the Roman historians'.[80] While it would be wrong to claim that he never makes a single mistake,[81] classicists and ancient historians are unanimous in their conviction that the detectable errors in his work are not only largely trivial but few and far between. Indeed, some of the errors might even be scribal.[82]

One area where Tacitus can be seen to have exercised especial care is that of titulature. Since his concern in the *Annals* is largely with the conduct of Roman public affairs, inevitably frequent references have to be made to the various public offices held by the elite – whether the traditional urban magistracies like the consulship, or the new prefect-ships, administrative and/or military, that came in with the Principate (e.g., the Praetorian Prefectship and the fleet-commands), or the increased number of provincial governorships brought about by either conquest or the absorption of client states. Despite the frequency with which he has to handle titulature, errors (with the sole possible exception of Pilate's title) appear to be non-existent. Certainly I have not been able to find any alleged mistakes, despite searching diligently to find them.

To be sure, Tacitus does not always present titles in the form in which they invariably appear in public inscriptions. *Legatus Augusti pro praetore*, the official designation for the governor of an imperial province,

interpolation. For the actual change of title under Claudius from prefect to procurator and the likely reasons for it, see Barbara Levick, *Claudius* (London: Batsford, 1990), 48–9. The change itself was not confined to Judaea.

78. See, for instance, Eddy and Boyd, *Jesus Legend*, 181–2 and Shaw, 'Myth of the Neronian Persecution', 86 (deliberate modernizing).

79. Goodyear, *Tacitus*, 36 and *Annals of Tacitus*, 1:22, where Tacitus is described as 'a meticulous and self-conscious stylist' with an 'obsessive concern to find words which are, for his purposes, exactly right in quality and tone'.

80. Ronald Mellor, *Tacitus* (New York: Routledge, 1993), 40.

81. See Syme, *Tacitus*, 2:746–8 (= Appendix 61) for a discussion of some of them.

82. Syme, *Tacitus*, 2:747.

for instance, never appears in his works.[83] Such clunky terminology would have been considered totally inappropriate for historiography, a genre requiring elegant prose.[84] What we find instead is an immense array of elegant variations for official titulature, *variatio* (variation) being a highly esteemed literary skill.[85] The title *praefectus praetorio*, for instance, is never used, despite the frequent appearance of praetorian prefects in the *Annals*, most notably Sejanus.[86] Instead, we find a number of sonorous variants for their title – e.g., *praetoriarum cohortium praefectus*.[87] And rather than refer to the commander of the imperial fleet based in the Adriatic as *praefectus classis*, Tacitus extravagantly describes him as *praefectus remigum qui Ravennae haberentur* ('the prefect of the oarsmen who are based at Ravenna').[88]

Given these examples, which could easily be multiplied, the conclusion seems inescapable that titulature was not a matter which Tacitus ever treated casually. That being the case, the accusations of carelessness and thoughtlessness so lightly levelled at him for referring to Pilate as a procurator would appear to be ill-conceived. The view that Tacitus had 'naively retrojected' later Claudian usage into an earlier period seems particularly ill-judged.[89] A less naïve writer than Tacitus it would be hard to find.

Also questionable is the idea that Tacitus deliberately used the anachronistic term procurator in the interests of user-friendliness – a concept wholly unknown in the ancient world. The hallmark of Tacitus's Latin is its deliberately engineered complexity. Not only is his syntax generally strained and unnatural but his vocabulary is designed to arouse interest

83. On Tacitus's total avoidance of this cumbersome title, see Syme, *Tacitus*, 1:343–4 – 'He will go to any lengths or contortions rather than denominate the governor of an imperial province by the exact title'.

84. Goodyear, *Tacitus*, 36.

85. On *variatio* in Tacitus, see Walker, *Annals*, 52–7 (both vocabulary and syntax) and Woodman, *Annals*, xx–xxi.

86. Especially in *Annals* 4-6. For the collected references to him, see Yardley, *Tacitus*, 527 under Aelius Sejanus, Lucius.

87. *Annals* 1.7.2. For other variants, see *Annals* 1.24.1 (*praetorii praefectus*) and 4.1.1 (*cohortibus praetoriis praefectus*). For general discussion, see Goodyear, *Annals of Tacitus*, 1:342–5 (Appendix 4).

88. *Annals* 13.30. Pliny, another noted stylist, similarly resorts to elegant periphrasis when referring to his uncle's position as commander of Rome's western fleet. See *Ep.* 6.16.4 – *erat Miseni classemque imperio praesens regebat* ('He was at Misenum and was exercizing command of the fleet in person').

89. Meier, *A Marginal Jew*, 1:100 n. 8.

and to challenge.[90] Tacitus seems to go out of his way to employ words
that were unusual, even obscure. Multiple instances of the rare, the poetic
and the archaic have been identified in his writings.[91] On the odd occasion,
he even revives obsolete terminology. Thus in several places we find him
'idiosyncratically' referring to the proconsuls as praetors,[92] the latter term
having been abandoned as a title for provincial governors as far back
as the time of Augustus.[93] Such a calculated use of the recherché surely
renders utterly implausible the idea that Tacitus opted to call Pontius
Pilate a procurator for reasons of easy comprehension.[94]

If, then, neither of the regular explanations for Tacitus's employment
of the term procurator in the passage under review is convincing, how is
it to be accounted for?

5.6. *Tacitus's Employment of the Term Procurator a Rhetorical Ploy?*

Throughout my analysis of Tacitus's brief portrayal of Christus, I have
consistently stressed its rhetorical character: through the skilful selection
of facts and the even more skilful placement of them, Tacitus succeeds in
depicting Christus as a somewhat unsavoury figure of very little consequence. Whereas Pliny allowed for some positive inferences about Christ
to be drawn from the behaviour of his adherents, not least their worship
of him as a god, Tacitus does not permit so much as a hint of the positive
about the author of 'Christianity' to appear.[95] Given this thoroughgoing,
calculated use of the tools of rhetoric to discredit Christ, it is surely not
unreasonable to assume that a similar motivation might well have been at
work in the dubbing of the man responsible for Christ's death a procurator.

90. Goodyear, *Annals of Tacitus*, 1:26; Martin and Woodman, *Annals IV*, 19–26
(Language and Expression).

91. For detailed analysis, see Syme, *Tacitus*, 2:724–77 (Appendix 52); for a brief
overview, see Kraus and Woodman, *Latin Historians*, 111.

92. E.g., *Annals* 1.74.1 and 4.15.2.

93. For this 'idiosyncratic archaism' on the part of Tacitus, see Woodman, *Annals*,
359 (Appendix A) and Syme, *Tacitus*, 1:343. For Tacitus's possible reason for using
it, see Martin and Woodman, *Annals IV*, 139 (note on *Annals* 4.15.2).

94. Although I flirted with this idea in my previous piece (see Keith et al., eds, *The
Reception of Jesus*, 3:67 n. 55), I now realize that it is not tenable.

95. On Tacitus's deliberate omission of the favourable in order to persuade his
audience/readership to conclude the worst about someone, see J. González, 'Tacitus,
Germanicus, Piso and the Tabula Siarensis', *AJP* 120, no. 1 (1999): 123–42 (especially, 128 and 140–1, where Tacitus's deliberate suppression of those parts of the
official record favourable to the emperor Tiberius is clearly set out).

Several considerations suggest that that was the case. Take, for a start, the very title procurator. That it was far less prestigious than *praefectus* is incontestable.[96] Whereas the latter, in origin the title for a military officer, was borne by some of the most important figures in the imperial administration (e.g., the commander of the Praetorian Guard and the chief of police force at Rome[97]), procurators for the most part were fairly lowly civil servants concerned mainly with financial matters. To be sure, some procurators had weighty fiscal responsibilities – men such as Julius Classicianus, who had to ensure that all the revenues due to Rome in post-Boudiccan Britain were efficiently collected.[98] Others, particularly in small provinces such as Judaea, Sardinia and the Alps, had the twin tasks of collecting the revenues and maintaining law and order.[99] But these types of procurator were few and far between. Most were little more than bailiffs and bean-counters. The very meaning of their title, literally caretaker, is indicative of the generally rather humdrum nature of their duties.[100]

Also of relevance here is their social status. All were recruited from the lower echelons of Roman society. Indeed, many procurators were actually freedmen – i.e., ex-slaves.[101] It is this latter fact that enables Tacitus, a social snob to the core, to distort the picture so disgracefully and to treat the whole procuratorial cohort with such contempt. Throughout the *Annals*, procurators are routinely accused of incompetence and/or corruption (often both). Further, they are invariably compared to their immense disadvantage with their social superiors, the governors and the military officers of senatorial rank, with whom they had to work.[102] Not a single procurator emerges with any credit from the pages of the *Annals*

96. Levick, *Claudius*, 48.

97. For these positions, see *OCD³*, *s.v.v. praefectus praetorio* and *praefectus urbi*.

98. For Classicianus, see *Annals* 14.38.3 and *RIB* 1.12 (his epitaph). Now in the British Museum, this inscription gives his full official title – namely, *procurator provinciae Britanniae*.

99. For these so-called praesidial governors, see *OCD³*, *s.v.* procurator, 1.

100. For these steadily proliferating minor imperial bureaucrats, see Dessau's index in *ILS* iii, 403–7 (*procuratores provinciarum*) and 426–32 (*procuratores Augustorum*).

101. The best discussion remains that of P. R. C. Weaver, *Familia Caesaris: A Social Study of the Emperor's Freedmen and Slaves* (Cambridge: Cambridge University Press, 1972), 267–81.

102. See, for instance, *Annals* 12.49; 12.54; 14.32 and 38. We can be absolutely certain that if, as proposed by Syme (n. 51 above), Tacitus had mentioned Pontius Pilatus in the missing Book 7 of the *Annals*, then he would have been compared very unfavourably with Lucius Vitellius, the senatorial legate of Syria, who dismissed him from his post and sent him back to Rome in disgrace.

or from the pages of the *Histories* either for that matter.[103] Unsurprisingly, given Tacitus's notorious antipathy towards high-flying freedmen in the imperial administration, it is Antonius Felix, the only man of libertine status to hold the governorship of Judaea, who is singled out for particular opprobrium. While at *Annals* 12.54.1 Tacitus alleges that Felix exploited his connections at court (his brother was the influential Claudian freedman, Pallas) to secure immunity for his evil deeds (*malefacta*), at *Histories* 5.9.3 he accuses him of using his quasi-regal power to indulge in grossly immoral behaviour – *per omnem saevitiam ac libidinem ius regium servili ingenio exercuit* ('wielding the power of a king with the instincts of a slave, he practised every kind of cruelty and lust').

With a readership/audience thus primed to believe the worst of Rome's second-tier administrators, is it surprising that Tacitus opted to go for the term procurator rather than prefect in characterizing the agent of Christ's execution? What better way could there be of demeaning the founder (*auctor*) himself of the deadly Christian superstition than to have him judged and condemned by such a contemptible functionary?

In using the term procurator for Pilate rather than the latter's preferred title, *praefectus Judaeae*, Tacitus almost certainly was technically incorrect. But the fact that he was not being strictly accurate here would not have bothered one jot either him or his listeners/readers, all of them rhetorically trained. The deliberate 'misuse' of words, especially for the purpose of denigration, was a recognized and approved rhetorical ploy. There was even a formal term for it which captures well its negative intent – it was called, in Latin, *abusio* (abuse) and, in Greek, *catachresis* (κατάχρησις).[104] Tacitus himself, universally recognized as a master rhetorician, can be seen to have been no slouch when it came to using this tactic. The most notorious example is his repeated misapplication of the loaded word *noverca* (step-mother) to Augustus's wife, Livia. Determined to blacken her name, Tacitus repeatedly and misleadingly applies this term to her, often placing it quite deliberately in the part of the sentence where it would cause her the maximum damage – i.e., at the very end.[105]

103. For the procurator Gessius Florus, whose maladministration precipitated the great Judaean revolt of 66 CE, see *Histories* 5.10.1.

104. Kraus and Woodman, *Latin Historians*, 111 and 118 n. 117. For this usage, see also *CGL*, *s.v.* καταχράομαι, 5.

105. See, for instance, Yardley, *Annals of Tacitus*, 398 on 'the deliberate, if imprecise, use of the negative term *noverca*' (comment on *Annals* 1.3.3) and 399 on 'the rhetorical use of "stepmother"' (comment on *Annals* 1.6.2). On Tacitus's willingness to choose words 'for their emotional impact rather than their strict meaning', see Walker, *Annals of Tacitus*, 123 (discussion of *Annals* 2.82.1).

From the foregoing, it can be seen that Tacitus's thumbnail sketch of Christus, far from being bland and merely descriptive, can be construed without any forcing of the evidence as being a subtle and thoroughgoing exercise in denigration. Nor is Tacitus's negativity about Jesus confined to this short sentence. His ensuing comments on the origins of the Christian superstition positively encourage further negative inferences to be drawn about its author (*auctor*).

5.7. *'Christianity's' Origins*

In the sentence just analysed, Tacitus does not disclose in which part of the empire the procurator responsible for authorizing Christ's execution had been operative. Now (in the words that immediately follow) he reveals that it was Judaea. It was there that the evil (*malum*) that was 'Christianity' had first come into being and from there that that 'deadly superstition' (*exitiabilis superstitio*) eventually had spread to Rome and infected Roman society – an inevitable development, given the imperial capital's propensity to attract to itself from everywhere anything that was 'abominable or shameful' (*atrox aut pudendum*).[106]

In focusing the attention of his listeners/readers on the Judaean origin of 'Christianity' Tacitus was once more, through malicious insinuation, encouraging them to think very negatively about Christ and the nature of the movement of which he had been the founder. Notwithstanding the fact that the population of the province of Judaea was ethnically quite varied,[107] elite Romans tended to treat the term Judaea as a kind of shorthand for 'land of the Jews',[108] a subject people they could rarely bring themselves to mention without resorting to disparagement.[109] Tacitus, himself, had

---

106. *Annals* 15.44.3. On the *topos* (literary commonplace) of Rome's centripetal pull on undesirable peoples and practices, especially from the East, see Ash, *Annals XV*, 206. In Livy's account of the suppression of the Bacchic cult, discussed above, attention is drawn at the very start to its eastern origin and hence to its inherently reprehensible character. See Livy, *History of Rome* 39.8.3.

107. On the ethnically mixed population of Caesarea Maritima, for instance, see Josephus, *War* 2.266-70 and *Ant.* 20.173-78.

108. See, for instance, Pliny, *Nat.* 13.46 and Dio, *Roman History* 37.16.5.

109. On the rarity of positive notices about the Jews in Latin literature in the period between Cicero and Tacitus, see Margaret H. Williams, 'Latin Authors on Jews and Judaism', in *The Eerdmans Dictionary of Early Judaism*, ed. John J. Collins and Daniel C. Harlow (Grand Rapids: Eerdmans, 2010), 870–5. Those of Flavian date, unsurprisingly, are entirely negative. See, for instance, Pliny, *Nat.* 13.46; Martial, *Epigrams* 9.94 and Quintilian, *Inst. Orat.* 3.7.21.

earlier (*Histories* 5.2-9) shown himself to be a master of this kind of denigration. In the ethnographic survey with which he had prefaced his account of the Flavians' final assault on Jerusalem in 70 CE and their 'capture' (i.e., subjugation) of Judaea, he had indulged to the full the (presumed) anti-Jewish prejudices of his audience. Greek and Latin literature abounds in anti-Jewish tropes.[110] All these and more are given a full airing in Tacitus's notorious overview of Jewish ancestral customs in *Histories* 5, the unforgettable punchline of which is that those customs are simply 'absurd and mean'.[111]

Given Tacitus's reputation at that time as Rome's premier rhetorician and man-of-letters and the popularity of *recitationes* (pre-publication public readings), this ethnographic tour de force[112] must have been known to many of his social peers.[113] Given their sophistication, most will easily have picked up the point he was bent on making here at *Annals* 15.44 – namely, that Christus and the adherents of this new Christian *superstitio* were no better than, indeed as pernicious as, those attached to the ancient Jewish *superstitio* of which they were a mere offshoot.[114] Lest any of them should be slow to do so, Tacitus provides a helpful prod by deliberately echoing the phraseology of that earlier ethnographic survey – just as the Jews in that piece (*Histories* 5.5.2) had been charged with being possessed of a hatred for all non-Jews (*adversus omnes alios hostile odium*), so the Christians here (*Annals* 15.44.4) are characterized by their hatred of the human race (*odio humani generis*).[115]

By implying that the Christians of Neronian Rome essentially were Jewish, Tacitus is, of course, being seriously misleading. As can be seen from Paul's letter to the Romans, generally dated to the mid- to late 50s CE,[116] the Christian community at Rome by that time was already comprised of both Gentiles and Jews.[117] Tacitus, a man clearly well

---

110. For a comprehensive survey of these, see Schäfer, *Judeophobia*.

111. *Histories* 5.5.5 – *Iudaeorum mos absurdus sordidusque*.

112. For a detailed literary analysis of this, see René S. Bloch, *Antike Vorstellungen vom Judentum. Der Judenexkurs des Tacitus im Rahmen der griechisch-römischen Ethnographie*, Historia Einzelschriften 160 (Stuttgart: Franz Steiner, 2002).

113. On a likely public reading at Rome of at least one part of the *Histories*, see Pliny, *Ep.* 9.27 (discussed above at Chapter 4 n. 66).

114. For Tacitus's references to Judaism as a *superstitio*, see *Histories* 5.5.2; 5.3 and 13.1; *Annals* 2.85.4.

115. For an illuminating discussion of the relationship between these two passages, see Schäfer, *Judeophobia*, 190–1.

116. James D. G. Dunn, *Romans 1–8*, WBC 38A (Waco: Word, 1988), xliii–iv.

117. For full discussion, see Lampe, *From Paul to Valentinus*, 69–79.

informed about cultic matters at Rome,[118] very likely will have known that too. However, it suits his rhetorical purpose in this passage to depict the movement founded by Christ as Jewish and therefore abhorrent – indeed so abhorrent that the Christians' punishment after the great fire was thoroughly merited (*novissima exempla meritos*), even if the formal charges brought against them had been, at least in part, bogus.

Tacitus's treatment of Christus, then, is far from being as straightforward as it is usually assumed to be. Here we have no simple statement of facts but a carefully wrought piece of prose by a master of rhetoric, the intention of which is to cast both Christus and his adherents in a very unfavourable light. In doing this, Tacitus clearly is at odds with Pliny, whose letter on the Christians he could well be critiquing very subtly here.[119] Whereas the latter had been prepared to admit that the *flagitia* with which the Christians were commonly associated (*flagitia cohaerentia nomini*) lacked any substance, Tacitus allows the popular belief that the Christians were prone to committing shameful acts (*flagitia*) to stand unchallenged. Whereas Pliny was ready to accept that Christus was, for his devotees at least, an object of worship, indeed a god, for Tacitus he is no more than a common Jewish criminal whose offences had been of sufficient gravity to merit the Roman official in charge of Judaea condemning him to death.

The reasons for these differences are not hard to guess. Partly they must be a consequence of each of these writers having a different target audience and a different purpose. Whereas Pliny needed to whitewash Christus and his devotees in order to secure from Trajan a favourable response to his plea for help,[120] Tacitus will have felt no compunction in pandering to the well-known prejudices of his elite audience. Prominent among those prejudices was an ingrained contempt for the Jewish superstition.[121]

---

118. Barrett, *Nero: A Guide to the Ancient Sources*, 166, deduces this from Tacitus's duties as a *quindecemvir sacris faciundis*.

119. That Tacitus knew, used and even critiqued Pliny's work is certain. For his indisputable use of Pliny's *Panegyricus*, see Whitton, 'Let us Tread', 349. On the close intertextual relationship between Tacitus's works and Pliny's letters, most notably *Ep.* 1.9, see Woodman, 'Tacitus and the Contemporary Scene', 34–5. That the clear verbal correspondences between *Annals* 15.44 and *Ep.* 96.10 are due to Tacitus's direct use of Pliny remains a distinct possibility. However, their common exploitation of Livy's Bacchic narrative cannot be ruled out altogether as an explanation. For Pliny and Tacitus' critiquing of each other's work, see especially Pliny, *Ep.* 7.20.1-3.

120. See Chapter 3 above and Corke-Webster, 'Trouble in Pontus'.

121. See n. 109 above. The centrality of the study of Cicero's orations in Roman rhetorical education (Quintilian, *Inst. Or.* 10.5.18-19) doubtless will helped foster

But a far more important factor surely must be the different dates of the composition of Pliny's letter about the cult of Christ (*ca.* 110 CE) and Tacitus's brief reference to it at *Annals* 15.44 (*ca.* 120 CE). Separating them were the devastating Jewish uprisings that had taken place in several of Rome's eastern provinces in 116/117 CE, most notably Egypt, Cyrene (modern Libya) and Cyprus. These had been on too grand a scale and caused too much destruction not to have caused the Roman establishment considerable anxiety. Indeed, the rising in Egypt must have been especially worrying given the importance of that province to the food supply (*annona*) in Rome.[122] Whether the Jews of Judaea also rose in actual revolt at that time is disputed.[123] However, it seems fairly certain that at the start of Hadrian's reign they were *at the very least* 'showing an eagerness for rebellion' (*rebelles animos efferebant*).[124] Clear proof of the deep anxiety about the loyalty of the Judaean Jews felt by the Romans then (i.e., at that time) is provided by their decision (either late in Trajan's reign or early in Hadrian's) to double the strength of their garrison in that province by stationing there a second legion – a huge military force for such a small area.[125]

Given this situation, it is hardly a surprise that the language Tacitus uses to describe the Christian superstition, whose Judaean origins he is careful to point out, is far more negative than that of Pliny,[126] and his portrayal of Christus himself altogether more hostile.

(and make respectable?) that prejudice. For Cicero's comments on the Jews, see Stern, *Greek and Latin Authors*, 1: nos. 68 (*Pro Flacco* 28:66-69) and 70 (*De prov. Cos.* 5:10-12).

122. On these rebellions, see M. Pucci Ben Zeev, *Diaspora Judaism in Turmoil, 116–117 CE: Ancient Sources and Modern Insights* (Leuven: Peeters, 2005) and 'The Uprisings in the Jewish Diaspora, 116–117', in *The Cambridge History of Judaism*, vol. 4, *The Late Roman-Rabbinic Period*, ed. S. T. Katz (Cambridge: Cambridge University Press, 2006), 93–104.

123. See the authorities cited at William Horbury, *Jewish War under Trajan and Hadrian* (Cambridge: Cambridge University Press, 2014), 259 n. 352.

124. For this description of the Jews of 'Palestine' (*Palaestina*) at the commencement of Hadrian's principate, see *HA*, Hadrianus 5.2. For an excellent, nuanced discussion of the extraordinarily challenging evidence for the Jews of Judaea around this time, see Horbury, *Jewish War*, 257–64.

125. Benjamin Isaac and Israël Roll, 'Judaea in the Early Years of Hadrian's Reign', *Latomus* 38, no. 1 (1979): 54–66, re-printed with Postscript in B. Isaac, *The Near East Under Roman Rule*, Mnemosyne, Supp. 177 (Leiden: Brill, 1998), 182–97.

126. See Furneaux's note on *exitiabilis superstitio* ('pernicious superstition') at *Annals* 15.44.3.

Sharing Tacitus's hostile attitude towards 'Christianity' is his younger contemporary, the scholarly, high-flying imperial bureaucrat, Gaius Suetonius Tranquillus (b. *ca.* 70 CE). As we saw earlier, for him, as for Tacitus, the cult of Christ is an evil, upstart superstition (*superstitio nova ac malefica*).[127] But what is his attitude towards Christ himself? Does he, in fact, voice any opinion about him at all? It is time for us to consider in depth this greatly under-estimated individual and to examine his much-disputed reference to Chrestus[128] in the light of not only his immense erudition but, more particularly, his notable expertise in the field of onomastics.

127. Suetonius, *Nero* 16.2.
128. *Div. Claud.* 25.4.

Chapter 6

SUETONIUS AND CHRESTUS: THE THIRD CLASSICAL WRITER TO REFER TO CHRIST?

6.1. *The Author and his Testimony: A Few Brief Observations*

The third classical writer to refer to the Christians and, in the opinion of many, to refer to Christ too is Gaius Suetonius Tranquillus, a younger contemporary by about ten years of Pliny and by about fifteen of Tacitus.[1] With Pliny, whose steady patronage he enjoyed,[2] Suetonius seems over time to have grown increasingly intimate.[3] Indeed, so close did their relationship become that most scholars now believe that in all likelihood Suetonius accompanied Pliny to Bithynia-Pontus *ca.* 109 CE as part of the latter's official entourage.[4] Some are also of the opinion that, following Pliny's presumed death in office there (*ca.* 111 CE), Suetonius may even have edited his official correspondence with Trajan.[5] A prominent part of

---

1. The scholarly consensus is that Suetonius was born *ca.* 70 CE. The arguments of Barry Baldwin, 'Suetonius: Birth, Disgrace and Death', *Acta Classica* 18 (1975): 61–70 (61–7), for a date around 61/62 CE, though hard to refute, do not appear to have gained traction.

2. Pliny, *Ep.* 1.24; 3.8; 10.94-95.

3. At *Ep.* 1.24.1 and again at *Ep.* 10.94.1 Pliny speaks of Suetonius as his *contubernalis* ('mess-mate'). On this (originally military) term which had come to be used of 'especially treasured individuals', see Gibson and Morello, *Reading the Letters*, 140–1.

4. The case for this, first argued by Syme at *Tacitus*, 2:779 and asserted more forcefully by him in 'The Travels of Suetonius Tranquillus', *Hermes* 109 (1981): 105–17 (107) is now generally accepted.

5. E.g., Syme, *Tacitus*, 2:660 ('Suetonius may have inherited (or sequestered) the papers of his friend and patron') and Williams, *Pliny the Younger*, 4 together with his commentary at *Ep.* 10.94.

this was, as we have seen, their exchange of letters about the Christians and Christus.

For Suetonius's relations with Tacitus there is no direct evidence. That the two were, at the very least, acquainted is highly probable. The parallelism of their literary careers makes it most unlikely that their paths never crossed: both started to make their mark in literary circles at Rome under the emperor Nerva (i.e., *ca.* 97 CE)[6] and both maintained their productivity into the early years, at the very least, of Hadrian's reign (117–138 CE).[7] Given the very public nature of literary activity at Rome, it surely can be safely assumed that both will have participated, whether as performers or listeners, in the *recitationes* that were such a feature of the age. Consequently both are likely to have had more than a passing acquaintance with the other's work.[8] The fact that Tacitus was of senatorial rank and Suetonius only of equestrian will have had no limiting effect upon their social interactions. It is clear from Pliny's letters that easy social relations existed between these two social orders.[9]

Politically, Suetonius appears to have rather more in common with Pliny than with Tacitus. Neither Suetonius nor Pliny seems to have harboured the deep reservations about the Principate to which Tacitus gave voice throughout his various works.[10] Although Pliny is found on a few occasions expressing mild regret that things are not as they used to be

6. By the time that Pliny had published his first book of letters (*ca.* 97 CE), Suetonius's literary reputation was already established. See Pliny, *Ep.* 1.24. For 97/98 CE as the date of the composition of Tacitus's earliest work, the biography of his father-in-law, Gnaeus Julius Agricola, see above Chapter 4 n. 10.

7. For the probable early Hadrianic date of the later books of Tacitus's *Annals*, see Chapter 4 above, nn. 15 and 16; for the Hadrianic date of at least the earliest of Suetonius's Lives of the Caesars, see John the Lydian, *De mag.*, 2.6, where he refers to their dedication to the early Hadrianic Praetorian Prefect, Septicius Clarus. For a full discussion of the problem of dating the Lives of the Caesars, see Gavin Townend, 'The Date of Composition of Suetonius' Caesares', *CQ* 9 (1959): 285–93. How far into the reign of Hadrian these two authors continued writing is not known.

8. That Suetonius knew the text of the *Annals* up to and including the books on Nero's reign has been inferred from certain implied criticisms that he appears to be levelling at it. For a list of these criticisms, see Donna W. Hurley, *Suetonius: Divus Claudius* (Cambridge: Cambridge University Press, 2001), 9 n. 33 and below 115.

9. Wallace-Hadrill, *Suetonius*, 100.

10. For Tacitus's views of the Principate, freedom (*libertas*) and despotism, see Ch. Wirszubski, *Libertas as a Political Idea at Rome during the Late Republic and Early Empire* (Cambridge: Cambridge University Press, 1950), 160–7.

under the Republic,[11] Suetonius appears to have had no regrets whatsoever about the replacement of that system of government by the rule of the Caesars.[12] The renown that he achieved through his distinguished career in the service of the emperors[13] would not have been possible for him under the Republic, given his very 'modest extraction'.[14] At the peak of his public career, when he held the important 'ministerial' post of *ab epistulis*, he not only had overall responsibility for the emperor's official correspondence[15] but he was also an intimate, an official 'friend' (*amicus*), no less, of the emperor Hadrian himself.[16]

In cultic matters, by contrast, Suetonius seems to have more in common with Tacitus than Pliny. Like Tacitus, he shows relatively little interest in the imperial cult.[17] Similarly conservative in matters of religion, Suetonius likewise is mainly concerned with the maintenance of traditional cults.[18] And, like Tacitus, he has no time at all for *superstitiones* – i.e., unauthorized cults of a non-Roman character and largely eastern origin. In his life of Augustus, he notes with approval how the latter deliberately snubbed the all-important cult of Apis while in Egypt (30 BCE) and how subsequently (1 BCE) he praised his grandson Gaius for not paying his respects at the Temple in Jerusalem when visiting Judaea (*Div. Aug.* 93). Throughout the

---

11. *Ep.* 3.7.14; 3.20.10-12. For discussion, see Thomas E. Strunk, 'Pliny the Pessimist', *G&R* 59, no. 2 (2012): 178–92 (187–90).

12. For Suetonius's admiration for Augustus and the Principate, see Wallace-Hadrill, *Suetonius*, 110–12 and Keith Bradley, 'Review Article: The Rediscovery of Suetonius', *CPh* 80, no. 3 (1985): 254–65 (265).

13. For the text and a translation of the fragmentary honorific inscription from Hippo Regius in north Africa (modern Annaba in Algeria) in which his principal public honours and offices are set out, see Appendix 1, C.

14. Ronald Syme, 'Pliny's Less Successful Friends', *Historia* 9, no. 3 (1960): 362–79 (364). For Suetonius's father, Suetonius Laetus, an officer of equestrian rank in Legio XIII, see Suetonius, *Otho* 10.1; for the possibility that his grandfather had been a Praetorian Guardsman, see Gavin Townend, 'The Hippo Inscription and the Career of Suetonius', *Historia* 10 (1961): 99–109 (105–6).

15. For full discussion of Suetonius's tenure of this important post, see H. Lindsay, 'Suetonius as *ab epistulis* to Hadrian and the Early History of the Imperial Correspondence', *Historia* 43, no. 4 (1994): 454–68 and below 112–14.

16. Suetonius, *Div. Aug.* 7.1 and Crook, *Consilium Principis*, 185.

17. On its striking absence from the Lives of the Caesars, see Wallace-Hadrill, *Suetonius*, 131. In Pliny's writings, by contrast, it is quite prominent. On the imperial cult as a *Leitmotif* of both the *Panegyricus* and the tenth book of the letters, see Woolf, 'Pliny's Province', in Gibson and Whitton, eds, *Epistles of Pliny*, 447.

18. Wallace-Hadrill, *Suetonius*, 132. For Tacitus's religious conservatism, see above 85–6.

rest of his Lives of the Caesars he consistently rates as meritorious any attempt on the part of an emperor to suppress 'foreign rituals' (*externae caerimoniae*). Tiberius's actions against the worshippers of Isis, the Jews and Jewish sympathizers at Rome (19 CE), for instance, are chalked up to his credit (*Tiberius* 36), as are the death sentences meted out by Nero to the Christians (*Christiani*) of the imperial capital, the devotees, in his view, of a superstition not only new but actually criminal.[19]

Given such an attitude towards the *Christiani* and their cult, one would not expect Suetonius to have anything very positive to say about Christ himself. Does he, however, have anything to say at all? A majority of scholars, especially those concerned with the early history of the Jesus movement at Rome, are of the opinion that he does. Their evidence? It is simply a brief entry in a short list of measures taken by the emperor Claudius in respect of individuals and communities of peregrine (i.e., alien), as opposed to (Roman) citizen, status.[20] In the Latin (for the moment deliberately left untranslated), the entry runs as follows: *Iudaeos impulsore Chresto assidue tumultuantes Roma expulit.*

Easy though it is to grasp the broad meaning of this piece of typically unflashy, down-to-earth Suetonian prose, producing a satisfactory translation of it, one that pleases the ear, reflects the essential meaning of the Latin and leaves no room for any misunderstanding, is another matter altogether. The one most commonly found in scholarly use is that of Rolfe in the Loeb edition of Suetonius: 'Since the Jews constantly made disturbances at the instigation of Chrestus, he (Claudius) expelled them from Rome'.[21] Although this translation meets the first criterion (readability) well, the same cannot be said in respect of the second (basic meaning) and third (unambiguity). Firstly, it fails to make sufficiently clear that the *impulsor* Chrestus was present *in person* in the events described – indeed, was actually fomenting the continuous riots which resulted in Claudius's

---

19. *Nero* 16.2 (*superstitio nova ac malefica*). For Tacitus's unrelenting scorn for foreign cults, see *Annals* 11.15 and 15.44.

20. For a translation of the full list and a discussion of its literary function and character, see Appendix 2.

21. J. C. Rolfe (trans.), *Suetonius*, LCL, 2 vols (London: William Heinemann, 1913–14; rev. ed. with a new introduction by K. R. Bradley, 1998), 2:53. For its widespread adoption, see, for instance, Stern, *Greek and Latin Authors*, 2: no. 307; Stevenson/Frend, *New Eusebius*, no. 2; Stephen Benko, *Pagan Rome and the Early Christians* (London: Batsford, 1985), 18 and 28 n. 41; Louis H. Feldman and Meyer Reinhold, eds, *Jewish Life and Thought among Greeks and Romans* (Edinburgh: T&T Clark, 1996), 332.

expulsion order.[22] Secondly, and more seriously, it permits those who have already convinced themselves that the sentence must contain a reference to (Jesus) Christ to take the translation, 'at the instigation of Chrestus', to mean 'through the influence of Christ' or even 'under the impulse of Christianity' – interpretations that are not at all obvious if Suetonius's text is read without such a preconception.[23]

Aware of these drawbacks, especially the blunting of the meaning of *impulsor*, Van Voorst decided to offer as an alternative to Rolfe's translation, 'He (*sc.* Claudius) expelled the Jews from Rome, since they were always making disturbances because of the instigator Chrestus'.[24] Although this definitely represents an improvement, it still does not quite catch the forcefulness and largely negative connotations of the word *impulsor*, a noun derived from the verb *impello*, meaning 'to drive forward, set in motion, urge on, impel'.[25]

Given this situation, I here offer as the basis for our discussion the following translation – 'The Jews who were constantly causing disturbances on account of Chrestus's incitement, he (Claudius) expelled from Rome'. Although this lacks the elegance of Rolfe's translation, it does make more explicit the ring-leading role played by Chrestus in the disturbances for which Claudius expelled at least some of Rome's Jews.

Translating the difficult phrase *impulsore Chresto* is not the only challenge, however, presented by Suetonius's 'Jesus' testimony. As is well known, this short sentence of Suetonius, for all the plainness of its Latin, has given rise to a number of intractable problems and, in consequence, generated a vast amount of scholarly literature.[26] Happily for us, there is no need to concern ourselves here with problems such as the date of the expulsion and the relationship between Suetonius's evidence and the other testimonia relating to Claudius's dealing with the Jews of

---

22. In standard Latin usage, an *impulsor* generally is not a remote influence but 'an individual who is present in the envisioned situation as a causal agent'. See Cook, *Roman Attitudes*, 20 for a thorough discussion of the evidence.

23. For the assumption that *Chrestus* is simply a synonym for Christianity, see the authorities cited at Slingerland, *Claudian Policymaking*, 206–9 and by L. V. Rutgers, 'Roman Policy toward the Jews: Expulsions from the City of Rome during the First century C. E.', in *Judaism and Christianity in First-Century Rome*, ed. Karl P. Donfried and Peter Richardson (Grand Rapids: Eerdmans, 1998), 93–116 (105 n. 50).

24. Van Voorst, *Jesus*, 30–1.

25. Lewis and Short, *A Latin Dictionary*, *s.v. impello*, I. B.

26. For a brief overview of both the problems and the bibliography, see Gruen, *Diaspora*, 38–41. For a comprehensive survey of scholarship on this passage from the fifteenth to the late twentieth century, see Botermann, *Das Judenedikt*, 72–95.

Rome, most notably Acts 18:2.[27] In this chapter our principal concern will be with the question of whether Suetonius is, or is not, making some kind of reference to (Jesus) Christ.

On the face of it, that seems rather unlikely. Not only is Christ's name misspelt[28] but the factual content of the passage is at odds with that found in all the other sources for Jesus, whether Jewish (Josephus) or Christian (the gospel narratives) or pagan (Tacitus). They are in agreement that it was under Tiberius (not Claudius) that Jesus met his end, and in Judaea, not Rome.[29]

Such difficulties, however, have not prevented most scholars from believing that this sentence probably does contain one of the all-too-rare, early pagan references to Christ. Indeed, some are so convinced of this that they insist that it lies with those who take an opposing view to prove their case. Thus we find Momigliano, for instance, bullishly declaring 'Those who deny that the "Chrestus" of Suetonius is Christ must undertake the onus of proving their view: the identification is undoubtedly more reasonable, and therefore more probable, than any other solution, and in fact no serious argument has yet been brought against it'.[30] Smallwood felt no less certain about applying an *interpretatio Christiana* to the passage: 'The only reasonable interpretation of Suetonius's sentence is that the reference is to Christianity [*sic*], though he was apparently under the misapprehension that "Chrestus" was a rabble-rouser present in person'.[31] In a later

27. For brief but thorough discussions of the evidence, see Smallwood, *Jews under Roman Rule*, 210–16; Irina Levinskaya, *The Book of Acts in its Diaspora Setting* (Grand Rapids: Eerdmans, 1996), 171–81; J. M. G. Barclay, *Jews in the Mediterranean Diaspora* (Edinburgh: T&T Clark, 1996), 303–6. Exhaustive explorations of the evidence are offered by Slingerland in *Claudian Policymaking*, 151–217 and by Botermann in *Das Judenedikt*, 50–102.

28. On the powerful support supplied by the MSS for Chrestus as the original reading, see Jobjorn Boman, 'Inpulsore Cherestro? Suetonius' Divus Claudius 25.4 in Sources and Manuscripts', *SBFLA* (2011): 355–76, who concludes that the few Christ-spellings that occur most likely are conjectures by Christian scribes or scholars. For Orosius's Christian makeover of *Div. Claud.* 25.4, see H. Dixon Slingerland, 'Suetonius, *Claudius* 25.4, Acts 18, and Paulus Orosius' *Historiarum adversum paganos libri VII*: Dating the Claudian Expulsion(s) of Roman Jews', *JQR* 83 (1992): 127–44. Besides quietly substituting Christus for Chrestus, Orosius also introduces the idea that the 'tumult' in which the Jews were engaged was caused by their opposition to Christ.

29. See above, 54.

30. Arnaldo Momigliano, *Claudius: The Emperor and His Achievement* (Cambridge: Heffer, 1961; reprint with corrections of the 1934 Clarendon ed.), 33.

31. Smallwood, *Jews under Roman Rule*, 211.

work, she goes even further than this, insisting that the real reason for the Chrestus-induced troubles was 'disturbances in the reopened synagogues caused by the advent of Christian missionaries – disturbances such as had resulted from Paul's attempts to evangelize in the synagogues (*sc.* of the eastern provinces)'.[32]

With backing as powerful as this from scholars of such eminence, it is hardly surprising that their view of the passage remains paramount notwithstanding the many decades that have passed since they wrote those words. Today both in textbooks and in works of a more popular character the equation, Chrestus = (Jesus) Christus, is taken virtually as a given. Theissen and Mertz dispose of the matter in a short footnote with these words: 'Chrestiani was a popular designation for Christians; a shift from the unknown "Christus" to the familiar name "Chrestus" is easily imaginable'.[33] The Christian apologist, A. N. Wilson, is even briefer, swatting aside those sceptical of the identification of *Chrestus* as *Christus* thus: 'Only the most perverse of scholars have doubted that "Chrestus" is Christ'.[34]

Given the general acceptance commanded by these views[35] and the failure of such challenges as have been mounted against them to gain significant support,[36] it is perfectly legitimate to ask whether there really is any point in my re-opening the question. The mere existence of this chapter shows that I am convinced that this will be a worthwhile undertaking. Let me now set out my reasons for this belief.

32. E. Mary Smallwood, 'The Diaspora in the Roman Period before CE 70', in *The Cambridge History of Judaism III: The Early Roman Period*, ed. W. Horbury, W. D. Davies, and J. Sturdy (Cambridge: Cambridge University Press, 1999), 176.

33. Theissen and Mertz, *Historical Jesus*, 84 n. 62.

34. A. N. Wilson, *Paul: The Mind of the Apostle* (London: Sinclair-Stevenson, 1997), 104.

35. Such scepticism as is expressed tends to come from non-biblical scholars – e.g., Koestermann, 'Ein Folgenschwerer Irrtum', followed by Heikki Solin, 'Juden und Syrer im westlichen Teil der römischen Welt', *ANRW* II.29.2 (1983): 659 and 690; J. Mottershead, *Suetonius: Claudius* (Bristol: Bristol Classical, 1986), 149–50.

36. On these alternative explanations, see discussion and bibliography at Slingerland, *Claudian Policymaking*, 205–6, to which add Stephen Benko, 'The Edict of Claudius of A.D. 49 and the Instigator Chrestus', *TZ* 25 (1969): 406–18. His hypothesis that Chrestus was a local Jewish political agitator, a Zealot, possibly with messianic leanings, is dismissed by Gruen (*Diaspora*, 271 n. 152) primarily on the grounds that there is not a hint in the sources of any militancy at any time on the part of the Jews of ancient Rome.

6.2. *The Recent Revolution in Suetonian Scholarship*

A notable and surprising feature of nearly all recent discussions of Suetonius's Chrestus text, especially those by biblical and ecclesiastical scholars, is the lack of knowledge or, indeed, of curiosity displayed about Suetonius himself. References to recent and not-so-recent scholarship (i.e., material published since the middle of the last century) are conspicuous by their absence. No use appears to have been made, for instance, of either of the monographs on Suetonius that appeared in 1983 – those of Baldwin and Wallace-Hadrill.[37] Equally unnoticed is Townend's essay on Suetonius, the standard introduction to Suetonius in English prior to those publications.[38] Discussions appear to be driven largely by the belief that Suetonius is a thoroughly incompetent operator. Accusations of ignorance, inaccuracy, carelessness and lack of judgement abound. All too typical is Van Voorst's judgement on Suetonius: 'Repeating a mistake in his sources is characteristic of Suetonius, who often treats them uncritically and uses them carelessly'.[39] On occasion, a reluctance to engage in solid research is also added to the charge-sheet,[40] as is a propensity on Suetonius's part to misunderstand the findings of such research as he happens to have carried out. Thus we find Leon, for instance, berating him for 'misinterpreting his source, *as he not infrequently did*'[41] – an accusation for which he supplies not a shred of supporting evidence.

If we ask why this has come to be the accepted view of Suetonius at least among biblical and ecclesiastical specialists concerned with the possibility of a Christian dimension to *Div. Claud.* 25.4, the reason seems to be a too-great readiness to take at face-value what earlier scholars said about him. The reliance of Lane, for instance, on an article by Janne, published in 1934, in which Suetonius is dismissed as a writer who merely reproduced his sources without attempting to evaluate them carefully,

37. Barry Baldwin, *Suetonius* (Amsterdam: Hakkert, 1983); Wallace-Hadrill, *Suetonius*.

38. G. Townend, 'Suetonius and his Influence', in *Latin Biography*, ed. T. A. Dorey (London: Routledge & Kegan Paul, 1967), 79–111.

39. Van Voorst, *Jesus*, 38.

40. As by F. F. Bruce, 'Christianity under Claudius', *BJRL* 44 (1961/62): 309–26 (316), who compares Suetonius unfavourably on this score with Tacitus.

41. Harry J. Leon, *The Jews of Ancient Rome*, rev. ed. (Peabody: Hendrickson, 1995), 25–6 (my italics). For a similar estimate of Suetonius's capabilities, see James D. G. Dunn, *Jesus Remembered* (Grand Rapids: Eerdmans, 2003), 142.

is one example of this.[42] Another is Van Voorst's approving citation of Howatson's contemptuous remarks about Suetonius: 'Suetonius followed whatever source attracted him, without caring much whether it was reliable or not'.[43]

This unquestioning acceptance of rather dated scholarship is truly unfortunate, since Suetonian studies have undergone a complete revolution during the last half-century or so.[44] The start of Suetonius's rehabilitation can be dated precisely to 1951 with the publication in that year of Steidle's mould-breaking monograph on him.[45] Since then the process of revisionism has gone on unabated. I know of no contemporary classicist or ancient historian who would for a moment subscribe to the contemptuous views, driven largely by moral disapproval,[46] so common in early twentieth-century scholarly writings about Suetonius. Instead of being dismissed as a literary lightweight with a regrettable penchant for the salacious and the trivial,[47] Suetonius is now regarded, as indeed he was throughout antiquity, as a man of wide and impressive learning, the main driving force of whose life was *doctrina* (the pursuit of learning).[48]

42. William L. Lane, 'Social Perspectives on Roman Christianity during the Formative Years from Nero to Nerva: Romans, Hebrews, 1 Clement', in Donfried and Richardson, eds, *Judaism and Christianity in First-Century Rome*, 196–244 (204). For the Janne study, see H. Janne, '*Impulsore Chresto*', in *Mélanges Bidez*, AIPHOS 2 (Brussels: Secrétariat de l'Institut, 1934), 531–53.

43. Van Voorst, *Jesus*, 38. For his bibliographical source for this quotation, see M. C. Howatson, *The Oxford Companion to Classical Literature*, 2nd edn (Oxford: Oxford University Press, 1989), 542. I note that this sentence has been removed from the Suetonius entry in the latest (3rd) edition of this handbook.

44. P. Galland-Hallyn, 'Bibliographie Suétonienne (Les "Vies des XII Césars") 1950–1988: vers une réhabilitation', *ANRW* 2.33.5 (1991): 3576–622.

45. W. Steidle, *Sueton und die antike Biographie*, Zetemata 1 (Munich: Beck, 1951; repr. 1963).

46. See, for instance, J. W. Duff, *A Literary History of Rome in the Silver Age* (London: Unwin, 1927), 508, who condemned the Lives of the Caesars for 'partak(ing) of the nature of a *chronique scandaleuse*'. What aroused his disgust was the explicit material relating to the sexual practices of some of the emperors, most notoriously the alleged perversions of Tiberius (*Tiberius* 43-44).

47. For Sir Paul Harvey, Suetonius was little more than an amusing anecdotalist. See *The Oxford Companion to Classical Literature*, 1st ed. (Oxford: Clarendon, 1937), *s.v.* Suetonius.

48. See Bradley, revised Loeb edition of Suetonius, 1:6. For a list of Suetonius's various biographical, antiquarian and lexicographical works, see Wallace-Hadrill, *Suetonius*, 43 n. 22.

How highly he was esteemed in antiquity is shown by the epithets applied to him by writers ranging in date from the early second to the sixth century CE. Thus we find Pliny describing him as *scholasticus* (scholarly) and *eruditissimus* (most learned),[49] Flavius Vopiscus, one of the pseudonymous authors of the *Historia Augusta* (late fourth century), characterizing him as *emendatissimus et candidissimus* (most correct and most truthful),[50] John the Lydian (sixth century CE) referring to him as *philologos* (lover of learning/studious of words)[51] and the Syrian chronicler, John Malalas of Antioch (also sixth century), rating him as *sophotatos* (most wise/learned).[52]

Unlike that more elegant stylist, Tacitus, whose writings enjoyed no enduring popularity perhaps because of the difficulty of their mannered Latin,[53] Suetonius's various works, especially his Lives of the Caesars (*De vita Caesarum*) and his Lives of Illustrious Men (*De viris illustribus*), continued to be widely appreciated.[54] Some of the greatest scholars of Late Antiquity mined them heavily for their contents. Thus we find, for instance, Jerome (fourth/fifth century CE) making extensive use of Suetonius's Illustrious Men when writing his expanded version of Eusebius's *Chronicle*[55] and Bishop Isidore of Seville (sixth/seventh century CE) no less energetically exploiting Suetonius's lexicographic treatises for his own lexicographical masterpiece, *Etymologiae*.[56] During the Carolingian period, Suetonius's Lives of the Caesars were especially admired. Most famously, the Frankish scholar and courtier, Einhard

49. Pliny, *Ep.* 1.24.4 and 10.94.
50. *HA*, Firmus, Saturninus, Proculus and Bonosus 1.1.
51. John the Lydian, *De mag.* 1.34.
52. Ioannes Thurn, ed., *Ioannis Malalae Chronographia* (Berlin: de Gruyter, 2000), 2:8.14 – ὁ σοφώτατος Σουετώνιος Τραγκύλλος.
53. Within a century and a half of his death (by the mid-270s CE), they were in danger of being lost altogether through lack of readerly interest (*lectorum incuria*). See *HA*, Tacitus 10.3.
54. Of the latter work which originally contained the biographies of about one hundred literary figures, divided into five categories (poets, orators, historians, philosophers, grammarians and teachers of rhetoric), only those in the final category have survived to any great extent. For an excellent commentary on these, see now Kaster's *C. Suetonius Tranquillus: De Grammaticis et Rhetoribus* (hereafter abbreviated as Suetonius, *DGR*).
55. Wallace-Hadrill, *Suetonius*, 51.
56. J. Wood, 'Suetonius and the *De vita Caesarum* in the Carolingian Empire', in *Suetonius the Biographer: Studies in Roman Lives*, ed. T. Power and R. Gibson (Oxford: Oxford University Press, 2014), 273–91 (284–8).

(ninth/tenth century CE), took Suetonius's life of Augustus as his model when composing his celebrated biography of Charlemagne (*Vita Karoli*).[57] In fact, it was not until Victorian times that his reputation plummeted and he became regarded as an author of little consequence.

If we ask why Suetonius's reputation has come to be restored and Suetonius himself to be regarded now as a figure worthy of serious attention, three reasons immediately suggest themselves. The first of these is the transformation of cultural values. Suetonius's descriptions of the sexual practices of the emperors, previously a major factor in his condemnation as an author, no longer evoke the feelings of disgust that they once did. It is hard for us now to appreciate the degree of outrage once caused by these passages which actually constitute a very small part of the Lives of the Caesars. Indeed, so feared was their potential for corruption that the most explicit of them (*Tiberius* 43-44) were even left untranslated in the original Loeb edition of Suetonius (1913) – a situation not reversed, amazingly, until the last quarter of the twentieth century. Also contributing to the low esteem in which Suetonius was held was his practice of incorporating in his lives vulgar material such as graffiti, lewd lyrics and crude quotations from anonymous satirical pamphlets. Once condemned as beneath the dignity of history,[58] they are now seen as providing rare, and therefore precious, evidence for non-elite views of the Caesars. Indeed, in this willingness to take popular culture seriously Suetonius can be said to be well ahead of his time.

The second factor in sparking a re-assessment of Suetonius was the publication in 1952 of an epigraphic find of unusual importance. Discovered in the main square (forum) of the town of Hippo Regius in northern Africa (modern Annaba, formerly Bône, in Algeria), it consisted of the remnants of a substantial text from a monument (probably a statue) set up by the citizenry in honour of Suetonius.[59] Yielding important new information about the latter's public honours and distinguished career as an imperial bureaucrat, this inscription sparked a revival of serious interest in him, especially among English-speaking scholars.[60] Clearly he

57. For a full discussion of this work, see Townend, 'Suetonius and his Influence', 98–106 and, more briefly, Wood, 'Suetonius and the *De vita Caesarum*', 280–3.

58. For Duff, *Literary History of Rome in the Silver Age*, 508, Suetonius was 'too keen upon petty and prurient detail to produce a scientific account of his subjects'.

59. For the *editio princeps* of this text, see E. Marec and H. G. Pflaum, 'Nouvelle inscription sur la carrière de Suétone', *CRAI* (1952): 76–85 = *AE* 1953, no. 73.

60. For early recognition of the significance of this text for re-evaluating Suetonius, see J. A. Crook, 'Suetonius "ab epistulis"', *PCPhS* NS 4 (1956/57): 18–22 and Townend, 'The Hippo Inscription'.

had been a far more significant figure in late Trajanic and early Hadrianic Rome than had hitherto been appreciated.

But most important of all for turning the Suetonian tide was the publication in 1983 of Wallace-Hadrill's seminal monograph on Suetonius.[61] Thoroughly researched, authoritative and highly readable, it succeeded in persuading a significant section of the classical establishment that Suetonius was indeed the serious scholar so revered by the ancients. Indeed, one reviewer was prepared to go as far as to conclude thus: 'Wallace-Hadrill has rescued Suetonius' scholarship'.[62]

How had he managed to bring this about? Fundamental to this rehabilitation was Wallace-Hadrill's success in convincing the classical world that Suetonius had to be judged *strictly on his own terms*, not those of others. Suetonius himself, after all, could not have made it clearer that he was not in the business of writing history in the manner of Tacitus, a genre which, as we have seen, had an overt moral purpose and demanded the use of elevated, highly wrought language and the avoidance of anything that smacked of the vulgar.[63] Consequently, to condemn him, as most classicists had been inclined to do, for not being as accomplished as Tacitus either as a Latinist or as an historian, was not just unfair, it was simply wrong. He had an entirely different agenda.[64]

Precisely what type of literary creation he had in mind Suetonius himself does not say, at least in the Lives of the Caesars, as they have come down to us. (The introductory section which might have yielded that information has not survived.) Nor does the work itself make that easy to determine. Not only do the twelve lives combine in an entirely novel way elements of the biographical and the historical[65] but they also display many of the features characteristic of antiquarian and lexicographic writing – plain, unvarnished prose, the unembarrassed use of technical and foreign words, especially Greek, and the extensive organization of material by category, the latter often marked by rubrics. Indeed, it is not

---

61. Coincidental with the publication of this monograph was Baldwin's more traditional study. For bibliographical details, see Chapter 1 n. 30 and n. 37 above. For an in-depth, joint review of these two 'totally distinct' but fortuitously complementary works, see Bradley, 'The Rediscovery of Suetonius'.

62. See J. Paterson, Review of Andrew Wallace-Hadrill, *Suetonius: The Scholar and His Caesars, G&R* 31 (1984): 218–19 (219).

63. For Suetonius's explicit statement about his own intended methodology in the Lives of the Caesars, see *Div. Aug.* 9.1.

64. Ash, *Tacitus*, 77.

65. See Tristan Power, 'Introduction: The Originality of Suetonius', in Power and Gibson, eds, *Suetonius*, 1–18.

uncommon to find set out under the various rubrics bald lists of illustrative examples in which no attention whatsoever is paid either to date
or context.[66] Small wonder that Wallace-Hadrill could come up with no
better definition of these hybrid compositions than 'not-history'.[67]

But irrespective of how the Lives are labelled, demonstrably they are
works, if not of great aesthetic appeal,[68] certainly of immense erudition.
The sheer amount of data garnered from an unusually wide range of
sources, not to mention their systematic organization and general accuracy,
speak for themselves. That the detectable errors in Suetonius's work are
remarkably few in number is the conclusion reached by all of those who
have written commentaries on his work.[69] The most serious criticism that
can be made of him in terms of accuracy is that sometimes, and particularly in the later lives, he reveals a tendency to over-generalize from a
single instance.[70] No surprise, then, that Wallace-Hadrill's insistence that
Suetonius should be viewed primarily as a scholar of stature, not as a
second-rate historian, is now generally accepted. A clear proof of how
influential his monograph has proved to be is the fact that the entries on
Suetonius in all the standard classical reference works have now been
re-written to reflect the views expressed in it.[71]

Given this situation, a big question mark surely needs to be placed
over the interpretation of the Chrestus sentence most favoured by those
whose expertise lies in academic areas other than classics, most notably
Historical Jesus research and ecclesiastical studies. Their conviction that

66. For a typical example of this presentational method, termed by Suetonius *per
species* ('by category'), see Appendix 2, where the 'Chrestus' section in its entirety is
set out and fully discussed.

67. Wallace-Hadrill, *Suetonius*, 9–10.

68. Bradley, 'Rediscovery of Suetonius', 265, conceding Suetonius's 'artistic
inferiority'.

69. See, for instance, John M. Carter, *Suetonius: Divus Augustus* (Bristol: Bristol
Classical, 1982), 9 and G. B. Townend, 'Introduction', in *Suetonius Divus Julius*,
ed. H. E. Butler and M. Cary (Bristol: Bristol Classical, 1982), xii–xv, whose judicious assessment ends thus: 'In this life (i.e., *Divus Julius*) as elsewhere, Suetonius
emerges as a conscientious, sensible and accurate reporter of the sources at his
disposal'.

70. For some examples, see Hurley, *Suetonius*, xxvii. For Tacitus's use of such
'generalizing plurals', see Ash, *Tacitus*, 67. He, however, is praised for using this
'hyperbolic and attention-grabbing' rhetorical device, rather than condemned for
historical inaccuracy!

71. See, for instance, the latest editions of the *Oxford Classical Dictionary* (1996)
and the *Oxford Companion to Classical Literature* (2011).

Suetonius has ignorantly misspelled Christ's name and carelessly reproduced a source that itself was probably confused[72] would appear to rest on
the shakiest of foundations.

Does this mean, then, that this interpretation, a staple component of all
sourcebooks and handbooks on the Historical Jesus and the early Christian
movement, simply must be jettisoned or can it be rescued somehow or
other? The latter would appear to be possible only if the current orthodoxy
in classical circles with regard to Suetonius can be shown to be unrea-
sonably positive. To see whether that might be the case, a closer look at
Suetonius clearly is essential. To that end I have selected three topics for
detailed examination – Suetonius's career, his handling of his sources and
his general treatment of personal names. Curiously, no attention is ever
paid to the last of these topics. That surely is a most regrettable omission,
given that the Chrestus problem basically is an onomastic issue.

6.3. Suetonius's Career and its Implications for the Chrestus Question

Prior to the publication of the Hippo inscription honouring Suetonius, our
main source for his life was Pliny's correspondence. In this, Suetonius, a
protégé and close friend of Pliny, features in no fewer than seven letters.
Four of these are addressed directly to him[73] and in the other three it is
concerns of his that form the subject matter of the correspondence.[74]

But for all the closeness of the relationship between Pliny and his
protégé,[75] the portrayal of Suetonius in these letters is hardly flattering.
He is presented as a serial non-achiever, an individual extremely reluctant
to take advantage of either his natural talents as a scholar and writer
(*Ep.* 5.10) or his training as a lawyer/advocate (*Ep.* 1.18). Even the
career opportunities secured for him by his patron Pliny he was loath to
exploit. In *Ep.* 3.8 we find him, to Pliny's barely suppressed annoyance,
refusing to take up the officership in the army in Britain that the latter
had gone to the trouble of securing for him. Instead, Suetonius suggests

---

72. For the long history of the hypothesis that Suetonius had allowed himself to
be led astray by police reports, themselves the consequence of misunderstanding, see
Slingerland, *Claudian Policymaking*, 208.

73. *Ep.* 1.18; 3.8; 5.10 and 9.34.

74. *Ep.* 1.24 (the purchase of a small property near Rome); *Ep.* 10.94 and 95
(securing the privilege of the 'right of three children' from the emperor Trajan).

75. On this, see n. 3 above.

that this position be offered to a kinsman.[76] Small wonder that Syme felt no hesitation in classifying Suetonius as one of 'Pliny's less successful friends'.[77] By 111 CE, the approximate date of the last Plinian letters in which he is mentioned (*Ep.* 10.94-95), Suetonius, now in his early forties, appears to have made very little of his life.

This protracted period of apparent non-achievement, however, was soon to give way to something very different. The 'game-changing' Hippo inscription reveals that before many years were out (certainly by the beginning of Hadrian's reign and quite possibly even under Trajan[78]) Suetonius had embarked upon a bureaucratic career in which he rapidly achieved considerable distinction: after serving as 'Minister for Studies' (*a studiis*)[79] and 'Minister for Libraries' (*a bibliothecis*),[80] he had gone on to occupy what was probably the most important position in the entire imperial bureaucracy – namely, the office known as *ab epistulis* ('Minister for Correspondence').[81] Illustrative of its importance and the prestige it conferred is the fact that in the Hippo inscription the title, *ab epistulis*, appears to have been given, uniquely, a whole line to itself, thus making it the focal point of the text.[82]

What exactly was this post? Why does it matter to us? From the fullest surviving literary source for the duties of the *ab epistulis*, a poem published in the 90s CE,[83] it is clear that this was the administrator who bore the ultimate responsibility for the emperor's voluminous and

76. That Suetonius had got as far as ordering the clothes requisite for the posting before getting cold feet is suggested by the text on a recently discovered writing tablet from Vindolanda, for which see Anthony R. Birley, *Garrison Life at Vindolanda: A Band of Brothers* (Stroud: Tempus, 2002), 139.

77. Syme, 'Pliny's Less Successful Friends', 362–79 (364).

78. For discussion of both scenarios, see Hurley, *Divus Claudius*, 3–4.

79. The precise nature of this post is disputed. For the suggestion that Suetonius could well have acted as some kind of literary adviser to the emperor, see Wallace-Hadrill, *Suetonius*, 83–6.

80. As 'Minister for Libraries' (*a bibliothecis*), he will have had overall responsibility for the various public libraries established at Rome by emperors and/or members of the imperial family, including the two recently founded by Trajan in his new forum. For an excellent survey of these early imperial libraries, see L. Casson, *Libraries in the Ancient World* (New Haven: Yale University Press, 2001), 80–98.

81. For these attractive translations of Suetonius's three official titles, see Catharine Edwards, *Suetonius: Lives of the Caesars*, Oxford World's Classics (Oxford: Oxford University Press, 2000), viii.

82. For an illustration of the reconstituted text (it has survived only in fragments), see the insertion between pages 104 and 105 of Townend's 'Hippo Inscription' article.

83. Statius, *Silvae* 5.1.83-100.

multifarious official correspondence. Given that Roman imperial government largely was 'government by correspondence',[84] that makes the *ab epistulis* a very important figure indeed. It was why, when the emperor travelled (as Hadrian himself did constantly[85]), the *ab epistulis* was always part of his retinue.[86] Quite simply, he was someone whom 'the ruler could not do without'.[87]

When we first hear of the post, in the early days of the empire, it was the preserve of freedmen in the imperial household – men like the notorious Narcissus under Claudius.[88] By Hadrian's day, however, it had become a coveted elite position filled exclusively by men of equestrian status.[89] On what basis were appointments to the post made? The essential qualification for this, as for Suetonius's two earlier 'ministerial' positions, was a well-established scholarly reputation.[90]

The post of *ab epistulis*, then, was no sinecure but a highly responsible job for a highly educated person. It certainly was not a job for a man disinclined either to read documents with care or to master their contents, the caricature of Suetonius found in most non-classical scholarship relating to the Chrestus sentence. The material over which he was required to exercise oversight and which, on occasion, he may even have composed[91] was far too important to be treated with anything but the greatest circumspection. It included imperial communications with all the individuals and organizations who ensured the smooth running of the state and the success of its undertakings – provincial governors, commanders in the field and the numerous city administrations which formed the backbone of the empire.[92] And it is even possible that some

---

84. The title of Fergus Millar's chapter about Pliny's Bithynian correspondence with Trajan in Gibson and Whitton, *Epistles of Pliny*, 419–41.

85. Fergus Millar in *The Emperor in the Roman World (31 BC–AD 337)* (London: Duckworth, 1977), 39 describes him as 'a sort of moving capital'.

86. Lindsay, 'Suetonius as *ab epistulis*', 463.

87. Syme, 'Travels of Suetonius Tranquillus', 110.

88. *OCD*³, *s.v.* Narcissus (2).

89. For this decisive shift which probably took place under Domitian, see Lindsay, 'Suetonius as *ab epistulis*', 456.

90. See Lindsay, 'Suetonius as *ab epistulis*', 458 and especially Cornell, 'The Citing Authorities', 1:126.

91. The extent to which the *ab epistulis* actually composed the emperor's letters is disputed. Wallace-Hadrill, *Suetonius*, 87–8, argues that it was considerable, since 'the crucial requirement (*sc.* for the post) was some sort of gift for composition'.

92. For these and the other responsibilities of the *ab epistulis*, see Wallace-Hadrill, *Suetonius*, 87.

matters of state security may have fallen within the remit of the *ab epistulis*.[93]

For Suetonius's performance in this role we have no evidence. Although at some point, possibly as early as 122 CE, he was dismissed from this post,[94] there is no suggestion that his sacking was for incompetence.[95] That Suetonius certainly possessed the requisite skills to carry out well the duties of the *ab epistulis* can be deduced from his scrupulous handling of source-materials in such of his works as have happened to survive.

6.4. *Suetonius's Handling of his Sources*

A particularly impressive example of Suetonius's discrimination in the handling of his source material is provided by his lengthy discussion at *Gaius* 8.1-5 about the birthplace of the emperor Gaius (Caligula), clearly a much-debated question at that time.[96] In a virtuoso display of source criticism unparalleled in ancient literature, we find Suetonius not only arguing cogently against each of the locations currently being promoted but settling the question outright by producing a piece of unimpeachable primary evidence – namely, the birth announcement itself as made in an official publication (*instrumentum publicum*). This announcement, Suetonius takes care to point out, he has actually seen with his own eyes,[97] thus preempting any objections that might be raised as to the authenticity of his

93. Lindsay, 'Suetonius as *ab epistulis*', 456 n. 20 – a point of considerable interest, given that Judaea clearly had come to be regarded by both Trajan and Hadrian as a security risk. See Isaac and Roll, 'Judaea in the Early Years of Hadrian's Reign' and discussion at 96 above.

94. The date is disputed. For a full discussion, see Crook, 'Suetonius "ab episp tulis"', 21, who argues against the consensus (122 CE) for a date no earlier than 128 CE. For a succinct discussion of the problem and the various solutions proposed, see Hurley, *Suetonius: Divus Claudius*, 4.

95. Allegedly it was for impropriety towards the empress, Sabina (*HA*, Hadrianus 11.3). However, the simultaneous fall from power of his patron, Septicius Clarus, and several others (ibid.), prompts the thought that the real reason may have been political.

96. For a translation of the greater part of this important passage, see Appendix 3.

97. *Gaius* 8.2 – *ego in actis Anti editum invenio* = '*I myself* find in the public record that he was born at Antium'. Note the emphatic use of *ego* (I myself) in the Latin. For the *acta diurna* (Daily Record), an official publication of important events, see above Chapter 4 n. 56.

testimony. As for the date he supplies for Gaius's birth (*Gaius* 8.1) – viz. *pridie Kal. Sept* ('the day before the Kalends of September' – i.e., 31 August), this has now been confirmed epigraphically.[98]

Far briefer but no less telling about Suetonius's care in handling his source materials is his discussion of Nero's youthful poetic compositions. Contradicting a writer (not named) who had claimed that Nero's work was not entirely his own, Suetonius writes as follows:

> There have come into my hands (*venere in manus meas*) note-books and papers with some well-known verses of his, written with his own hand (*ipsius chirographo*) and in such wise that it was perfectly evident that they were not copied or taken down from dictation, but worked out exactly as one writes when thinking and creating; so many instances were there of words erased or struck through and written above the lines. (*Nero*, 52 [trans. Rolfe])

That Suetonius is quietly correcting Tacitus here is generally agreed.[99] At *Annals* 14.6, the latter had indeed suggested the opposite. Nor is this the only place where Suetonius uses his greater mastery of documentary sources to score points off his more eminent contemporary. At *Tiberius* 21.4-7, he produces multiple verbatim quotations from the private letters of Augustus to Tiberius to contradict outright Tacitus's claim that the former regarded the latter with deep contempt.[100]

From these examples, it can be seen quite clearly how discriminating Suetonius could be in the handling of his sources. He thus fully justifies the glowing tribute recently paid him by the distinguished ancient historian, T. J. Cornell. Viewing Suetonius from the perspective of ancient historiography in general, Cornell writes as follows:

> Suetonius is, by ancient standards, rather generous in citing his sources.... he was particularly thorough and scrupulous in the study of works written by his subjects, including the Caesars.... It is fair to say that Suetonius, unlike most ancient historians and some of their modern successors, understood the fundamental distinction between primary and secondary sources.

---

98. For this evidence – namely, extracts from two official calendars – see Victor Ehrenberg and A. H. M Jones, *Documents Illustrating the Reigns of Augustus and Tiberius*, 2nd edn (Oxford: Clarendon, 1955), 51.

99. See, for instance, Townend, 'Suetonius and his Influence', 88–90, followed by, *inter alios*, Wallace-Hadrill, *Suetonius*, 10; Edwards, *Suetonius*, xxviii.

100. For this and other instances of Suetonian one-upmanship vis-à-vis Tacitus, see Hurley, *Divus Claudius*, 9 n. 33.

He cited primary documents frequently, often quoting them verbatim, in order to provide positive evidence (in contrast to the normal practice of ancient historians, who name only secondary sources, if they name any at all, and then only to disagree with them).[101]

In light of the above, it surely must be concluded that the hypothesis so popular with New Testament scholars in particular that the multiple errors in Suetonius's 'Christus' testimony can be attributed to simple carelessness on his part or to his uncritical copying of a source that was itself confused lacks all credibility. As Cornell so correctly observes, the standards by which Suetonius can be seen to operate in the handling of source-materials were far higher than those normally adopted in the ancient world.

6.5. *Suetonian Expertise in Onomastics (the Study of Names)*

It is not just in the handling of source-materials, however, that Suetonius displays a rare scrupulousness. Also unusual – and of the greatest relevance to us – is the close attention he pays to nomenclature. A marked feature of his oeuvre is the clutch of (now lost) lexicographical works devoted expressly to names of one kind or another – *On Names and Types of Clothing*; *On Names of Seas and Rivers*; *On Names of Winds*.[102] In addition to these, his partially extant mini-treatise in Greek, *On Abusive Words, or Insults and their Derivation* (Περὶ δυσφήμων λέξεων ἤτοι βλασφημιῶν καὶ πόθεν ἑκάστη), consists in large part of onomastic material, since a surprising number of Greek names have rather rude meanings. The remains of this work, scanty as they are,[103] illustrate with a remarkable clarity Suetonius's scholarly methodology – after discussing the meaning of each insulting name or word (these have already been grouped according to type), he proceeds to illustrate its usage by citing a selection of the literary passages in which it occurs.[104] This method, of course, is the same as that still employed by all compilers of serious dictionaries.

But it is not only in lexicographical treatises that his fascination with names and close attention to onomastic detail are revealed. In both of his main surviving works, Lives of the Caesars and On Grammarians and

101. Cornell, 'The Citing Authorities', 126–7.
102. Wallace-Hadrill, *Suetonius*, 43 n. 22.
103. For these, see Taillardat, *Suétone. Περὶ βλασφημιῶν*.
104. For some examples of his methodology, see Wallace-Hadrill, *Suetonius*, 44 and Power, 'The Originality of Suetonius', 9–10.

Rhetoricians,[105] the onomastic element is substantial. In large part this is because personal names, especially nicknames, can be quite revealing about the individuals and, where they become hereditary surnames (*cognomina*), also about the families that bore them. Sometimes, though, it must simply have been because a name intrigued Suetonius and he loved doing the etymological research into it and sharing the fruits of his learning. It is hard to account otherwise for some of the onomastic material included in his works. One of the best examples of this is provided by his detailed investigation into the cognomen, Galba, hereditary in the aristocratic family of Nero's short-lived successor, Servius Sulpicius Galba, and unique to it. To discover its origin and meaning, Suetonius consults no fewer than three authorities, as the precision of his Latin at *Galba* 3.1 makes clear.[106] After considering each one carefully, a process that involves the close examination of words of Greek, Latin and Gallic origin, he is content to leave the matter open, concluding thus: 'It is uncertain why the first of the Sulpicii who bore the surname Galba assumed the name, and whence it was derived'.[107] Given the brevity of Suetonius's life of Galba, the amount of space given over to this inconclusive discussion of his surname truly is disproportionate.[108]

Much of the onomastic information supplied by Suetonius is found in no other literary source, raising questions as to its reliability. However, documentary sources of one kind or another can be used to check his data for accuracy. From these comparisons, Suetonius emerges with flying colours. His detailed comments upon the distinctive onomastic practices of Nero's paternal family, the Domitii Ahenobarbi, for instance, receive extensive confirmation from the epigraphic evidence relating to that family.[109] Similarly with the emperor Galba, every single one of the various changes that Suetonius claims he made to his nomenclature (*Galba*

---

105. For the latest commentary on *De grammaticis et rhetoribus* (*DGR*), see Chapter 1 n. 31 above.

106. *Quidam putant; alii (putant); nonnulli (putant)* = Some think; others (think); others (think). Of note too is the elegant variation of Suetonius's Latin here.

107. *Galba* 3.1. So much for Suetonius's alleged inability to make editorial judgements! For this, see Cook, *Roman Attitudes*, 21.

108. Neither Plutarch nor Tacitus, whose respective accounts of Galba's short reign both survive, pay any attention at all to Galba's surname. For detailed commentary on Suetonius's etymological research at *Galba* 3.1, see David Shotter, ed., *Suetonius: Lives of Galba, Otho and Vitellius* (Warminster: Aris & Phillips, 1993), 101–2.

109. K. R. Bradley, *Suetonius' Life of Nero: An Historical Commentary*, Collection Latomus 157 (Brussels: Latomus, 1978), 27–8.

3.1 and 4.2) can be independently confirmed. Galba's switch under the will of his step-mother, Livia Ocellina, to the name, Lucius Livius Ocella (*Galba* 4.1), for instance, is confirmed by the Fasti Ostienses (the official calendar of Ostia) for 33 CE.[110] For his resumption of his birth-name after he became emperor, there is support not only from coins and inscriptions but even from papyri as well.[111]

It was not just the nomenclature of the imperial families, however, that interested Suetonius. His mini-biographies of grammarians and rhetoricians, men of humble extraction who made their living by teaching 'letters' and the art of public speaking, are packed with onomastic material too. Indeed, some of them consist of little more than a discussion of personal names, since the social obscurity of those individuals was such that very little hard information about their lives and achievements had made it into any written record. We will present only one case here, that of Aurelius Opil(l?)us,[112] since it will suffice to illustrate Suetonius's extraordinary attention to detail in research matters generally and onomastic questions in particular.

With regard to this particular individual, Suetonius knows no more about him than that he 'first taught philosophy, then rhetoric and finally grammar' before accompanying his patron, Rutilius Rufus, into exile at Smyrna (92 BCE), where he resided for the rest of his life. What interests Suetonius about Aurelius Opil(l?)us, however, is not so much his life as, firstly, the reason for the curious titles of the various learned books that he wrote in exile and, secondly, the precise spelling of his name.

The solution to the first puzzle Suetonius gratifyingly finds in a statement made by Opillus himself (*Opillus ait* = Opillus says). As for the second problem, Suetonius's satisfaction is unconfined when he turns up evidence that Opillus himself had spelled it with two LLs, not one. Where does he find this evidence? It is in an acrostic, no less, that Opillus himself had written in one of his own works, a treatise called Pinax or the Tablet: *Huius cognomen in plerisque indicibus et titulis per unam L litteram animadverto, verum ipse id per duas effert in parastichide libelli, qui inscribitur 'Pinax'* (I observe that his surname is given in numerous

---

110. Ehrenberg and Jones, *Documents*, 43.

111. For full discussion of the evidence, see Shotter, *Lives of Galba*, 104–5 (comm. on *Galba* 4.1), where *CIG* III, 4947, however, should be read as *CIG* III, 4957.

112. Suetonius, *DGR* 6. Other onomastically interesting grammarians are Lucius Aurelius Praeconinus Stilo and Lucius Ateius Philologus, for whom, see *DGR* 3.1-2 and 10 with Kaster's commentary.

catalogues and titles with a single L, <u>but he himself writes it with two in an acrostic</u> in a little book of his called 'Pinax') (trans. Rolfe).

Given such close attention to detail in onomastic matters, it surely is extremely unlikely that the scholarly Suetonius will have committed the elementary, risible error of confusing the names, Christus and Chrestus.[113] As someone who is on record as referring to the Christians as *Christiani* (*Nero* 16.2),[114] he will have taken it for granted, given the way that the Latin language works, that their name was derived from a founder-figure known as Christus. To be sure, many individuals did make the mistake of thinking that the Christians were called *Chrestiani* and that Christ's name was Chrestus.[115] They, however, tended to be the uneducated and the ignorant.[116] That Suetonius, a deeply erudite individual and a demonstrable onomastics expert, was guilty of committing this common error surely is inconceivable.

If the foregoing arguments about Suetonius's professionalism whether as a high-ranking imperial bureaucrat or as a scholar are accepted, the conclusion is inescapable that he simply cannot have had Christ in mind when he made his notorious reference to the urban agitator, Chrestus. Although Momigliano claimed that the burden of proof in this matter rested upon those who did not accept the identification of Suetonius's Chrestus with Christ,[117] the opposite surely is the case. Contra Momigliano, such an identification is not the only 'reasonable' explanation of this passage, nor is it even the 'most probable'. Whoever Chrestus was,[118] he must have been someone other than Christ – both his Claudian date and his Roman location, not to mention the standard meaning of *impulsor* and Suetonius's proven track-record as an onomastics expert, all combine to render the matter beyond doubt.

---

113. On the linguistic reasons for this confusion, see Van Voorst, *Jesus*, 34–6 and above Chapter 4 n. 92.

114. Although Wells (*Did Jesus Exist?*, 41) and the mythicists cited at Carrier, 'Prospect of a Christian Interpolation', 269 claim that this statement is a likely Christian interpolation, there is not a shred of evidence to support this. See B. H. Warmington, *Suetonius: Nero* (Bristol: Bristol Classical, 1977), 73 (comm. on *Nero* 16.2).

115. E.g., the common people (*vulgus*) of Rome at the time of Nero. Tacitus, *Annals* 15.44.2. See above, 68.

116. Of relevance here is the testimony of Lactantius (early fourth century CE) who at *Divine Institutes* 4.7.5 speaks of 'the error of the ignorant who by a change of letter are accustomed to call him (viz. Christus) Chrestus'.

117. Momigliano, *Claudius,* 33 and above, 103.

118. For some speculation on this subject, see Appendix 4.

6.6. *Suetonius and Christ*

But even if Suetonius makes no reference to Christ either at *Div. Claud.* 25.4 or anywhere else in his surviving works, that does not necessarily mean that he will have known nothing or have had no opinions about him. From the fact that for many years he moved in the same social and literary circles as Pliny and Tacitus, was acquainted with their writings and, in the case of Pliny's official letters, may even have been their posthumous editor, it surely must be safe to infer that his knowledge about Christus will have been, at the very least, in no way inferior to theirs.

If, as is generally believed, Suetonius was part of Pliny's entourage in Bithynia-Pontus,[119] then it seems inconceivable that he will not have been involved in the discussions that must have taken place about the cult of Christ and its devotees, the *Christiani*. One of the reasons for a governor such as Pliny inviting his friends to accompany him to his province was to benefit from their advice in administrative and jurisdictional matters.[120] Such friends were not there purely for social reasons. Since it was the worshippers of Christus, active and lapsed, particularly the latter, who presented Pliny with the most difficult problem he had to deal with during the entirety of his governorship, it surely is most unlikely that Suetonius, as a member of Pliny's unofficial advisory committee, knew nothing of the latter's investigations into their activities, the conclusions he reached and the line he proposed to take in his letter to Trajan on this subject. If, as some believe, he even edited Pliny's correspondence with Trajan, he will have had an intimate knowledge of that celebrated text (*Ep.* 10.96) in which the name of Christ, Christus, crops up no fewer than three times.

From Tacitus also he could have learned something about Christ. If, as has been suggested, Suetonius both read and critiqued the *Annals,*[121] then he will have been apprised (or perhaps reminded) of the basic facts of Christ's life by Tacitus's comments at *Annals* 15.44.3 – namely, that it was under Tiberius (*Tiberio imperitante*) and in Judaea that Christ had been executed by the Roman authorities.

But Suetonius may not have had to wait until Pliny and Tacitus produced their respective texts mentioning Christus before learning something about him. As someone who had been resident in Rome during the autocracy of Domitian, he could well have picked up information about the cult of Christ at that time. Both 'Christianity' and its parent religion, Judaism,

119. See n. 4 above.

120. Pliny, *Ep.* 10.87.2 with Sherwin-White, *Letters*, comm. ad loc.

121. Suggested by the polemical tone of, among other passages, *Tiberius* 21.4-7 and *Nero* 52. For discussion of these passages, see above, 115.

were very much 'in the news' then largely on account of the emperor's cultic rigorism.[122] Trials of Christians there are mentioned by Pliny,[123] and Suetonius himself tells us of his own attendance at an anti-semitic trial in which he witnessed a nonagenarian being stripped by an imperial agent to see *an circumsectus esset* ('whether he was circumcised').[124]

Unlike Tacitus and Pliny, both of whom showed complete contempt for the 'sordid plebs',[125] Suetonius recognized the evidential value of the products of popular culture. Hence his use of contemporary graffiti and anonymous pamphlets to provide more rounded portraits of the various Caesars, including Domitian.[126] Given this openness to the culture of Rome's non-elite, not to mention his insatiable appetite for facts, some 'early learning' on his part about the latest 'foreign superstition' to hit the capital and to gain a footing among the plebs is not improbable.

All this is, of course, speculative. Where we are on firmer ground is in deducing Suetonius's likely opinion of Christ. In his solitary reference to the *Christiani* (*Nero* 16.2), Suetonius describes their cult as 'new' (i.e., revolutionary) and 'evil-doing' (i.e., criminal). Now, the ancients generally tended to draw a tight connection between the adherents of any movement and its founder. A classic example of this is to be found in Tacitus's notorious Jewish excursus where the most distinctive and (to a conservative Roman) unattractive characteristics of present-day Jewry are attributed to their founder, Moses.[127] Consequently, when Suetonius describes the Christian 'superstition' (itself a pejorative term) as 'revolutionary and criminal' (*nova ac malefica*), the clear implication is that he thought that its originator (*auctor*) will have been no different.

In using such strong words about 'Christianity', Suetonius is very much echoing (or at least taking the same line as) Tacitus, for whom the cult itself was an evil (*malum*), its devotees prone to criminality and Christ himself not only an offender against Rome authority (whence his execution by Pilate) but a disrupter of Jewish society too. As the founder

122. See above, 32.
123. Pliny, *Ep.* 10.96.1, with Sherwin-White's discussion ad loc.
124. Suetonius, *Domitian* 12.2. Suetonius's reference to himself as a stripling at that time (*me adulescentulum*) puts the date of the incident somewhere between 85 and 88 CE. See Heemstra, *Fiscus Judaicus*, 27.
125. Tacitus, *Histories* 1.4. Cf. Pliny, *Ep.* 9.6.3-4.
126. See *Domitian* 13.2 for his citation of a punning Greek *graffito* and 14.2 for his quotation of several verses, again in Greek, from an anonymous pamphlet (*libellus*) mocking Domitian.
127. *Histories* 5.4.1. For other examples of this way of thinking, see Quintilian, *Inst. Or.* 3.7.21 and Juvenal, *Satires* 14.100-104.

of a breakaway Jewish movement, Jesus had done something of which Romans thoroughly disapproved – he had gone against ancestral practice, the *mos maiorum* (the customs of the ancestors), and thus threatened to de-stabilize society.[128]

That Suetonius should hold views similar to those of Tacitus about 'Christianity' and view the Christians and their cult rather less complaisantly than it had suited Pliny to do[129] should not surprise.[130] His Lives of the Caesars reveal him as both a thoroughgoing traditionalist in religious matters[131] and a person who had no reservations whatsoever about the current political dispensation.[132] As someone who had done well out of the Augustan system, Suetonius clearly had no time for those whose activities might undermine it. Since Christians with their refusal to recognize the divinity of any god other than Christ had the potential to do just that, clearly they were to be regarded as a bad thing, as must the man who had brought them into existence – namely, Christ himself.

128. For the development of this line of attack by Celsus, see below, 180.

129. See above, 46–8.

130. Quite possibly he was deliberately distancing himself from his erstwhile patron. Even during Pliny's lifetime, Suetonius had not been afraid to take an independent line. See Pliny, *Ep.* 3.8.

131. Wallace-Hadrill, *Suetonius*, 131–2.

132. Bradley, for one, sees the Lives of the Caesars as 'a loyalist work, in which none of Tacitus' political rancour is to be found, nor anything of opposition to the current dispensation'. See his 'Rediscovery of Suetonius', 265.

Chapter 7

LUCIAN OF SAMOSATA:
A SATIRICAL TAKE ON JESUS

7.1. *Introduction*

With our next classical source for Jesus, Lucian (in Greek, Loukianos),[1] we move to a different part of the Roman world, a rather different cultural environment and a very different type of literary composition.[2]

Born *ca.* 120 CE on the very edge of the Roman Empire in the Syrian (mainly Aramaic-speaking?) town of Samosata on the middle Euphrates,[3] Lucian, a self-identifying Syrian or Assyrian,[4] ended up leading anything but a marginal life. For the greater part of his adulthood, he was, if his own portrayals of his career are to be believed,[5] extremely active on

---

1. *Suda, s.v.* λ 683.

2. The bibliography on Lucian is vast. The two general studies of his works which I have found most useful are Robinson, *Lucian and his Influence* and C. P. Jones, *Culture and Society in Lucian* (Cambridge, MA: Harvard University Press, 1986). My immense debt to the latter will become obvious in what follows.

3. For Samosata as Lucian's birthplace, see his *How to Write History*, 24. For its likely cultural character, see Millar, *Roman Near East*, 454–6.

4. For his self-identification as Syrian, see, *inter alia*, *Twice Accused* 14 and 25-34; as Assyrian, ('a more affected version of Syrian'), see *Twice Accused* 27; *On the Syrian Goddess* 1; Millar, *Roman Near East*, 454–5 (source of the quoted material). What Lucian might have meant to imply by using these terms is disputed. For a thorough discussion and extensive bibliography on this point, see now J. L. Lightfoot, *Lucian: On the Syrian Goddess. Edited with Introduction, Translation, and Commentary* (Oxford: Oxford University Press, 2003), 205, who cautiously inclines to the view that Lucian most likely was implying that his first language was not Greek but either Aramaic or Syriac.

5. These are to be found mainly in *Twice Accused* and *The Dream*. However, Lucian's allegorical, highly literary treatment of his career in these works makes the interpretation of this material extremely difficult. The most balanced assessment of the evidence known to me is that of Jones, *Culture and Society*, 6–23.

the international cultural scene where he was, among other things, both a teacher of rhetoric and a public entertainer in that art-form. Highly educated, with an intimate knowledge of archaic and classical Greek literature, he produced in the course of his lengthy literary career[6] a substantial number of stylish compositions, almost all of them written in an Attic Greek admired to this day for its purity and elegance.[7] Indeed, one of the reasons for the survival of so much of his oeuvre, notwithstanding the deep disapproval of it in Late Antiquity by Christian scholars, is the exceptional quality of his Attic Greek.[8]

Where Lucian acquired the skills to produce work of such sophistication is not known. Certainly it is unlikely to have been Samosata itself. The part of Syria in which that town was located, the former kingdom of Commagene, remained something of a cultural backwater throughout its history. Described by Millar as 'a world of villages',[9] it seems always 'to have been isolated from the general stream of Greco-Roman culture'.[10] In Lucian's day, such importance as Samosata had lay in its status as a Roman military town: it was the permanent base of one of the legions (XVI Flavia Firma) guarding Rome's eastern frontier on the Euphrates.[11] Far more likely as the place where he acquired his advanced Greek education is Ionia (now western Turkey).[12] At that time several of the ancient Greek cities there, most notably Ephesus and Smyrna, were hot-houses of Greek learning and culture. Throughout the Graeco-Roman world they enjoyed a reputation, second only to Athens and Alexandria, for being, in effect, university cities of excellence.

From such works of Lucian's as can be dated,[13] it would appear that Lucian's most productive period as a writer (viz. the 160s and 170s CE)

6. He was still writing as late as 180 CE, as his reference at *Alex./False Prophet* 48 to the emperor Marcus Aurelius as deified, and therefore dead, shows.

7. For a short discussion of Lucian's language and style, see Neil Hopkinson, ed., *Lucian: A Selection* (Cambridge: Cambridge University Press, 2008), 6–7.

8. See Edwards, 'Lucian of Samosata', 143.

9. Millar, *Roman Near East*, 456.

10. Jones, *Culture and Society*, 7.

11. On Samosata's geographical position and strategic importance, see Kevin Butcher, *Roman Syria and the Near East* (London: British Museum Press, 2003), 114 and 129.

12. Deducible from Rhetoric's words at *Twice Accused* 27 – περὶ τὴν Ἰωνίαν .... πλαζόμενον .... ἐπαίδευσα, 'I gave him his (rhetorical) education...as he roamed around Ionia'.

13. These comprise only a tiny minority. For a comprehensive list of the dating clues detectable in his oeuvre, see Jones, *Culture and Society*, 167–9 (Appendix B).

coincided very closely with the heyday of the so-called Second Sophistic, the cultural 'movement' in which pride of place was given to declamation – more specifically, declamation as practised during the 'Great Age of Athens' by orators such as Demosthenes.[14] In Lucian's day, the most celebrated practitioners of that art-form enjoyed almost 'rock-star' status in elite circles. Performances of epideictic (i.e., exhibition) oratory by sophists such as Herodes Atticus and Aelius Aristides were major cultural events, attracting vast audiences from among the so-called *pepaideumenoi*, the highly educated.[15] But even rhetoricians of lesser eminence, in whose ranks Lucian almost certainly should be placed,[16] could make a satisfactory living by exploiting that popular form of elite entertainment. A significant part of Lucian's career appears to have been spent as a peripatetic, crowd-pleasing performer at such gatherings in various parts of the Roman Empire.[17] His surviving works, generally reckoned to be about eighty in number,[18] are thought largely to have been composed for such occasions. Unfortunately we have very little idea as to precisely when and for which particular audience most of these works were written.

Given that Lucian figures so prominently in so many of these compositions, generally either as a kind of 'master-of-ceremonies'[19] or as an active participant in his comic dialogues, he remains a strangely elusive figure: ever ready to ridicule the opinions of others, he keeps his own views on virtually everything tightly under wraps.[20] And no less hard to pin down

14. For this so-called 'movement', in reality a construct of his own, see Philostratus, *Lives of the Sophists*.

15. For the Second Sophistic, see G. W. Bowersock, *Greek Sophists in the Roman Empire* (Oxford: Clarendon, 1969); E. L. Bowie, 'The Importance of Sophists', *YCS* 27 (1982): 29–59; G. Anderson, *The Second Sophistic: A Cultural Phenomenon in the Roman Empire* (London: Routledge, 1993); Tim Whitmarsh, *The Second Sophistic*, New Surveys in the Classics 35 (Oxford: Oxford University Press, 2005).

16. This is implied by Philostratus's failure to include him in his *Lives of the Sophists*.

17. Jones, *Culture and Society*, 14–15. For the various places in which Lucian says he performed, see Robinson, *Lucian*, 3. The fact that these were 'hardly the most fashionable parts' (Robinson, ibid.) rather underlines Lucian's second-rate status.

18. For the Greek text of these works, see Matthew D. Macleod, *Luciani Opera*, 4 vols (Oxford: Clarendon, 1972–87). For both text and translation, see *Lucian*, trans. A. M. Harmon and others, LCL, 8 vols (London: William Heinemann, 1921–67).

19. Many of Lucian's short pieces are classed as *prolaliai*, chatty introductions in which he seeks to commend himself to his audience. On this literary form, see Hopkinson, *Lucian*, 109.

20. This point, first made by the ninth-century CE Christian scholar, Photius, still finds frequent expression today. See, for instance, C. D. N. Costa, *Lucian: Selected*

are the works themselves.[21] Extraordinarily varied in character, they have proved to be notoriously difficult to categorize, since a feature of so much of his oeuvre is the highly original and wholly unexpected way in which he combines in a single composition multiple literary forms. An excellent example of this is the composition on which we shall be focusing in the main body of this chapter because of the material it contains on Jesus and the Christians – namely, *On the Death of Peregrinus*. Inside an epistolary casing, a personal letter written by Lucian to a friend, we are presented with a dazzling pair of antithetical speeches given by, respectively, an admirer and a severe critic of the Peregrinus of the title, a Cynic philosopher contemporaneous with Lucian himself. While the first is a parody of an encomium, a type of composition taught in the schools of rhetoric,[22] the second is a textbook example of *prosopopeia*, the putting of an imaginary speech into the mouth of an invented character.[23]

No less varied than the forms of Lucian's writings is their tone. Unsurprisingly, given Lucian's invention of the comic dialogue and his favouring of that hybrid form,[24] most of his works of that type are humorous and mildly satirical,[25] as indeed are the vast majority of his non-dialogic pieces. However, some of his writings are rather different – indeed, in a few instances so different that their very authenticity has been questioned. The unusual warmth with which Lucian, a writer not known for a sympathetic approach to religion, treats the cult of Atargatis in *De Dea Syria* (On the Syrian Goddess), has caused many scholars to conclude that Lucian cannot be its author.[26] And no less surprising, given Lucian's widely held

Dialogues, Oxford World Classics (Oxford: Oxford University Press, 2006), x–xi. For Photius's critique of Lucian, see J. H. Freese (trans.), *Photius, Biblioteca, Vol. I* (London: SPCK, 1920), 215–16 (= section 128).

21. On the problems of classification, see Robinson, *Lucian*, 13–20.

22. For a wonderful example of Lucian's virtuosic handling of this type of composition, see his 'fifteen-minute show-piece talk', *In Praise of the Fly*. For a recent commentary on this ingenious parody of an encomium, see Hopkinson, *Lucian*, 142–50. For a translation, see Costa, *Lucian*, 3–6.

23. On this type of composition, also taught at an advanced level in the schools of rhetoric, see below, 160.

24. On Lucian's reasons for inventing this form with its Platonic structure and Aristophanic tone, see his explanation at *Twice Accused* 34.

25. See, for instance, the four sets of dialogues that comprise vol. 7 of the Loeb edition of Lucian: *Dialogues of the Dead, the Sea-Gods, the Gods* and *the Courtesans*.

26. For a recent, powerful defence, however, of the Lucianic authorship of this parody of Herodotus, written in Ionic Greek rather than Lucian's habitual Attic, see Lightfoot, *Lucian: On the Syrian Goddess*, 184–208 ('The Authorship of *De Dea Syria* Revisited').

reputation as a satirist, are the two thoroughly sycophantic essays, *Images* and *In Defence of Images*.[27] Written in the early 160s CE in praise of Lucius Verus's mistress, an Ionian courtesan by name of Pantheia, these works represent brazen attempts on the part of Lucian to ingratiate himself with that emperor, on the fringes of whose court he happened to be at that time.[28]

Notwithstanding these immense variations in form and tone, however, in a few areas Lucian displays considerable consistency. His treatment of the ancient Greek gods, for instance, is never anything other than mocking.[29] Indeed, his persistent ridicule of the Olympians, especially Zeus,[30] clearly was an important factor in the preservation of so much of his work: Christian apologists found this constant, Aristophanic lampooning an extraordinarily useful weapon in their defence of the cult of Christ against its pagan critics.[31] And despite exhibiting a very positive attitude towards the Platonist Nigrinus[32] and the Athens-based Cynic, Demonax, allegedly his former teacher,[33] Lucian generally treats philosophers, in his day a rather unpopular species of humanity,[34] rather roughly. It is not without considerable justification that Dickie has described them as 'one of his bugbears'.[35] And Lucian tends to come down heavily on

27. The works in question are to be found in the Loeb edition of Lucian, vol. 4 (trans. Harmon), 255–335, under the titles, *Essays in Portraiture* and *Essays in Portraiture Defended*.

28. This was probably at Antioch. For Verus's presence there during Rome's war with Parthia (162–66 CE), see HA, *Verus*, 7. For a general discussion of Lucian's relations with Verus's court, see Jones, *Culture and Society*, 68–77.

29. For his relentlessly comic treatment of them, see Tim Whitmarsh, *Battling the Gods: Atheism in the Ancient World* (London: Faber & Faber, 2016), 221–7. What Lucian's own beliefs (if any) were is impossible to say.

30. As in *Zeus Catechized and Zeus Rants* (Loeb. vol. 2) and many of the *Dialogues of the Gods* (Loeb vol. 7).

31. Jones, *Culture and Society*, 22.

32. For a useful discussion and a translation of Lucian's piece on this philosopher, see Costa, *Lucian*, 61–73.

33. *Demonax* 1. For a discussion of this short, entirely favourable biography of that philosopher, see Jones, *Culture and Society*, 90–8, Diskin Clay, 'Lucian of Samosata: Four Philosophical Lives (Nigrinus, Demonax, Peregrinus, Alexander Pseudomantis)', *ANRW* 2.36.5 (Berlin: de Gruyter, 1992), 3406–50 and Helen K. Bond, *The First Biography of Jesus: Genre and Meaning in Mark's Gospel* (Grand Rapids: Eerdmans, 2020), for whom it forms an important literary model for Mark.

34. See Jones, *Culture and Society*, 32.

35. So Matthew W. Dickie, 'Lucian's Gods: Lucian's Understanding of the Divine', in *The Gods of Ancient Greece: Identities and Transformations*, ed. J. N. Bremmer and A. Erskine (Edinburgh: Edinburgh University Press, 2010), 348–61 (352).

those individuals whom he regards as charlatans and hypocrites.[36] For them, he reserves his fiercest satire. One of the best examples of this type of composition is, once again, *On the Death of Peregrinus*. A satiric treatment of the life (as well as the death) of the celebrated Cynic philosopher and one-time Christian leader, Peregrinus of Parium, also known as Proteus, it is of particular relevance and importance to us. Not only does it contain the earliest surviving references to Jesus in a Greek text of pagan authorship but it provides the fullest portrait of him and his devotees so far encountered in a piece of classical writing. Hence our focus on this text in the rest of this chapter.[37]

7.2. Setting the Scene for Jesus:
A Short Introduction to the Peregrinus

Written in the aftermath of the Olympic Games of 165 CE,[38] Lucian's satire on Peregrinus takes the form of a personal letter from Lucian to his friend, Cronius,[39] in which the latter is regaled with a blow-by-blow account of Peregrinus's spectacular self-immolation at that prestigious religious festival. Lucian, allegedly having been present during the build-up to

36. Since Lucian tends to be our sole or principal source for most of these indi‑viduals, the reliability of his treatment of them is hard to establish. On the difficulties of assessing the historicity of, for instance, his highly satirical portrait of Alexander, founder of the new oracular cult of the snake-god, Glycon, at Abonuteichus, see Robin Lane Fox, *Pagans and Christians* (London: Viking, 1986), 243–4 (part of an extended discussion of Lucian's *Alexander or the False Prophet*).

37. For this work, see Macleod, *Luciani Opera* 3, no. 55 (Greek text only); Harmon, Loeb edition of Lucian, vol. 5, 1-51 (text and translation); Costa, *Lucian*, 74–87 (translation only). Among recent studies of this work that I have found useful of note are Peter Pilhofer, Manuel Baumbach, Jens Gerlach and Dirk Uwe Hansen, *Lukian: Der Tod des Peregrinos. SAPERE IX* (Darmstadt: Wissenschaftliche Buch‑gesellschaft, 2005); Jan N. Bremmer, 'Peregrinus' Christian Career', in *Flores Florentino: Dead Sea Scrolls and Other Early Jewish Studies in Honour of Floren‑tino García Martínez*, ed. Anthony Hilhorst, Émile Puech and Eibert J. C. Tigchelaar (Leiden: Brill, 2007), 729–47; Jason König, 'The Cynic and Christian Lives of Lucian's Peregrinus', in Brian C. McGing and Judith Mossman (Swansea: Classical Press of Wales, 2006), 227–54.

38. For a detailed discussion of the date of the *Peregrinus*, see Jones, *Culture and Society*, 124–5. Although it is certain that the piece was written after 165 CE, how long after cannot be determined.

39. Generally thought to have been a minor Platonist. See, for instance, Harmon's note at *Peregr.* 1 (Loeb ed.) and Jones, *Culture and Society*, 20 and 117.

Peregrinus's self-cremation and an eye-witness of it,[40] now wishes to share with his friend both something of the amusement that he had derived from watching that 'melodramatic publicity stunt'[41] and also something of the outrage that he alleges he had felt at having had to witness such a gross display of hypocrisy. Although Peregrinus had claimed that his self-immolation was intended to be a simple object-lesson in how best to cope with suffering and death,[42] his actions suggested that his purpose had been altogether different. His advance notice of his planned self-cremation (he had announced it four years earlier at the previous Olympics![43]), his choice of venue and time (the climax of the most prestigious, and therefore 'the most crowded of the Greek festivals'[44]), not to mention his rumoured networking activities throughout Greece in the run-up to the event,[45] had left little doubt as to what his aim really had been – it had been to secure for himself everlasting glory and quite possibly even cultic status through the erection throughout the Greek world of statues in honour of himself.[46] That a leading light of a philosophy that placed such great stress on the importance of treating public opinion with indifference should go to such lengths to win posthumous fame seemed to Lucian quite insupportable. Hence his decision to compose a satirical piece targeting Peregrinus's insatiable and utterly hypocritical appetite for glory. In the process of denouncing and ridiculing this defect in Peregrinus's character Lucian does not overlook other aspects of his behaviour incompatible with his alleged commitment to Cynicism – namely, his materialism and physical cowardice. These, however, are not deemed worthy of more than the odd jibe.[47] The main emphasis throughout this piece is on Peregrinus's all-consuming preoccupation with the enhancement of his reputation – a constant feature of his life.[48]

40. For the view that his attendance may simply be a convenient literary fiction, see Stephen Halliwell, *Greek Laughter: A Study of Cultural Psychology from Homer to Early Christianity* (Cambridge: Cambridge University Press, 2008), 468.

41. Halliwell, *Greek Laughter*, 466.

42. *Peregr.* 23 and 33.

43. *Peregr.* 20.

44. *Peregr.* 1.

45. See *Peregr.* 41 for the letters and envoys he is said to have sent to almost all Greek cities of note.

46. On the cult-statue of him erected after his death in his home town of Parium, see Clay, 'Lucian of Samosata', 3432. Allegedly it delivered oracles.

47. See *Peregr.* 16 (materialism) and 43 (cowardice).

48. For the glory (*doxa*) motif that runs right through the work, see *Peregr.* 1 (*bis*); 2; 4 (*bis*); 12; 14; 18; 20; 22; 30; 34 (*bis*); 38; 42; 44.

But what, it may well be asked, has this to do with Jesus? Spectacular as the ending was that Peregrinus had engineered for his life, this showy death was just one out of a clutch of grand, limelight-seeking gestures that he had performed in the course of his colourful, shape-shifting career. Whatever circumstances he had found himself in, he had always done his utmost to manipulate them in order to win prestige. Now at one stage in his protean career Peregrinus allegedly had joined, and then come to lead, a Christian community in Palestine, in which position he had found himself arrested and imprisoned by the Roman authorities. No surprise then, given the kind of person he was, to find that he had tried to exploit those experiences for the purpose of enhancing his reputation and winning glory. And no surprise either that Lucian decided to use that all-too-typical behaviour on Peregrinus's part as a rod to beat his back. In the process of that beating not only do contemporary Christians, depicted as Peregrinus's dupes, come in for satiric treatment, but their founder, the 'crucified sophist' (i.e., Jesus), also has ridicule heaped upon him. Although it was not strictly necessary at this point for Lucian to satirize the Christians' 'first law-giver', the chance of raising a laugh at the expense of a low-class founder[49] of a strange new mystery religion (καινὴν τελετήν) was too good to miss.[50]

This exploitation of the comic possibilities of the Christian phase of Peregrinus's life is to be found in the second of the speeches about him allegedly delivered in the run-up to Peregrinus's long trailed self-immolation.[51] That particular speech, it will be recalled, had been given by a critic of the celebrated Cynic. Although Lucian does not reveal the name of that individual, the scholarly consensus is that he is none other than Lucian himself.[52] Certainly in its contempt for the hypocrisy of philosophers, the fraudulence of cult-leaders and its mockery of the credulity of the uneducated, this speech is at one with Lucian's other works.

The critic's speech itself is quite substantial. It accounts, in fact, for approximately half of the text of the *Peregrinus*. Here I provide, as an aid to our discussion, a translation of those sections relevant to Lucian's satirization of the Christians and Christ. The material relating specifically to Jesus is printed in bold.

49. Implied by the fact that he had been crucified. On crucifixion as punishment reserved largely for slaves, see Hengel, *Crucifixion*, 51–63.

50. On 'new' as a term of disapprobation, see above, Chapter 5, 85–6.

51. *Peregr.* 7-30.

52. See, for instance, Harmon, *Lucian*, 1 and 8 n. 2; Robinson, *Lucian*, 34 ('a barely disguised *alter ego*'); Jones, *Culture and Society*, 119 – 'This person is a double of Lucian'.

7.3. *Lucian's Satire on the Christians and Jesus:* Peregrinus *10-14*

What Peregrinus did to his father, however, is altogether worth hearing. Indeed, you all know it, for you have heard how he throttled the old man, unable to endure the fact that he was already over sixty years old. Then when the crime had become well known and truly broadcast, condemning himself to exile, he wandered about, at different times exchanging one country for another (10).

It was then that he gained a thorough mastery of the astounding wisdom (τὴν θαυμαστὴν σοφίαν) of the Christians by associating with their priests and scribes in Palestine. And – guess what? – in no time at all he made them look like children (παῖδας); for he was a prophet (προφήτης), cult leader (θιασάρχης), convener of the congregation (ξυναγωγεύς), all by himself. Of their writings, some he interpreted and explained, but many he actually composed himself (πολλὰς δὲ αὐτὸς καὶ συνέγραφεν). In consequence, they revered him as a god (ὡς θεόν), employed him as a lawgiver (νομοθέτην), and made him their official leader (προστάτην), **admittedly in second place to that man whom they still worship, the fellow who was crucified (literally, impaled) in Palestine because he introduced this new mystery cult into the world** (μετὰ γοῦν ἐκεῖνον ὃν ἔτι σέβουσι, τὸν ἄνθρωπον τὸν ἐν Παλαιστίνῃ ἀνασκολοπισθέντα[53], ὅτι καινὴν ταύτην τελετὴν εἰσῆγεν ἐς τὸν βίον) (11).

Arrested on account of this (that is, his prominence as a Christian), Peregrinus was thrown into prison, an experience that furnished him with no little credibility for his subsequent career and for the charlatanry and the craving for celebrity (δοξοκοπίαν) of which he was enamoured. Well, when he had been imprisoned, the Christians, considering the incident a calamity, left nothing undone in their efforts to rescue him. Then, as this proved impossible, every other form of attention was shown him, not casually but with zeal. From the very break of day, old women, widows and orphan children were to be seen waiting by the prison, while their officials even slept inside with him, having bribed the guards. Then fancy meals were brought in and their sacred texts were read aloud and excellent Peregrinus – for he still went by that name[54] – was called 'The New Socrates' by them (12).

53. On the Greek terminology for crucifixion, see David W. Chapman, *Ancient Jewish and Christian Perceptions of Crucifixion*, WUNT 2/244 (Tübingen: Mohr Siebeck, 2008), 9–13.

54. Precisely when Peregrinus took the name Proteus is unknown. From the fact that the original Proteus, a minor sea-god first mentioned by Homer, was famous for his ability to turn himself into, among other things, fire (*Odyssey* 4. 418), it is a reasonable assumption that he took the name at the time of his announcement of his intended self-immolation. See Jones, *Culture and Society*, 126–7.

Indeed, people came even from the cities of Asia, despatched by the Christians at communal expense, to succour the man and to speak in his support and to supply encouragement. They show incredible speed whenever any such public action is taken; for at once they give their all. And so in the case of Peregrinus a great deal of money accrued to him from them on account of his incarceration, and he made for himself a considerable income from it. The poor souls (κακοδαίμονες) have convinced themselves, first and foremost, that they are going to be immortal and will live for ever, in consequence of which they despise death and most of them give themselves up of their own free will.[55] **Furthermore, their first lawgiver persuaded them that they are all brothers of one another once they have transgressed by denying the Greek gods, worshipping the crucified sophist himself and living according to his laws** (ἔπειτα δὲ ὁ νομοθέτης ὁ πρῶτος ἔπεισεν αὐτοὺς ὡς ἀδελφοὶ πάντες εἶεν ἀλλήλων, ἐπειδὰν ἅπαξ παραβάντες θεοὺς μὲν τοὺς Ἑλληνικοὺς ἀπαρνήσωνται, τὸν δὲ ἀνεσκολοπισμένον ἐκεῖνον σοφιστὴν αὐτὸν προσκυνῶσιν καὶ κατὰ τοὺς ἐκείνου νόμους βιῶσιν). Therefore they despise all things equally and consider them common property, accepting such ideas without any hard proof. So if any charlatan and clever operator capable of exploiting the situation comes among them, immediately he becomes wealthy by making a mockery of (these) simple (i.e., uneducated) creatures (ἰδιώταις ἀνθρώποις) (13).[56]

However, Peregrinus was freed by the then governor of Syria, a man with a fondness for philosophy. Perceiving Peregrinus's idiocy (ἀπόνοιαν) and his willingness to die so that he might leave behind a glorious reputation (δόξαν) on this account, he freed him, not even considering him worthy of punishment (14).

– trans. Margaret Williams

7.4. *Analysis of* Peregrinus *10-14*

At the outset of our analysis of *Peregr.* 10-14, it should be pointed out that there are virtually no scholars who have not expressed at least some reservations about the historicity of the Lucianic material to be considered in this section. Most take with a pinch of salt the allegation of

55. The Greek here is rather ambiguous and so gets interpreted differently. While some (e.g., Harmon, Loeb ed. *ad loc.*) take it to mean that the Christians willingly 'give themselves into custody', others (e.g., Van Voorst, *Jesus*, 59) take it as an allusion to the Christians' willingness to lay down their lives for the faith. The translation offered here deliberately preserves the ambiguity of the Greek.

56. On the Christians' gullibility and their willingness to take ideas on board without any evidence or reasoned discussion, see Celsus, as quoted by Origen at *Contra Celsum* 1.9.

parricide in the first paragraph of the translation above. Drawn from the common stock of ancient invective, this allegation is frequently used by those formally trained in rhetoric as a way of smearing their opponents.[57] Rather more contentious is the main episode described in the passage translated above – namely, Peregrinus's career as a Christian. Unattested elsewhere,[58] it is considered by some simply to be an invention on Lucian's part.[59] However, a Christian phase in Peregrinus's life is not in itself implausible: if, as some scholars hypothesize, a kind of 'marketplace in religions' existed at that time,[60] then a degree of 'shopping around' by the religiously curious or needy is not unlikely. One is reminded here of the one-time Christians in Pontus with whom Pliny had had to deal (*Ep.* 10.96.6). Temporary religious allegiances such as theirs surely are likely to have been quite common. Given this situation, it seems only reasonable to conclude that while Peregrinus's membership of a Christian community does not 'compel belief', it does not 'strain belief' either.[61] By the mid-second century, after all, 'Christianity' had begun to attract serious interest from educated pagans, the most notable of the converts to it being Justin (later Martyr).

But even if Peregrinus's Christian career is pure invention on Lucian's part and no more than a ruse for satirizing elite conversion to 'Christianity' and the literary activities of those converts,[62] that does not mean that this particular section of *On the Death of Peregrinus* has no historical value. His portrayal of that alleged episode in Peregrinus's life still reveals quite a lot about the extent of elite (pagan) knowledge about the Christians,

57. Jones, *Culture and Society*, 121. Similar in kind are the accusations of pederasty and adultery made earlier by Lucian against Peregrinus (*Peregr.* 9). For further examples in Lucian of these typical insults, see Robinson, *Lucian*, 18–19.

58. For a catalogue of the ancient passages referring to Peregrinus, see Clay, 'Lucian of Samosata', 3430–3.

59. See, for instance, Robinson, *Lucian*, 58–9, who regards the entire composition as 'a highly fictionalised invective' and Halliwell, *Greek Laughter*, 468. On Lucian's capacity for invention, see his own confession of making things up at *Peregr.* 39 and the successful literary fraud with which Galen credits him. For this, see *OCD*[3], *s.v.* Lucian.

60. See John North, 'The Development of Religious Pluralism', in *The Jews among Pagans and Christians in the Roman Empire*, ed. Judith Lieu, John North and Tessa Rajak (London: Routledge, 1992), 174–93 and especially 178–9 and the *Encyclopedia of Early Christianity*, *s.v.* Justin Martyr.

61. See Mark Edwards, 'Satire and Verisimilitude: Christianity in Lucian's Peregrinus', *Historia* 38, no. 1 (1989): 89–98 (89).

62. On the flood of Christian apologetic writing produced by those converts during the latter half of the second century CE, see Hurtado, *Lord Jesus Christ*, 490–1.

'Christianity' and Christ in the latter part of the second century CE. The fact that Lucian thought that he could play those subjects for laughs, and could do so in quite an allusive manner (it will have been noticed that he does not actually name Jesus in his satire), speaks volumes for his assumptions about the likely level of the knowledge possessed by his audience on Christian matters.

About both the Christians and Christ, Lucian himself appears to be better informed than any other early classical writers so far dealt with in this monograph. He knows, for instance, that 'Christianity' is a cult in which the reading and interpretation of texts is central (*Peregr*. 11 and 12); that an important aspect of Christian identity is the provision of financial and moral support to distressed members of the Christian community, such as individuals held in Roman custody (*Peregr*. 12 and 13), and that in Christian communities the elderly women, widows and orphans enjoy unusual prominence (*Peregr*. 12). None of these aspects of the Christian movement features in any of the earlier classical references to it.[63]

With regard to the author of that movement (i.e., Jesus), he is more informative than earlier classical writers too. Tacitus, for instance, tells us nothing about the manner of Christ's death even though he puts on record the fact that Pontius Pilate ordered his execution.[64] And he is far from specific about where in the empire Pilate passed that judgement. The attentive reader is merely left to infer that it was Judaea.[65] Lucian, by contrast, is very precise on both these points. He clearly states that the founder of the Christian cult met his end 'in Palestine' (ἐν Παλαιστίνῃ), the official name in Lucian's day for territory previously known as Judaea. Further, in the two sentences where he focuses directly upon Christus (*Peregr*. 11 and 13), he stresses that his death came about through that most humiliating of punishments, crucifixion. Tacitus fastidiously omits to spell this out, that gruesome penalty being considered beneath the dignity of history.[66]

And Lucian is also far more informative than Pliny about the founder of the Christian cult. Although it emerges from the latter's celebrated letter to the emperor Trajan that by the early second century Christus had come to be worshipped as a god (*Ep*. 10.96.7), about the earthly life of Christus Pliny has nothing to say. Lucian, however, not only refers, mockingly, of

---

63. Although these features seem worthy to us, probably they were included by Lucian because they 'were doubtless thought amusing at the time'. See Robinson, *Lucian*, 58.

64. *Annals* 15.44.3.

65. *Annals*, ibid.

66. See above, 82.

course, to the didactic role played by Jesus, the first time that this has been alluded to in a classical text, but he even gives some idea as to the nature of the instruction offered by the Christians' 'first lawgiver' (ὁ νομοθέτης ὁ πρῶτος),[67] the 'crucified sophist'. According to Lucian, the most important lesson that he imparted to his followers was that all those who renounced traditional religion and became initiates of the new mystery cult that he had founded purely for the worship of himself would become brothers. From that tenet, so Lucian would have it, everything else flowed. Since all the converts to this new mystery religion effectively constituted one large family, it naturally followed that, in the first place, their possessions were to be regarded as common property, in the second, those assets were to be drawn upon when any family member was in need and, thirdly, moral support should be offered by the rest of the Christian family when any of its members was in distress. Although Lucian also mentions the Christians' peculiar and, in his opinion, insane willingness to lay down their lives in the belief that they will live for ever,[68] his main emphasis is on the economic and social consequences of Jesus's teaching.

This picture of the life and teaching of the founder of 'Christianity', although the most comprehensive to be found so far in a classical text, cannot but strike the reader whose knowledge of Jesus is based on early Christian sources, particularly the Synoptic Gospels, as decidedly unbalanced, distinctly lacunose and in places simply incredible. Although the term 'brother' did figure occasionally in Christ's discourse, as reported in the Gospels,[69] by no stretch of the imagination can the brotherhood of all Christians be considered the central tenet of Jesus's teaching. That surely 'revolved around the Kingdom of God',[70] the imminence of the Endtime[71] and the need to be prepared for that dramatic upheaval of the world order. But about those matters, Lucian is wholly silent (because wholly ignorant?). Nor does he have anything at all to say about Jesus's main claim to fame – his prowess as a healer. Instead, he attributes to

67. With Harmon (note on *Peregr.* 13 in Loeb ed. of Lucian), Bremmer ('Peregrinus's Christian Career', 740) and Pieter van der Horst (review of Pilhofer et al., *Lukian: Der Tod des Peregrinos, BMCR* 2005.11.16), I am baffled by those who think that 'the first lawgiver' was not Christ but either Moses or Paul. Both the context and Lucian's language clearly imply that it was Christ himself.

68. *Peregr.* 13 and 14.

69. See Mt. 23:8 πάντες δὲ ἀδελφοί ἐστε.

70. At least as far as the Synoptic Gospels were concerned. On the centrality of this idea to Jesus's teaching, see Bond, *Historical Jesus*, 89.

71. Paula Fredriksen, *When Christians Were Jews: The First Generation* (New Haven: Yale University Press, 2018), 68–73.

him injunctions that are pure fantasy – Jesus could not have required his would-be followers to renounce the worship of the gods. Since his ministry was confined to the Jews (on this all the gospels are in agreement[72]), that issue would not have arisen. And it is simply inconceivable that Jesus, an observant Jew until the day he died,[73] would have demanded of his followers that they worship him as a god.

More important for us, however, than the accuracy of Lucian's facts, which, given the satirical nature of *On the Death of Peregrinus*, inevitably will have been subject to distortion, is the manner of Lucian's portrayal of Christ. To Lucian's way of thinking, 'Christianity' was in essence little different from the cult of the snake-god Glycon.[74] In other words, it was an exploitative racket set up by a clever trickster with the express aim of deceiving and defrauding the ignorant and the gullible. Consequently, if this scam was to be successfully exposed, then those who operated it had to be revealed for what they were—bogus intellectuals on the take.

Since Lucian's main target in this work is Peregrinus, inevitably it is against him, rather than against the actual founder of the Christian movement, that his most explicit criticism is directed. Jesus, however, does not escape. As the *prodromos* of Peregrinus, he is, by implication, no less guilty than the rogue who eventually took up his baton. When, therefore, Lucian writes at the end of *Peregr.* 13 'if any charlatan and clever operator capable of exploiting the situation comes among them, immediately he becomes wealthy by making a mockery of [these] ignorant creatures (ἰδιώταις ἀνθρώποις)',[75] it is not just Peregrinus but Jesus also whom he has in his sights.

For Lucian, however, merely implicating Jesus in the Christian fraud was not enough. If the cult was to be thoroughly discredited, then Jesus himself had to be explicitly discredited too. Hence the pointedly negative treatment of 'Christianity's' founder at *Peregr.* 11 and 13.

Worth noting, in the first place, is the fact that Lucian never actually dignifies the founder of 'Christianity' by referring to him by name. Whereas Tacitus and Pliny refer to Jesus of Nazareth as Christus, which

---

72. Fredriksen, *When Christians Were Jews*, 80–1.

73. Even Celsus, Lucian's contemporary, knew that. See Origen, *Contra Celsum* 2.6.

74. Viciously satirized in *Alexander or the False Prophet*.

75. For other instances of ἰδιώται being used as a term of mockery, see Acts 4:13 and Celsus, as cited at Origen, *Contra Celsum* 1.9; 1.27; 3.75. In all these cases, the word and its cognates (e.g., ἰδιωτεία) are used to underline the Christians' lack of formal education and hence their ignorance.

they appear to think was his personal name,[76] for Lucian he is simply 'that man, the fellow who was crucified in Palestine' (ἐκεῖνον..., τὸν ἄνθρωπον τὸν ἐν Παλαιστίνῃ ἀνασκολοπισθέντα).

Then there is the repeated emphasis on the fact that 'Christianity's' founder underwent crucifixion—the most shameful of punishments and one that was largely reserved for slaves.[77] Such was the hideousness of that punishment that elite Latin authors tended to resort to euphemism when talking about the subject.[78] Hence Tacitus's rather colourless description of Christus's fate – *supplicio affectus* (lit., 'affected by punishment').[79] Lucian, however, shows no such restraint but simply revels in the fact of Christ's crucifixion, twice using a term for it routinely avoided by Christian writers of the time on account of its offensiveness to them – namely, *anaskolopisis* (lit., 'impalement').[80]

Coupled with the term *anaskolopisis* we find the word *sophistes*— a combination so offensive to the Christian ear that it produced in the great Christian scholar, Arethas of Caesarea (9th–10th centuries CE), an outpouring of vitriol against Lucian unparalleled elsewhere in his marginalia.[81] But what exactly did Lucian mean to convey by his use of the word *sophistes*? Jan Bremmer has claimed that it is hard to know how to understand this word here, 'as it is sometimes used favourably and sometimes unfavourably by Lucian'.[82] Undoubtedly it is the case that in Lucian's day *sophistes* could be used either as a term of approbation or abuse.[83] That had long been so. Already in fifth-century BCE Greece, when the sophist first emerged as an identifiable social type (he was, primarily, an elite, peripatetic teacher of rhetoric), the term had been applied *both* to individuals of towering intellect and universally acknowledged integrity *and* to the intellectual second-raters who flocked to Athens at that time to instruct well-off youngsters in the art of public speaking and, according

---

76. Tacitus, *Ann.* 15.44.4 and Pliny, *Ep.* 10.96.7. There is no hint that either of them was aware of its messianic implications or of the phenomenon of messianism itself.

77. Hengel, *Crucifixion*, 51–63.

78. Hengel, *Crucifixion*, 38.

79. *Annals* 15.44.3.

80. Significantly, there are no entries in W. Bauer, W. F. Arndt and F. W. Gingirich, *Greek-English Lexicon of the New Testament*, for either ἀνασκολοπίζω (I impale/crucify) or ἀνασκολοπίσις (impalement/crucifixion).

81. Clay, 'Lucian', 3437 n. 74.

82. Bremmer, 'Peregrinus' Christian Career', 740.

83. Whitmarsh, *Second Sophistic*, 17–18.

to their critics, to cheat and corrupt them too![84] In which of these senses is the word being used by Lucian?

Bremmer himself ducks this question, opting instead for a rather neutral interpretation of *sophistes*: 'If we look at the contemporary soph-ists, who were rhetors and teachers of younger pupils, often moving from one place to the next, it is not difficult to see that Lucian could have interpreted Jesus' activities in this particular manner'.[85] The logic of the passage, however, shows that this interpretation cannot be right, for it demands that the term *sophistes* be seen in a negative light. For not only is Christ's wisdom, his θαυμαστὴν σοφίαν, introduced with heavy irony,[86] but the consequences of that wisdom are shown to be dire for the simple souls (lit., 'idiots') who take it on trust. Not only do these poor creatures (κακοδαίμονες) needlessly throw their lives away in the crazy conviction that they will live for ever but, as the final sentence of *Peregr*. 13 makes clear, they end up being cheated out of their money too.

But it is not just the logic of the passage that compels this interpretation of *sophistes*. So does the nature of Lucian's art as well. The latter's satire, produced by a πεπαιδευμένος (a cultured, classically educated member of the elite) for an audience consisting largely of other πεπαιδευμένοι made a point of flattering that audience by frequent allusions to works in the classical canon, especially the tragedies and comedies of the great fifth-century BCE Athenian dramatists.[87] The play most cited by Lucian for its amusement was Aristophanes's *Clouds*,[88] a deadly satire on sophists and sophistry—so deadly that Socrates, who, for comic purposes, was portrayed in it as a leading sophist, blamed it in large part for his subse-quent prosecution for impiety.[89] When, therefore, Lucian calls Christus a sophist, his audience automatically will have been reminded of that work and the central role played in it by the fraudulent teachers of the academy of higher learning (Φροντιστήριον/Thinkery) presided over by Socrates.[90]

---

84. *OCD*[3], *s.v.* sophists; Whitmarsh, *Second Sophistic*, 15–16.

85. Bremmer, 'Peregrinus' Christian Career', 740. That is assuming, of course, that Lucian was acquainted with the gospel narratives of Jesus's life, which he may not have been.

86. So correctly, Jones, *Culture and Society*, 121 n. 19.

87. On the literary tastes and 'performance culture' of Lucian's day, see Jones, *Culture and Society*, 149–59 and Whitmarsh, *Second Sophistic*, 23–40.

88. Jones, *Culture and Society*, 13 n. 36 and 151; F. W. Householder, *Literary Quotations and Allusion in Lucian* (New York: King's Crown, 1941), 4.

89. Plato, *Apol*. 18b-d.

90. For a lucid introduction to this play and a translation of it, see Alan H. Sommerm stein, *Aristophanes: Lysistrata and Other Plays* (London: Penguin, 2002), 63–130.

To a man, those *sophistai* were total frauds, not only intellectually dishonest but morally and financially corrupt as well.

Nor is *Clouds*, however, the only play to which there is an allusion at *Peregr.* 13. When Lucian oxymoronically mocks Christ as 'that crucified sophist',[91] his audience will have been reminded of *Prometheus Vinctus* too,[92] a play so well known that Lucian could make it the subject of one of his comic dialogues.[93] For at several points in the original play but most notably the opening scene in which Prometheus is being crucified by Hephaestus and his two henchmen, Strength and Violence (Κράτος καὶ Βία), the humbled Titan is openly jeered at precisely for being a *sophistes*, a man who for all his cleverness and his name (it meant foresight!) could neither foresee nor escape from the terrible, humiliating punishment being inflicted on him: 'Then pin down that other arm safely too', orders Strength, 'so he'll learn, this intellectual (*sophistes*), that Zeus is cleverer than he is'.[94] Small wonder that Arethas reacted so strongly to the phrase τὸν δὲ ἀνεσκολοπισμένον ἐκεῖνον σοφιστήν. Satire could hardly get any more savage.

But, deliberately distorted as Lucian's treatment of Jesus and his followers is, it is not uninformed. This raises the question – from where did he get his information? That it was derived from direct study of Christian texts such as the Synoptic Gospels seems extremely unlikely. Although a small number of coincidences between the gospels and *Peregr.* 10-14 can be identified,[95] these are vastly outnumbered by the differences.[96]

That Lucian should display little or no first-hand acquaintance with Christian texts is unsurprising. Clever and immensely inventive as he clearly was, he does not come across as an especially scholarly individual. Unlike Suetonius, for instance, whose enduring passion for research can be seen clearly in his surviving works and easily deduced from the titles

---

91. The incongruity lies in the fact that, while crucifixion was inflicted only on the lowest of society, sophists belonged to the educated elite.

92. Generally this play is attributed to Aeschylus but its authorship remains a matter of dispute. See Mark Griffiths, *The Authenticity of Prometheus Bound* (Cambridge: Cambridge University Press, 1977).

93. For his *Prometheus*, a burlesque on the opening (crucifixion) scene of *Prometheus Vinctus*, see Loeb edition of Lucian, vol. 5, 241–65.

94. For this translation, see Alan H. Sommerstein, *Aeschylus: The Persians and Other Plays* (London: Penguin, 2009), 169.

95. In addition to the reference to brothers (see n. 69 above), also relevant is the reference at Mt. 25:35 to the meritoriousness of helping one's fellows in captivity.

96. For a useful discussion, see Van Voorst, *Jesus*, 63–4.

of the many that are lost,[97] Lucian would appear to have been content for the most part to draw upon and manipulate the texts that he had studied and internalized in the course of his education (*paideia*), most notably, the Homeric epics, Herodotus's *Histories* and selected items from the respective oeuvres of Plato, Aristophanes and Euripides.[98] For new material, he appears to have relied largely upon either his own observation of current intellectual, cultural and religious developments[99] or information gleaned through interaction with his social and intellectual peers, the *pepaideumenoi*. As a fully engaged member of that 'supra-regional' cultural elite,[100] the Greek world's 'chattering class', he will have been very aware of the kinds of issues that attracted its interest and/or concern. Since by his day 'Christianity' had become sufficiently well known for it to have become a subject for elite discourse,[101] picking up potentially useful information about it from that source will not have been difficult for him. Such information as the elite possessed about 'Christianity', however, is unlikely to have come from Christian texts: by and large educated pagans did not bother to read such material, as Tertullian was to observe somewhat ruefully several decades later.[102] More probably it will have derived from what was 'in the air' at that time.[103] By the middle of the second century, 'Christianity' had become such a widespread phenomenon that the more distinctive practices of its adherents (e.g., their refusal to participate in civic cults and their eagerness to die for their beliefs) can hardly have gone unnoticed or unremarked by non-Christians.

That Lucian's own knowledge about the Christian cult was not 'book-based' is clear from the nature of his comments about it. None of the features of it that he singles out for ridicule are to be found in texts describing Jesus's earthly ministry.[104] Most, however, are well attested in

97. Wallace-Hadrill, *Suetonius*, 43.

98. For a full list of works either quoted or alluded to, see Householder, *Literary Quotation and Allusion in Lucian*, 1–40.

99. The recently established, highly popular oracular cult of Glycon at Abonuteichus in Paphlagonia is a case in point. There seems to be no reason to doubt Lucian's claim (*Alex./False Prophet* 55-57) that he had made a deliberate detour whilst en route from Syria to Greece to check out this new cult. See Lane Fox, *Pagans and Christians*, 243.

100. Millar, *Roman Near East*, 455.

101. Hurtado, *Lord Jesus Christ*, 488–92.

102. Tertullian, *Testimonio Animae* 1 – (*litterae*) *ad quas nemo venit nisi iam Christianus* ('writings to which no one comes unless he is already a Christian').

103. Meier, *A Marginal Jew*, 1:92.

104. The pooling of private property, satirized at *Peregr.* 13, for instance, was a short-lived, post-resurrection phenomenon (Acts 2:44-45 and 4:32-37).

Lucian's own period – e.g., 'Christianity's' familial character, its attraction to widows and orphans, its prominent charitable activities, its 'bookishness'.[105] And the picture that Lucian paints of Jesus likewise is derived largely from pagan knowledge about *current* Christian behaviour: because contemporary Christians, most of them gentiles, were notorious for their abandonment of the old gods and their insistence upon worshipping Christ alone, Lucian suggests, quite wrongly, that it was Christ himself, 'the crucified sophist', who had ordained those practices.

But even if this anachronism had been spotted by any in Lucian's original audience, it is unlikely that they would have been at all troubled by it. They, after all, had come to his performance expecting to be entertained. With his lively, wide-ranging satire on Peregrinus, and his side-swipes at the latter's Cynic admirers, his one-time Christian devotees and their charlatan of a founder, the crucified sophist, Lucian will not have disappointed them. All those targets would have been regarded as fair game, with 'Christianity' deserving, at the very least, some gentle ribbing. In the eyes of the majority of those belonging to 'the polished and enlightened orders of society',[106] 'Christianity' was simply an idiotic (in all senses of the word) superstition and its crucified founder, a so-called man of wisdom (*sophistes*), an object of contempt.

7.5. *Final Observations*

But favourable as the immediate reception of *On the Death of Peregrinus* is likely to have been, its subsequent fate was very different. What had been calculated to go down well with an audience of pagan sophisticates at the height of the Second Sophistic, gravely affronted scholarly Christian readers in Late Antiquity. Over-compensating perhaps for their guilty pleasure in having read that text at all, they peppered the margins of their copies of the work with the vilest insults they could imagine.[107] The anonymous Christian author of the entry on Lucian in the great tenth-century Byzantine encyclopedia, the Suda, went even further, predicting that this 'blasphemer or slanderer, or more accurately, this atheist', would 'in the next world inherit eternal fire with Satan' because of 'his attack

---

105. On the phenomenal literary output of Christians in the latter half of the second century, see Hurtado, *Lord Jesus Christ*, 490–1. On the confirmation that Lucian's depiction of the Christians receives from contemporary or near-contemporary Christian sources, see Bremmer, 'Peregrinus' Christian Career', 740–1.

106. For this elegant description of Lucian's audience, see Gibbon, *Decline and Fall*, 1:30.

107. For some examples, see Edwards, 'Lucian in Christian Memory', 148–9.

on Christianity and his blasphemy of Christ Himself'.[108] Later Christians went still further again: in the early medieval period the offending sections of *On the Death of Peregrinus* were actually excised from certain manuscripts of that work[109] and during the sixteenth century such was the abhorrence felt for Lucian's atheistic and slanderous compositions in Catholic circles that by its end (1590) his entire oeuvre found itself placed on the Inquisition's *Index of Prohibited Books*.[110]

But offensive as Lucian's remarks about Christ undoubtedly were found to be, they do need to be kept in proportion. In the whole of his very extensive oeuvre, it is in *On the Death of Peregrinus* alone that Jesus is a satirical target[111] and, even then, Lucian's attack on him is relatively restrained. He is spared the vitriolic treatment meted out to, for instance, that other cult-founder satirized by Lucian, Alexander of Abonuteichus. Further, it should be noted that Lucian's treatment of the Christians is not invariably hostile: at *Alex./False Prophet* 25 and 38 he refers to them quite approvingly. Because the target of his satire in that work, Alexander of Abonuteichus, loathes the Christians, it suits Lucian's comic needs to treat them favourably. All this should remind us that much (most?) of what Lucian writes should be taken with a pinch of salt. His opinions shifted according to the exigencies of the moment, the need to make his audience laugh always being of paramount importance to him.[112] Consequently, what he really thought about anything, 'unless his opinion is that one can know nothing for certain',[113] is impossible to establish.

Not all of Lucian's contemporaries, however, were as mentally flexible as he. With our final author, Celsus, we find ourselves dealing with an individual with very decided beliefs indeed, a committed pagan not prepared to put expediency above principle.

---

108. For an excellent translation of the full Suda entry on Lucian, see Turner, *Lucian*, 7.

109. Clay, 'Lucian of Samosata', 3436 n. 73 and MacLeod, *Luciani Opera* 3, 188.

110. Robinson, *Lucian*, 98.

111. Although Christian scholars in Late Antiquity were convinced that Lucian's mockery of 'the Syrian from Palestine' who performed exorcisms for a fat fee was a satire upon Jesus, that interpretation of *Lover of Lies* 16 is improbable, not least because that exorcist clearly was a contemporary figure known to the speaker. See the commentaries of Harmon (Loeb ed. of Lucian, vol. 3, 345 and Costa, *Lucian*, 265). For the prevalence of religious charlatans of one kind and another in late second-century Palestine, see the eye-witness testimony of Celsus as cited at Origen, *Contra Celsum* 7.9.

112. For the three completely different ways in which he portrays Socrates, see Robinson, *Lucian*, 14–15.

113. Photius, as quoted at Edwards, 'Lucian of Samosata', 151.

Chapter 8

CELSUS: THE FIRST SERIOUS PAGAN CRITIC OF JESUS

8.1. *Introduction*

With Celsus, broadly a contemporary of Lucian,[1] we encounter a step-change in the treatment accorded Jesus by classical writers. As we have seen, none of the authors so far discussed pays very much attention to him. Indeed, none of the Latin writers appears even to know that his personal name was Jesus and that Christus, in origin at least, was no more than a title meaning 'anointed one' – i.e., messiah. Although the Greek author Lucian provides us with a few personal details about Jesus, most notably that he was a teacher of some kind, he still has far more to say about Jesus's followers than about Jesus himself. With Celsus, however, we find ourselves for the first time in the presence of a classical writer who is not only extremely well informed about Jesus (he always refers to him by his 'correct' name and deliberately refrains from calling him Christus[2]) but so concerned about his growing influence across the Roman world that he decides to devote a large part of a substantial treatise, the anti-Christian polemic, *Alethes Logos* (literally, True Word),[3] to destroying his credibility and, with it, that of Christianity too.

1. Celsus's dates are unknown. The likely date of his anti-Christian polemic, *Alethes Logos*, will be considered later in this chapter.

2. A reflection of his conviction that Jesus was not the long-promised messiah. For Celsus's arguments against Jesus's messianic status, see 170–2 below.

3. Since there is no universally accepted English translation of Celsus's title for this work (*True Word/Account/Discourse/Reason/Doctrine/Teaching* are all found), I have decided simply to use the original Greek title – namely, *Alethes Logos*. For Origen's use of this title, see *Contra Celsum* 3.1; 4.62 and 84. Please note that from now on the *Contre Celsum* will be referred to only by its book and chapter numbers – e.g., 3.1; 4.62 etc.

Truth, for Celsus, is the worship, in accordance with established custom, of both the traditional 'great' gods and the various minor deities and spirits, all of whom (and they include the Roman emperor himself) have been appointed to their respective spheres of influence by the Supreme Deity – i.e., God (8.67-68). On this reckoning, the upstart cult of Christ, being based on no more than Jesus's own deceitful claim to divinity (1.28), has no legitimacy whatsoever. The purpose of the *Alethes Logos*, then, is to demonstrate, using a variety of rhetorical strategies, the out-and-out falsity of this dangerous new arrival on the religious scene and to dissuade his readers from having anything to do with it.

Celsus, it should already be clear, did not regard Christianity as a subject for humorous treatment – in this, differing greatly from Lucian. Some of his concerns were traditional: as a loyal subject of Rome, he regarded the Christians' refusal either to worship the traditional gods or to acknowledge the divinity of the emperor as posing a direct threat to the well-being of the state.[4] But newer concerns had now arisen too for which he provides the earliest surviving pagan testimony. One was the growing tendency on the part of Christians to refuse to engage in public life, whether as soldiers, magistrates or administrators. Clearly this had the potential to diminish the general effectiveness of Roman rule (8.75). But even more worrying were the effects of Christian propagandizing, the main target of which were the empire's non-elite inhabitants – individuals snobbishly referred to by Celsus as vulgar, uneducated and gullible (1.9; 1.27 and 6.14). Because of the susceptibility of these 'idiots' to Christian pressure tactics,[5] patriarchal authority was being challenged, families were being divided and societal cohesion, in consequence, was being put at risk.[6]

No surprise, then, that Celsus's stated aim in composing the *Alethes Logos* was to convince these simple souls of their wrong-headedness (1.9). However, given the length and complexity of his treatise, it is highly unlikely that it even reached, let alone was appreciated by, such people.

---

4. For a good discussion of the passages in Celsus relating to this topic, see Michael B. Simmons, 'Graeco-Roman Philosophical Opposition', in *The Early Christian World*, ed. Philip F. Esler, 2 vols (London: Routledge: 2000), 2:840–68 (859–60).

5. For Celsus's frequent application of the word 'idiot' to Christians, see Marcel Borret, *Origène: Contre Celse*, 5 vols (Paris: CERF, 1967–76), 5:416. For Lucian's application of this word to Christians, see *Peregr.* 13.

6. The *locus classicus* for Christian propagandizing is 3.55. Translations of this famous passage are to be found at Stevenson/Frend, *New Eusebius*, 135 (no. 116) and Whittaker, *Jews and Christians*, 182.

Only those who had the means to afford such a work and the education to understand it are likely to have felt any urge to obtain a copy and read it.[7] Celsus's text with its innumerable literary references and allusions, most notably to Homer, Herodotus and Plato,[8] pre-supposes a readership that had acquired considerably more than a basic education.

Whether those who did manage to get hold of Celsus's treatise were converts to the new religion,[9] sympathetic to it but not quite convinced[10] or, like Celsus himself, strongly opposed to it, we have no means of knowing. But if Hurtado is correct in his observation that 'apologists for or against any cause may formally address their opponents, but they are typically and mainly read by those already aligned to their position',[11] then it would be fair to conclude that Celsus's readership consisted largely of individuals much like himself – i.e., highly educated elite pagans (*pepaideumenoi*), who shared his antipathy towards this newfangled cult and saw a need for a serious intellectual challenge to be mounted against it.[12]

For the task of delivering on this, Celsus was unusually well equipped. To a thorough training in the art of rhetoric and a conventional schooling in philosophy, he could add a slightly freakish interest in contemporary Christianity in all its startling heterogeneity[13] and a wholly exceptional (for a pagan) knowledge of both Christian and Jewish texts. No difficulty for him, then, to produce a well-informed, well-crafted attack on Jesus and to demonstrate the philosophical weakness of the chief claims being made for the latter – namely, that he was God's son by a human mother, had risen from the dead after his humiliating execution by the Roman authorities and, by so doing, had virtually guaranteed to those who believed in him a similar bodily resurrection at the end of time.

---

7. Michael Frede, 'Origen's Treatise Against Celsus', in *Apologetics in the Roman Empire: Pagans, Jews and Christians*, ed. M. Edwards, M. Goodman and S. Price (Oxford: Oxford University Press, 1999), 131–55 (152).

8. See Borret's index of pagan authors at *Contre Celse*, 5:284–99.

9. Johannes Quasten, *Patrology* (Westminster: Christian Classics, 1983–88), 52.

10. Frede, 'Origen's Treatise', 152.

11. Larry W. Hurtado, *Destroyer of the Gods: Early Christian Distinctiveness in the Roman World* (Waco: Baylor, 2016), 30.

12. For a similar conclusion about Celsus's likely readership, see James Carleton Paget, 'The Jew of Celsus and *adversus Judaeos* Literature', *ZAC* 21, no. 2 (2017): 201–42 (207 n. 30) – 'Its circle of readers may have been limited to Celsus' acquaintances, very few of whom would have been Christians'.

13. See Ramsay MacMullen, 'Two Types of Conversion to Early Christianity', *VC* 37 (1983): 174–92 (177), who characterizes him as 'a minor oddity'.

Whether Celsus's polemical treatise against Christianity was the first such work to be composed by a pagan writer is disputed.[14] Certainly it is the earliest that has come down to us. And even then, we have it only at second hand and in a very fragmented form. For it is only through the quotations taken from by the great third-century Christian scholar, Origen, that we have access to what Celsus himself wrote.[15] However, so extensive are those quotations[16] that it is possible to get a reasonably good idea of the broad structure and general character of Celsus's original composition. How much of the latter has been omitted by Origen in the course of fulfilling his brief from his patron, the 'God-loving' Ambrose, is impossible to determine. Although the most common estimate is about a third,[17] far more may be missing if Origen confined himself simply to refuting Celsus's anti-Christian charges.[18] Certainly, it is striking how little of a positive nature Celsus has to say on the stated subject of his discourse – namely, the 'true word'. But regardless of how much of

14. Although it is generally claimed that Cornelius Fronto, the one-time tutor of Marcus Aurelius, wrote at an earlier date an *entire* (now almost completely lost) speech against the Christians (*Oratio contra Christianos*), this view has been powerfully and, in my opinion, convincingly challenged by Champlin. He sees Fronto's indisputably anti-Christian remarks, preserved by the third-century Christian apologist, Minucius Felix, as simply asides in a work devoted to another topic altogether – namely, his rhetorical masterpiece, the *In Pelopem* (Against Pelops). For full discussion, see Edward Champlin, *Fronto and Antonine Rome* (Cambridge, MA: Harvard University Press, 1980), 64–6. For an entirely different view of the matter, however, see C. P. Bammel, 'Die erste lateinische Rede gegen die Christen', *ZKG* 104 (1993): 295–311. For translations of the Fronto passages themselves, see Whittaker, *Jews and Christians*, 173–6.

15. The bibliography for Origen's massive refutation of Celsus, the *Contra Celsum*, is vast. Works that I have found particularly useful in writing this chapter are Henry Chadwick, *Origen: Contra Celsum* (Cambridge: Cambridge University Press, 1953); Borret, *Origène: Contre Celse*; Michael Frede, 'Celsus philosophus Platonicus', *ANRW* 2.36.7 (1994): 5183–5213; Horacio E. Lona, *Die Wahre Lehre des Kelsos. Übersetzt und erklärt* (Freiburg: Herder, 2005).

16. As can be perceived easily from their italicization in Chadwick and Borret (previous note) and the use of bold type for them in Miroslav Marcovich, *Origenes Contra Celsum: libri VIII* (Leiden: Brill, 2001).

17. See, for instance, Simmons, 'Graeco-Roman Philosophical Opposition', 842.

18. See the pertinent remarks of James Carleton-Paget, Review of Horacio E. Lona, *Die Wahre Lehre des Kelsos. Übersetzt und erklärt (Freiburg: Herder, 2005)*, *JEH* 58, no. 2 (2007): 297–9 (297). The number of places where Origen can be seen clearly to have compressed or omitted material from the *Alethes Logos* is actually very small.

Celsus's text has been lost, certainly enough has survived for at least nine scholars to have attempted a reconstruction of it.[19] These reconstructions are extremely valuable both for enabling us to read Celsus's text independently of Origen, something that the scale and seriousness of his enterprise undoubtedly merit, and for helping us to appreciate better the passion that drove Celsus to embark upon this enterprise.[20] Origen's decision to refute Celsus point by point and so to break up his text into a vast mass of fragments makes this virtually impossible.[21]

From these introductory remarks, it can be seen that in this chapter we shall be dealing with an entirely new kind of work and a writer completely different from any hitherto considered in the volume. Rightly does Carleton Paget describe the *Alethes Logos* as 'a bolt from the blue'.[22] Of the concerns that drove Celsus to produce this polemic, we have already spoken. But what of the man himself? Who was he? Where did he come from? When exactly or approximately was he writing? Before we get to grips with his assault upon Jesus, we need to address these questions and attempt to contextualize Celsus, a writer largely ignored by classicists and deserving far more attention than he currently receives.[23]

8.2. *Celsus: His Identity and Provenance*

Notwithstanding Celsus's importance to us as the first serious pagan critic of Jesus, pinning down who he was and where he came from is extraordinarily difficult. That he probably flourished in the second half of the second century seems a reasonable inference from Origen's statement in

---

19. For the full list, see Lona, *Die Wahre Lehre*, 486. The most easily accessible of these, for the English-speaking reader at least, is that of R. Joseph Hoffmann. For this, see his *On the True Doctrine: A Discourse against the Christians* (New York: Oxford University Press, 1987).

20. Hoffmann (previous note), it seems to me, succeeds triumphantly in achieving this through the simple (but surely justifiable) tactic of replacing with direct speech much of the reported speech used by Origen in his citations of Celsus.

21. On Origen's justification for proceeding in this manner, a shift from his original plan, see *Praef.* 6.

22. Carleton-Paget, Review of Horacio E. Lona, 299.

23. I am hopeful that the very recent publication of *Celsus in His World: Philosophy, Polemic and Religion in the Second Century*, ed. James Carleton-Paget and Simon Gathercole (Cambridge: Cambridge University Press, 2021) will help to transform this situation. Regrettably, this work appeared too late for me to take account of it in this monograph.

his preface that he had long been dead.[24] (It was in the late 240s CE that Origen embarked upon his great refutation of the *Alethes Logos*.[25]) Who Celsus was, however, is a far more difficult question to answer, since Origen, our sole source for him, appears not to have known himself. Initially, he thought that the Celsus with whom his patron had required him to engage[26] must be one or other of the two early imperial Epicurean philosophers bearing that name. Thus at 1.8 we find him writing, 'It has come down to us that there were two Epicureans called Celsus, the earlier one a contemporary of Nero, while the other lived in Hadrian's time or later'. As he worked on his refutation, however, it became increasingly clear to him that 'his' Celsus could be neither of those individuals since the *Alethes Logos* manifestly had been written by someone who nowhere admitted to being an Epicurean (5.3), whose outlook was unmistakeably Platonic (4.83) and whose views concerning God, providence and the soul were completely incompatible with the basic tenets of Epicureanism.[27] Given such uncertainty on Origen's part as to the identity of 'his' Celsus,[28] plus the absence of any new evidence that could clarify the issue for us, it just has to be accepted that we simply do not know who Celsus was.

In addressing the question of Celsus's likely provenance, however, we have considerably more evidence with which to play around. We know for certain, for instance, that he enjoyed some kind of personal connection with southern Syria. At 7.9 he produces a scurrilous description, clearly derived from personal observation, of the practices of the (often) beggarly prophets who traipsed around the cities and military camps of Phoenicia and Palestine. At 7.11 he even claims to have interrogated some of those charlatans and heard 'with his own ears' (αὐτήκοος) their admissions of fraudulence.

While this shows that Celsus almost certainly had spent time in those areas, it does not reveal in what capacity he had been there. Schwartz's suggestion that he might have been a high-ranking Roman official ('*haut*

---

24. *Contra Celsum*, Praef. 4.

25. For the date, see Eusebius, *Hist. eccl.* 6.36.2 and Chadwick, *Contra Celsum*, xiv-xv.

26. *Contra Celsum*, Praef. 1 and 3 ('the task which you have set us').

27. For Origen's changing views and growing puzzlement as to Celsus's philosophical allegiance, see 1.10 and 20; 2.60; 3.80; 4.4, 54 and 75; 5.3. For a useful discussion of these passages, see Stern, *Greek and Latin Authors*, 2:225. For Celsus's particular brand of Platonism, see Frede, *Celsus philosophus Platonicus*, 5192.

28. On the likely reason for this uncertainty, see M. Frede, 'Celsus's Attack on the Christians', in *Philosophia Togata II*, ed. Jonathan Barnes and Miriam Griffin (Oxford: Clarendon, 1997), 216–40 (223–7).

fonctionnaire en exercice en Syrie') certainly cannot be dismissed out of hand.[29] Proof, however, is impossible. It could simply be the case that Celsus was a permanent resident in that part of the Roman Empire, having originated, as did his close contemporaries, Lucian and Justin Martyr, from one of Syria's many flourishing towns and cities.[30] Although Celsus's political loyalties clearly lay with Rome (8.73 and 75), in terms of cultural identity he was proudly (it could even be said, arrogantly) Greek.[31]

Southern Syria, however, is not the only area that has been suggested for Celsus's provenance. Egypt and, more specifically, its capital, Alexandria, also have their champions.[32] That Celsus mentions Egypt more than any other part of the Roman world is an undeniable fact. Although many of his references to that country, especially its religious practices, consist of material drawn from Herodotus,[33] he is not reliant solely on that classical author. He knows a certain amount about, for instance, the relatively new cult of Antinoos, the deified catamite of the emperor Hadrian who drowned in the Nile in 130 CE (3.36 and 5.63), is well informed about Egyptian demonology (8.58) and among his oral informants at least one individual of Egyptian extraction is to be found (6.41). Suggestive as these multiple references to things Egyptian are, they do not prove either an Egyptian or an Alexandrian provenance for Celsus. Indeed, against the likelihood of the latter, one might cite Origen's ignorance about Celsus. Had he come from Alexandria, one might have expected Origen, himself

29. Jacques Schwartz, 'Du Testament de Lévi au Discours véritable de Celse', *RHPhR* 40 (1960): 126–45 (144 n. 93). Wilken's claim (*Christians as the Romans Saw Them*, 95), that 'unlike Pliny, he [Celsus] is not a politician or a civil official' seems to me to be a trifle dogmatic. Many Roman officials (e.g., Pliny the Elder and Arrian) managed simultaneously to be both government officials and writers. For Lucian's employment late in life as a Roman administrator, see Jones, *Culture and Society*, 20–1.

30. On the vigour of urban life in Roman Syria in the early Roman imperial period and the many literary and philosophical figures of distinction that Syria produced at that time, see Maurice Sartre, *The Middle East under Rome*, trans. Catherine Porter and Elizabeth Rawlings (Cambridge, MA: Harvard University Press, 2005), 151–205 and 284–91.

31. Shown by his remarks at 1.2 and 6.1 about the natural superiority of Greeks to barbarians.

32. M. Niehoff, 'A Jewish Critique of Christianity from Second-Century Alexandria: Revisiting the Jew Mentioned in *Contra Celsum*', *JECS* 21, no. 2 (2013): 151–75 (154–5 and 168). Although Chadwick, *Contra Celsum*, xxviii–ix, also inclines to this view, he does not fully commit to it.

33. See, especially, the long quotation at 5.34 from Herodotus, *Histories* 2.18.

a citizen and one-time resident of that city, to have had a clearer idea as to his identity.[34] That Celsus, like so many elite young Hellenes, had been educated in that 'university city' remains, however, a distinct possibility. His brand of Platonism apparently was the type that had been developed and was studied there.[35] Further, the Logos-theology of Hellenistic Judaism with which Celsus was well acquainted likewise had been formulated in that city.[36]

Less likely is a Roman provenance for Celsus. Although some have suggested that he might have come from the imperial capital[37] or at least visited it,[38] the evidence for this is far from compelling. One of the arguments for a sojourn on Celsus's part in the capital is his undoubted knowledge about Gnosticism and Marcionism, both of which flourished greatly there around the middle of the second century.[39] Rome, however, was not the only place in the Graeco-Roman world where these 'heretical' varieties of Christianity were to be found. Justin, writing shortly after 150 CE, states that Marcion's doctrine has spread among all the nations of the world.[40] Celsus's knowledge of Gnosticism has been used to support an Alexandrian provenance for him![41]

Niehoff and Lona both seek to explain the evidence (such as it is) by suggesting that Celsus came from Alexandria and visited Rome, possibly spending a fair bit of time in the latter.[42] They justify this by pointing to the mobility enjoyed by Greek intellectuals during the second century.[43]

34. So, persuasively, John Whittaker in Richard Goulet, ed., *Dictionnaire des philosophes antique*, 5 vols (Paris: CNRS 1994–), *s.v.* vol. 2, C. 70.

35. See Niehoff, 'A Jewish Critique', 155.

36. W. H. C. Frend, *Martyrdom and Persecution in the Early Church* (Oxford: Blackwell, 1985), 297 n. 56, following Chadwick.

37. See, for instance, Frede, 'Celsus philosophus Platonicus', 5190–1.

38. Niehoff, 'A Jewish Critique', 154 – 'he must also have travelled to Rome'.

39. For Valentinus, see Ismo Dunderberg, 'Valentinian Teachers in Rome', in *Christians as a Religious Minority in a Multicultural City*, ed. Jürgen Zangenberg and Michael Labahn, JSNTSup 243 (London: T&T Clark, 2004), 157–74 (158). For Marcion, see S. Moll, *The Arch-Heretic Marcion* (Tübingen: Mohr, 2010), 43–5.

40. *Apol.* 1.26.5 ('he has persuaded many from every race of humankind'). For its strong presence in Syria, see Sartre, *Middle East under Rome*, 340 and 541 n. 266.

41. Chadwick, *Contra Celsum* xxviii–ix.

42. Niehoff, 'A Jewish Critique', 154; Lona, *Die Wahre Lehre*, 56–7.

43. See the bibliography cited at Niehoff, 'A Jewish Critique', 155 n. 12. On this point, see also Simon Goldhill, 'Rhetoric and the Second Sophistic', in *The Cambridge Companion to Ancient Rhetoric*, ed. Erik Gunderson (Cambridge: Cambridge University Press, 2009), 228–41 (230).

This tidy explanation may be right. However, the fact remains that the only areas with which Celsus is explicitly associated are Phoenicia and Palestine. Consequently, Frend's cautious conclusion, now endorsed wholeheartedly by Simmons,[44] that both Celsus's work and Celsus himself probably emanated from 'the broad area between Alexandria and Antioch' seems to me to represent a sounder estimate of the evidence.[45]

If rock-solid biographical data about Celsus are almost impossible to come by, that does not mean that nothing can be known about him. Much can be safely inferred about him from the remains of his work, as preserved by Origen. From this material we can work out, in the first place, approximately when Celsus felt driven to fire his broadside against the Christians and Jesus.

8.3. *The Compositional Date of the* Alethes Logos

Although it has been claimed recently that no dating more precise than 'the second century' can be established,[46] Celsus's text actually offers several clear pointers of an historical nature to the likely date of its composition – a fact noted by one of the earliest scholars to attempt a reconstruction of his work, Theodor Keim (1873).[47] A striking feature of the closing section of the *Alethes Logos* is the author's clear anxiety about the threat currently posed by the barbarians to both the empire and its rulers. Thus at 8.68, for instance, we find him addressing the Christians in these words – 'If everyone were to do the same as you [i.e., refuse to support the emperor], there would be nothing to prevent him from being left, alone and abandoned, while earthly things [i.e., the empire] would fall into the hands of the most lawless and most savage barbarians, and nothing more would be heard among men of either your cult or the true wisdom'. And he follows this up by envisaging an even

44. Simmons, 'Graeco-Roman Philosophical Opposition', 844.

45. Frend, *Martyrdom*, 297 n. 56 and *The Rise of Christianity* (Philadelphia: Fortress, 1984), 177.

46. John Granger Cook, 'Celsus', in Keith et al., eds, *The Reception of Jesus*, 3:3–29 (3). For an even wider time-span (viz. from the middle of the second century to the beginning of the third), see K. Pichler, *Streit um das Christentum. Der Angriff des Kelsos und die Antwort des Origenes* (Frankfurt, 1980), 97.

47. For a discussion of Keim's dating (178 CE), which he broadly endorses, see Lona, *Die Wahre Lehre*, 54–5. For Keim's treatise itself, see Theodor Keim, *Celsus's Wahres Wort. Aelteste Streitschrift antiker Weltanschauung gegen das Christentum, vom Jahr 178 n. Chr.* (Zürich, 1873).

worse scenario – namely, the possibility that 'those who now reign over us' (οἱ νῦν βασιλεύοντες ἡμῶν) could even be taken prisoner (8.71).

Such concerns, inconceivable under the stable, unthreatened regimes of Trajan, Hadrian and Antoninus Pius, reflect the loss of confidence widely felt by the inhabitants of the empire during the reign of Marcus Aurelius (161–80 CE), especially its latter half. It was then that the empire's northern defences, already weakened by plague brought back from Mesopotamia by returning units of Lucius Verus's army, buckled and gave way under the pressures exerted by migratory tribes from the interior of the continent. The result had been the first 'barbarian' invasion of Italy since the late second century BCE and the penetration by the Costoboci, a trans-Danubian tribe, into the very heart of Hellas (170/71 CE). There they had ended up sacking one of the most revered religious sites in the whole Graeco-Roman world, the sanctuary of Demeter at Eleusis, home of the Mysteries.[48] The shockwaves created throughout the Greek world by that outrage can still be felt in the threnody (lament) for Eleusis delivered at Smyrna in the immediate aftermath of the disaster by Aelius Aristeides, one of the leading sophists of the day.[49]

For the empire's inhabitants, people who had come to take the Augustan peace for granted, these were indeed extraordinarily unsettling times. Adding to the general sense of insecurity was the knowledge that the emperor himself, a man with only minimal military experience, had decided to take to the field in person in order to face down the barbarian threat. Although in due course he did enjoy some successes, enough to secure him the title Sarmaticus (conqueror of the Sarmatians) and a triumph in Rome (celebrated in 176 CE), the barbarian problem was far from being solved. The closing years of Aurelius's reign (178–180 CE) saw him once again battling the barbarian on Rome's Danube frontier and so exposing himself to danger.[50]

It is this period, the closing years of 170s CE, then, that would appear to be the most likely time for the composition of the *Alethes Logos*.[51] The phrase, 'those who now reign over us' (8.71), if interpreted strictly, would support this view, since those years (177–80 CE) did indeed see the joint rule of two emperors, Marcus Aurelius and his sole surviving

---

48. For the dating of these events, see Birley in *OCD*[3], *s.v.* Aurelius, Marcus.

49. For the date and location of the delivery of this still extant speech (*Oratio* 22), see C. A. Behr, *Aristides and the Sacred Tales* (Amsterdam: Hakkert, 1968), 110.

50. Birley, ibid. for the details.

51. Keim's dating of the work precisely to 178 CE (n. 47 above) seems unnecessarily restricted.

son, Commodus.[52] That the work was composed under either Hadrian[53] or Antoninus Pius,[54] strikes me as improbable, given the largely peaceful nature of their reigns and the fact that the northern barbarians were not yet posing an active threat to the empire. Equally uncompelling is the suggestion that the *Alethes Logos* may have been composed *ca.* 200 CE during the joint reign of Septimius Severus and his elder son, Caracalla.[55] Although those emperors did embark together on a war at that time, that was by choice rather than necessity, and the possibility of their being captured by the enemy is not so much as hinted at in our sources.[56]

It is not just about the dating of Celsus's literary activity, however, that the surviving remnants of his work provide clues. They also have much to tell us about the scope of his scholarship and his educational background.

8.4. *Celsus's Knowledge and Handling of Christian Sources*

For the task of waging war upon Jesus and Christianity, Celsus was unusually well equipped. Generally the only people who read (or listened to) Christian writings were the Christians themselves, as we know from Tertullian.[57] While the difficulty of gaining access to these in-group texts clearly will have been one reason for this state of affairs, lack of interest on the part of pagans, plus a distaste for the relative crudity of Christian writings,[58] probably played a much larger part. To this general indif-

---

52. There is nothing to prevent this interpretation, even though some scholars prefer to take the phrase as no more than a generalized reference to Roman imperial rule. See, for instance, H.-U. Rosenbaum, 'Zu Datierung von Celsus' ΑΛΗΘΗΣ ΛΟΓΟΣ', *VC* 26 (1972): 102–1; Frede, '*Celsus philosophus Platonicus*', 5188–9; Cook, 'Celsus', 3.

53. For the recent suggestion of a Hadrianic date, see discussion at Carleton Paget, 'The Jew of Celsus', 202 n. 6.

54. See Schwartz, 'Du Testament de Lévi', 137 and 'Celsus Redivivus', *RHPhR* 53 (1973): 399–405 (399), who argues for such a date on purely literary grounds.

55. J. W. Hargis, *Against the Christians: The Rise of Early Anti-Christian Polemic* (New York: Peter Lang, 1999), 20–3.

56. See A. Birley, *Septimius Severus: The African Emperor* (London: Eyre & Spottiswoode, 1971), Chapter 14.

57. *Testimonio Animae* 1. For text and translation, see above Chapter 7, n. 102.

58. Wolfram Kinzig, 'Pagans and the Bible', in *The New Cambridge History of the Bible 1: From the Beginnings to 600*, ed. James Carleton Paget and Joachim Schaper (Cambridge: Cambridge University Press, 2013), 752–74 (752).

ference, however, Celsus proves to be a rare exception.[59] With him, we find ourselves for the very first time dealing with a well-educated pagan who has taken it upon himself to search out and to engage seriously with what 'the enemy' has written. And such is the zeal with which he carries out this self-imposed task that he ends up reading a far greater variety of Christian texts than most Christians in his day almost certainly will have done.

Celsus was only too aware that the contemporary Christian movement was not a single, monolithic entity.[60] He knew that many different forms of Christianity existed, each with its own distinctive beliefs about Jesus[61] and, in some cases, very different practices too.[62] Being without any attachment to Christianity himself, Celsus could view the movement's various splinter groups with complete impartiality. Hence his willingness to read all sorts of Christian writings and his readiness to press into service any Christian text that could further his polemical purpose. The works he searched out included not just texts that subsequently were to become canonical but sectarian writings later to be condemned as heretical and so for the most part lost to us. *The Celestial Dialogue* from which he quotes briefly at one point (8.15) is one such work.[63] The Gnostic (Ophite?) text with its elaborate cosmological diagram, discussed at considerable length by Origen at 6.24-38, is another.[64] With early Christian apologetic writings too he had some familiarity.[65] Whether these included Justin Martyr's

---

59. Hence MacMullen's characterization of him, cited at n. 13 above, as a 'minor oddity'.

60. On the schismatic nature of contemporary Christianity, see, for instance, 3.10 – 'At the beginning, they were few and of one mind. Having spread and multiplied greatly, they are divided (τέμνονται) and split (σχίζονται) and each wants to have his own faction (στάσις)'.

61. At 5.62 he lists quite a few of these sects – e.g., the followers of, respectively, Marcellina, Salome, Mariamme, Martha and Marcion. For Celsus's use of Marcionite source materials, see 5.54; 5.62; 6.52 and 53; 6.74 and 7.18.

62. At 5.64, for instance, he alludes to the ritual branding practised by some Christians. From the rather fuller account of Irenaeus (*Against the Heresies* 1.25.6), we learn that it was the Carpocratians, a Gnostic sect originating in Alexandria, who did this.

63. On this probably Marcionite text, so obscure that apparently it was unknown to Origen, see Howard M. Jackson, 'The Setting and Sectarian Provenance of the Fragment of the "Celestial Dialogue" Preserved by Origen from Celsus's Ἀληθὴς Λόγος', *HTR* 85, no. 3 (1992): 273–305.

64. On this, see A. J. Welburn, 'Reconstructing the Ophite Diagram', *NovT* 23 (1981): 261–87.

65. See Chadwick's note at 3.43.

celebrated defence of Christianity remains a matter of dispute.[66] However, there can be no doubt that he had read the *Dialogue of Papiscus and Jason*, a work that he viewed with undiluted contempt (4.52).[67]

Identifying precisely the Christian writings utilized by Celsus in the *Alethes Logos* is far from easy, which is why the lists drawn up by different scholars can vary so much.[68] Sometimes this is because the evidence is so meagre: Celsus's use of the *Epistle of Barnabas*, for instance, rests on two distinctive, possibly significant, epithets applied to Jesus's disciples at 1.63. While for some, they are enough to show that Celsus did indeed consult that work,[69] others remain unconvinced.[70] But the biggest obstacle to identification is caused by Celsus's practice, standard among classical writers of the period, of rarely naming the sources upon which he is drawing.[71] Consequently, it is only when he is making generous use of (those few) texts that have happened to come down to us that anything approaching complete certainty is possible.

Fortunately for us, the Christian texts of which Celsus makes the greatest use are the narrative accounts of Jesus's life which in due course became canonical – i.e., the gospels of Matthew, Mark, Luke and John. So extensive is his use of these texts, particularly the gospel of Matthew,[72]

---

66. See Gary T. Burke, 'Celsus and Justin: Carl Andresen Revisited', *ZNW* 76 (1985): 107–16 who challenges the once widely accepted hypothesis that the *Alethes Logos* was a direct response to Justin. For the hypothesis itself, see Carl Andresen, *Logos und Nomos. Die Polemik des Kelsos wider das Christentum* (Berlin: de Gruyter, 1955), 308–72.

67. For a recently discovered fragment of this mid-second-century Christian apologetic work, once thought to have been lost for ever, see François Bovon and John M. Duffy, 'A New Greek Fragment from Ariston of Pella's "*Dialogue of Jason and Papiscus*"', *HTR* 105, no. 4 (2012): 457–65, who attribute its neglect after the fourth/fifth century CE to its mediocrity.

68. While Frend, for instance (*Rise of Christianity*, 177) credits Celsus with use of the *Protevangelium of James*, John Granger Cook, following Borret, disallows this. See his monograph, *The Interpretation of the New Testament in Greco-Roman Paganism*, STAC 3 (Tübingen: Mohr Siebeck, 2000), 25. On Celsus's use of Paul, by contrast, the situation is reversed.

69. E.g., Simmons, 'Graeco-Roman Philosophical Opposition', 846 and Niehoff, 'A Jewish Critique', 165.

70. See, for instance, Borret, *Contre Celse*, 5:273.

71. See 63–5 above.

72. For Origen's explicit comment on this, see 1.34. For confirmation of Origen's opinion, see Borret's New Testament index at *Contre Celse*, 5:260–72 which shows that Celsus used Matthew far more than any other gospel.

that we can form a very good idea of the quality of his scholarship. Two features of this are worth pointing out here.

The first is Celsus's mastery of these sources. Indeed, such is his control of them that, when discussing the key events of Jesus's life, he knows instinctively which gospel will serve his polemical purpose best. That is why, for instance, when dealing with the discovery of the empty sepulchre on Easter morning, he privileges John's account over those of the other evangelists – something that he rarely did.[73] In order to convince his readership that Jesus's resurrection was a mirage, Celsus needs to cite the version of that event which provides the weakest eyewitness testimony. Since John has the smallest number of initial witnesses, just one,[74] and that witness is 'a hysterical woman' (γυνὴ πάροιστρος),[75] unerringly he favours John's version. On the basis of his account, Celsus can argue very plausibly that the resurrection is unsupported by any reliable evidence. It should not be forgotten that Celsus's readers, largely educated males steeped in the forensic oratory of classical Athens, would have been pre-conditioned to discount female testimony.[76]

The second feature of Celsus's scholarship worth emphasizing is his accuracy. Although a favourite tactic of Origen for undermining Celsus is to accuse him of misunderstanding his sources and getting his facts wrong,[77] very few errors can be laid to his account.[78] Indeed, on some

73. On the rarity with which Celsus uses John (five times less than Matthew), see Borret, *Contre Celse*, 5:264–5 and Cook, *Interpretation*, 25. In fact, almost all of Celsus's Johannine references are to the Easter morning events.

74. Mary of Magdala – Jn 20:1. By contrast, Matthew (28:1) has two witnesses, Mark (16:1), three, and Luke (24:10) three named witnesses plus an unspecified number of anonymous women.

75. See 2.55. The epithet, πάροιστρος (in a frenzy; out-of-control; beside oneself), will have reminded Celsus's readers of the Euripidean classic, the *Bacchae*, in which cognates of this word are used several times to denote the frenzied, out-of-control state of Dionysus's followers, the Maenads. See, for instance, *Bacch.* 32; 119; 665.

76. In classical Athens, the period most admired by the educated Greek elite, the *pepaideumenoi*, women could not even give evidence on their own behalf in court. A man had to do it for them. See R. Just, *Women in Athenian Law and Life* (London: Routledge, 1989), 34–6 and S. Blundell, *Women in Ancient Greece* (London: British Museum Press, 1995), 114.

77. For muddle, see, for instance, 1.62; 1.69; 2.10 and 8.16; for invention, 6.35; for lying, 7.11.

78. Rare cases are the trivial mistakes of referring to Herod as a tetrarch, rather than a king (1.58), and to the Carpocratians, a Christian splinter group in Egypt, as Harpocratians (5.62). On the reason for the latter slip, see Borret, *Contre Celse*, note *ad loc.*

of the occasions when Origen berates Celsus for inaccuracy, it is Origen himself who can be seen to be in the wrong. Thus his claim at 1.58 that Celsus has failed to mention the star that appeared at the time of Jesus's birth is disproved by the latter's explicit reference to the star at 1.34. And his accusation at 6.35 that Celsus is guilty of manufacturing his evidence is regarded by most modern commentators not only as unfounded[79] but even 'absurd'.[80]

That is not to say that Celsus never manipulates his texts for polemical purposes. Some of the subtle changes that he introduces, such as referring to Jesus's birthplace as a village rather than a city (1.28), and to some of the disciples as sailors rather than fishermen (1.62 and 2.46), are deliberately denigratory. If challenged about those tweaks to the gospel texts, doubtless he would have defended himself by saying that what he was doing was no different from what the gospel writers themselves habitually did. He had no illusions about the apologetic nature of their writings and the fact that the gospel texts, far from being set in stone, were constantly being re-shaped in order to counter the objections of critics (2.27).[81]

8.5. *Celsus's Knowledge and Handling of Jewish Sources*

It was not just Christian writings, however, that Celsus made a point of reading. Aware of the way in which Christians exploited the sacred writings of the Jews for apologetic purposes,[82] Celsus made an effort to acquaint himself (via the LXX) with at least some of the Hebrew scriptures too. How many of those writings he read at first hand is disputed. Burke's careful study has shown that Genesis is the only book where evidence of literary dependence is indisputable.[83] Some scholars, however, claim that he had consulted the Pentateuch more widely.[84] Certainly he does make reference occasionally to Exodus (twice) and Deuteronomy (eight times)[85] and he is sufficiently well acquainted with the teaching of Moses to be able to exploit for polemical purposes certain differences between

79. See, for instance, Hoffmann, *Celsus*, 139 n. 136.
80. Jackson, 'Setting and Sectarian Provenance', 277 n. 7.
81. For detailed discussions of this important passage, see Niehoff, 'A Jewish Critique', 160–2 and Lona, *Die Wahre Lehre*, 138–40.
82. For his criticism of them on this score, see, for instance, 1.50 and 2.28.
83. Gary T. Burke, 'Celsus and the Old Testament', *VT* 36, no. 2 (1986): 241–5. For a similar conclusion, see now Kinzig, 'Pagans and the Bible', 758.
84. E.g., Frend, *Rise of Christianity*, 177 – 'He knew the Pentateuch'.
85. For these references, see Borret's OT index at *Contre Celse*, 5:252–3.

Moses's precepts and those of Jesus.[86] But whether those references were gleaned from personal reading or acquired only at second hand is disputed. There is a similar difficulty with Jonah and Daniel. Although he knew the stories of Jonah and Daniel well enough to use them polemically against Jesus (7.53), whether he had read the books of Jonah and Daniel either whole or in part cannot be determined.

Celsus's knowledge of Jewish texts was not confined, however, to the books of the Old Testament. He was familiar with later Jewish writings too. With 1 Enoch, an apocalyptic work that played an important role especially in Gnostic speculation,[87] he appears to have been closely acquainted.[88] And he was well informed too about the current Jewish pushback against Jesus,[89] as the first two books of the *Contra Celsum* show very clearly. The precise form originally taken by this hostile Jewish material is a matter of debate.[90] While some believe that Celsus was using a written source or sources,[91] others think that he was drawing upon oral testimonies that were to assume a written form only at a very much later date.[92] That Celsus could indeed

86. After pointing out some of these differences (7.18), Celsus asks rhetorically 'Who is lying? Moses or Jesus?'

87. For this text, also known as the Ethiopic *Apocalypse of Enoch*, see George W. E. Nickelsburg, 'Enoch, Books of', in Schiffman and VanderKam, eds, *Encyclopedia of the Dead Sea Scrolls*, 1:249–53. For its later popularity with the Church Fathers, see E. Schürer, *The History of the Jewish People in the Age of Jesus Christ*, rev. and ed. Geza Vermes, Fergus Millar and Martin Goodman, 3 vols (Edinburgh: T&T Clark, 1973–87), 3:261–4.

88. See Chadwick's note at 5.52.

89. To be seen most clearly at Justin, *Dialogue with Trypho* 108.2. Tertullian, *On the Spectacles* (*De spectaculis*) 30.6, though slightly later in date (196–97 CE), is also relevant here. On this passage as evidence for 'current Jewish anti-Christian polemic', see William Horbury, *Jews and Christians in Contact and Controversy* (Edinburgh: T&T Clark, 1998), 176–9. That Jesus's mother had been a whore (*quaestuaria*) is prominent in the calumnies directed at him.

90. See Cook, *Interpretation*, 27 n. 51; Lincoln Blumell, 'A Jew in Celsus' *True Doctrine*? An Examination of Jewish Anti-Christian Polemic in the Second Century C. E.', *SR* 36, no. 2 (2007): 297–315 (299–301) and Carleton Paget, 'The Jew of Celsus', *passim*.

91. For the extreme (and, in my view, unconvincing) hypothesis that Celsus was doing little more than plagiarizing a work written by a second-century CE Alexandrian Jew, see Niehoff, 'A Jewish Critique'.

92. For these, see P. Schäfer, *Jesus in the Talmud* (Princeton: Princeton University Press, 2007). For an older and briefer treatment of the Talmudic material relating to Jesus, see R. Joseph Hoffmann, *Jesus Outside the Gospels* (Buffalo: Prometheus, 1984), 39–53.

have been pressing into service ideas picked up either through talking to Jews[93] or through his familiarity with Jewish-Christian disputation[94] is not at all unlikely. But really there is no need for the matter to be viewed in such binary terms. It is entirely possible that the contemporary Jewish material used by Celsus could have been a mixture of the oral and the written, given the wide-ranging nature of his investigations.[95]

8.6. *Celsus's Rhetorical Skills*

All this reading and collecting of Christian and Jewish material would have availed Celsus little, however, had he not possessed the analytical and rhetorical skills, the latter taught in the third and final stage of the Graeco-Roman educational system, to exploit the material itself effectively. These he obviously did have. What emerges with great clarity from his work, notwithstanding the fragmented state in which we meet it, is that Celsus, besides having a good brain and an indefatigable appetite for research, had also mastered the core techniques necessary for success in the art of persuasion. Acquired through an intensive course of mental gymnastics known as *progymnasmata*, these preliminary rhetorical exercises were designed to ensure effectiveness as much in writing as in speech. To quote Theon, the author of a popular textbook on the *progymnasmata*:

> Training in the *progymnasmata* is absolutely necessary not only for those who are going to practise rhetoric, but also if one wishes to undertake the function of poets or historians *or any other writers*. These exercises are, as it were, *the foundation of every kind of discourse*, and, depending on how one instils them in the minds of the young, necessarily the results make themselves felt in the same way later.[96]

How many of the fourteen graded exercises that traditionally made up the *progymnastic* course Celsus completed is not known.[97] Given the

93. Quite likely given his time spent in Palestine and Phoenicia (7.11).

94. See, for instance, 3.1 and 4.23, where these disputations are given full satirical treatment.

95. See the sensible remarks on Celsus's likely sources at Morton Smith, *Jesus the Magician* (Wellingborough: Aquarian, 1985), 58–9.

96. For this quotation and an excellent survey of *progymnasmata* in imperial times, see Robert J. Penella, 'The "Progymnasmata" in Imperial Greek Education', *CW* 105, no. 1 (2011): 77–90 (88–9 for the quotation; the italics are mine).

97. For brief discussions of the fourteen traditional exercises, see George A. Kennedy, *A New History of Classical Rhetoric* (Princeton: Princeton University Press, 1994), 203–7 and Penella, 'Progymnasmata', 80–2. Although detailed evidence for

length and the expense of the training, only a minority who embarked on the course are thought to have finished it and so reached the point where they could begin to compose original declamations, so-called *meletai* (μελέται).[98] That Celsus had taken this training to a very advanced level is shown by his apparent mastery of the exercise traditionally numbered 11 – i.e., *prosopopeia* or the personification of an imaginary character. A significant part of his polemic against Jesus, as we shall see in the next chapter, is the brutal attack that he places in the mouth of a nameless Hellenized Jew. Whether that individual is an invented character or an historical person is a hugely disputed and ultimately insoluble question, as Carleton Paget's recent, in-depth study of the matter shows.[99] The position adopted here is identical to that of Origen himself, who writes of Celsus (1.28) that 'he uses *prosopopeia* in the manner of a child introducing a figure of rhetoric'.[100] In other words, the anonymous Jew is a made-up figure created by Celsus to function as his mouthpiece rather like Lucian's anonymous critic in *On the Death of Peregrinus* 7-30.[101]

Given Celsus's mastery of this advanced exercise, there can be no surprise to find him competently executing several of the more elementary exercises in the progymnastic training programme – namely, *anaskeue*, or refutation (no. 5); *psogos*, or invective (no. 9) and *synkrisis*, or comparison (no. 10). In his execution of the last of these, *synkrisis*, Celsus showed himself particularly skilled. By comparing Jesus unfavourably with a variety of individuals, divine, semi-divine and human, he aims to portray Jesus as an inferior god, a second-rate hero and a derivative thinker.[102]

this scheme does not pre-date the fourth century CE, it is generally accepted that the scheme itself was already 'widely regarded as authoritative in the middle and late Roman Empire'. See Penella, 'Progymnasmata', 80. For some of the textbooks themselves, see George A. Kennedy, *Progymnasmata: Greek Textbooks of Prose Composition and Rhetoric*, Writings from the Greco-Roman World 10 (Atlanta: SBL, 2003).

98. On the low completion rate and the likely reasons for it, see Raffaella Cribiore, *Gymnastics of the Mind: Greek Education in Hellenistic and Roman Egypt* (Princeton: Princeton University Press, 2001), 224.

99. Carleton Paget, 'The Jew of Celsus'.

100. For further references by Origen to Celsus's use of *prosopopeia*, see *Praef.* 6; 1.32, 34 and 49; 2.1.

101. For the scholarly consensus that this was Lucian himself speaking, see above, Chapter 7 n. 52.

102. For examples of this comparative material, see 2.34 (Dionysus); 3.24 (Asclepius); 1.67 (Perseus and various other demi-gods); 7.53 (Hercules); 5.20 (Zeno, the founder of Stoicism); 6.16 (Plato). Not all figures with whom Celsus compares Jesus are derived from Greek culture. At 7.53 he compares Jesus unfavourably with Daniel.

Even as a wonder-worker Jesus is not allowed to shine: at 1.68 we find Celsus placing him on a par with the common-or-garden magicians who ply their dubious 'trade' in the market-places (*agorai*) of the Greek world.

Such in outline is the man who has made it his mission to destroy the credibility of Jesus and, with it, that of his distressingly popular cult. Our next task is to see how he puts this into operation. Celsus's plan of action falls into three parts. In the first, we see him conjuring up an anonymous Jew to attack Jesus personally (1.28-71); in the second, using that same character to berate those Jews who foolishly have abandoned the customs of their ancestors (i.e., true wisdom) for Christianity, a low class, upstart cult that has no legitimacy whatsoever (2.1-79). Finally, in the third part of his discourse (Books 3-8), we meet Celsus, speaking in his own voice and as a Platonist. Here he seeks to demonstrate why the main beliefs that underpin this Jesus-worship, most notably, his incarnation as the son of God and resurrection, are philosophically untenable.

Chapter 9

CELSUS'S TRIPARTITE ASSAULT ON JESUS

9.1. *An Anonymous Jew Attacks Jesus in Person*

To make an impact upon his readers/audience, Celsus will have been taught by his instructors in rhetoric that an arresting start is absolutely essential.[1] Hence the truly breathtaking manner in which he opens his case against Jesus. Conjuring up an anonymous Jew and casting him in the role of, as it were, counsel for the prosecution, he launches an extraordinarily vituperative attack on Jesus, charging him with being nothing more than a low-class liar, bastard and braggart. Since the flavour of this attack is best captured by Hoffmann,[2] I here reproduce his sparkling version of Celsus's text, notwithstanding the reservations I have about the looseness of his translation in some places. For a thoroughly literal, and therefore rather leaden, rendition of Celsus's text at 1.28, the reader should consult Chadwick.[3]

> Is it not true, good sir, that you fabricated the story of your birth from a virgin to quiet rumours about the true and unsavory circumstances of your origins? Is it not the case that far from being born in royal David's city of Bethlehem you were born in a poor country town, and of a woman who earned her living by spinning? Is it not the case that when her deceit was discovered, to wit, that she was pregnant by a Roman soldier named Panthera,[4] she was driven away by her husband – the carpenter – and convicted of adultery? Indeed, is it not so that in her disgrace, wandering

1. On the importance of crafting effective beginning and end sections to a discourse, see 78 above.
2. See his *Celsus*, 57.
3. Chadwick, *Origen: Contra Celsum*, 28.
4. Although this phrase does not appear in the Jew's harangue as given by Origen at 1.28, clearly it was part of it, as Origen's second, fuller citation of the harangue at

far from home, she gave birth to a male child in silence and humiliation? What more? Is it not so that you hired yourself out as a workman in Egypt, learned magical crafts, and gained something of a name for yourself which you now flaunt among your kinsmen?

Notwithstanding the considerable liberties taken by Hoffmann in producing this reconstruction of Celsus's text, it remains valuable for the way that it conveys so well, indeed better than any of the more literal translations available, just how powerful a polemicist Celsus could be and how well trained he was in the art of rhetoric. What we are presented with here is, in effect, a textbook example of invective (in Greek, ψόγος [*psogos*]; in Latin, *vituperatio*).

For a piece of invective to pass muster, it had to cover certain topics, the main ones being a person's origins (crucially, where he came from and who his parents were) and his upbringing. Under the latter heading matters to be dealt with included skills acquired (*technai*) in the process of reaching maturity and principles of conduct.[5] Each of these topics accordingly is addressed in the passage set out above. No prescription, however, was made as to how much space should be given to each topic. Nor was the order in which they should be addressed set in stone. As can be seen from examples of *psogos* in contemporary literature such as the writings of Lucian, much play tended to be made of sexual impropriety, whether that of the person under direct attack or that of those closely associated with him.[6] Indeed, often this particular topic was given the top billing and treated far more extensively than any of the others.[7] No surprise then to see Celsus giving such prominence to the adultery of Jesus's (here unnamed) mother. It served several purposes – besides, besmirching Jesus by association and destroying the extraordinary claims he allegedly was making about his birth, it will also have titillated his readership in the way they had come to expect.

In laying this charge against Jesus's mother, Celsus did not have to resort to fabrication himself, as was so often the case with those engaging

---

1.32 shows. Consequently, Hoffmann is entirely justified in including it in his reconstruction at *Celsus*, 57. Origen's quotation at 1.32 shows exactly where this offensive material should be placed.

5. For an example of the prescriptions laid down for invective, see Kennedy, *Progymnasmata*, 108.

6. For some examples, see Lucian, *Peregr.* 9 and *Alex./False Prophet* 5 and 42.

7. On sexual slander as a prominent element in classical invective, see Jones, *Culture and Society*, 107 and 121.

in formal invective.[8] His sources provided him with ready ammunition. While two of the gospel writers, Matthew and John, clearly hint that doubts existed about Jesus's paternity,[9] the Jewish counter-narratives against Jesus with which Celsus was familiar were very explicit on this point – not only did they refer to Jesus's mother as an adulteress but they even supplied the name of her paramour![10]

Whether Jesus's natural father really was a soldier called Panthera[11] or whether the Panthera figure was just a mischievous fiction, his name possibly being a pun on *parthenos*, the Greek word for maiden, is a matter into which there is no need for us to go.[12] The question that we do need to address and attempt to answer, however, is why Celsus decides to supply his name at all. Strikingly, it is the only one to be supplied in this passage, notwithstanding the fact that Celsus was not ignorant of either the name of Jesus's mother[13] or that of his native village.[14] Why, then, this exception?

If we ask ourselves what associations Celsus was trying to evoke in the minds of his elite Greek readers by drawing attention to the name Panthera (= a panther), a reasonable answer is not hard to produce. The panther featured prominently in both Greek mythology and Graeco-Roman art, especially in mosaics and on sarcophagi.[15] As a well-known familiar of the god Dionysos, this animal was depicted regularly in the latter's orgiastic retinue alongside satyrs and other convention-defying figures (e.g., maenads).[16] Given that Celsus's purpose in this passage is to impugn Mary's sexual conduct and to emphasize Jesus's bastardy,

8. On the hackneyed allegations of pederasty, calculated to produce laughter rather than indignation, see Jones, *Culture and Society*, 120–1.

9. The defensive tone of Mt. 1:18-25, in which Mary's suspicious pregnancy is attributed to the action of the Holy Spirit, suggests that doubts must have been raised about Jesus's paternity. At Jn 8.41, Jesus's opponents clearly imply that he, unlike them, had been 'born of fornication' (ἐκ πορνείας).

10. For detailed analysis and discussion of the Talmudic evidence for Ben Pandera/Pantera, see Schäfer, *Jesus in the Talmud*, 24–9.

11. This allegation is found only in Celsus (1.32). As with the allegation about Mary's adultery, it almost certainly had its origins in Jewish anti-Christian polemic. See Schäfer, *Jesus in the Talmud*, 28.

12. For this idea, found widely in the scholarly literature, see L. Patterson, 'Origin of the Name Panthera', *JThS* 19 (1917): 79–80 and the authorities cited at Lona, *Die Wahre Lehre*, 101 n. 442. Plausible as this suggestion is, it is not susceptible of proof.

13. Supplied by him in material quoted by Origen at 5.52.

14. See 7.18, where Jesus is referred to as 'the man of Nazareth'.

15. See, for instance, Iain Ferris, *Cave Canem – Animals and Roman Society* (Stroud: Amberley, 2018), 148–9.

16. Ferris, *Cave Canem*, Plates 77-79.

his decision to focus on a name that could be guaranteed to conjure up instantly images of sexual abandon is easily understood. He was simply doing what teachers of Greek rhetoric recommended – namely, using nomenclature for the purpose of diminishing his opponent.[17]

Lest this idea should appear fanciful, it should be pointed out that it is not solely through the inclusion of the suggestive name, Panthera, that Celsus hints at Mary's loose morals and Jesus's likely bastardy. His quotation of a phrase from Homer to describe the manner in which Mary gave birth to Jesus, namely, σκότιον ἐγέννησε (literally, 'she gave birth in secret'), also points in that direction. As Celsus's readers, many of whom will have known the *Iliad* by heart, almost certainly will have been aware, those words are used at *Iliad* 6.24 to describe the birth of a bastard – namely, Priam's illegitimate elder brother, the Trojan prince, Boukolion.[18]

Adultery and bastardy, though undoubtedly the most colourful of the allegations made by Celsus in this opening attack, are far from being the only negative comments that he makes about Jesus and his mother. To the rhetorically trained listener/reader, no piece of invective would appear wholly satisfactory unless it contained also certain stock aspersions such as originating from a village (κώμη) as opposed to a city (πόλις), being of low social status and having to work for one's living.[19] While manual work of any kind was despised,[20] working for another person, and, what is more, doing so for pay (μισθός), was regarded as beneath contempt.[21] Given these elite cultural values (prejudices?) and the elite character of Celsus's audience/readership, it is hardly surprising that we see him denigrating both Jesus and his mother on all three counts. Both

---

17. On the use of names and nicknames for the purposes of eulogy and invecv tive, see Kennedy, *Progymnasmata*, 51 (textbook of Theon). For Lucian's use of the suggestive, probably indecent name Coconnas (pomegranate seeds = ? testicles), see *Alex./False Prophet*, 6 and Costa, *Lucian*, 261.

18. For commentary on this passage, see M. M. Willcock, *Homer – Iliad I–XII* (London: Bristol Classical/Duckworth, 1996), 242. For full discussion of the adjective σκότιος (in the dark; in secret – i.e., unlawful), see Lona, *Die Wahre Lehre*, 99.

19. On the stock ingredients of invective, see Jones, *Culture and Society*, 107 nn. 28 and 29; 121 and 135.

20. For the view that the life of a man who subsists through the work of his hands (χερνήτης) was only marginally better than that of a slave, see Aristotle, *Pol.* 1277a38.

21. To be employed as a day-labourer (μισθαρνέω), the verb Celsus uses to describe Jesus's employment in Egypt, was to be the lowest of the low. See Aristotle, *Pol.* 1296b29, where, in the hierarchy of occupations, day-labourers come at the very bottom, lower even than manual workers.

are mocked equally for their rusticity,[22] for their poverty[23] and for the fact
that they had to work for others in order to secure the wherewithal for
their survival. The extremely rare word used by Celsus to describe Mary's
occupation, χερνῆτις, is intended to draw attention to her extremely low
socio-economic status: it indicates, according to the entry in LSJ, that she
was 'a woman that spins for daily hire'.[24] And the word chosen by Celsus
to describe Jesus's own manner of employment (μισθαρνήσας) could
scarcely be more pejorative: the most common application of this verb in
classical literature (it means to hire oneself out for pay) is to prostitutes.[25]

In alleging that both Jesus and his mother were lowly wage-earners,
Celsus may well have been making things up, fabrication being a common
and accepted feature of invective.[26] Certainly, these particular accusations
(of being, respectively, a spinner and a wage-earner in Egypt) are found in
no other surviving source, either Christian or Jewish. Their manufacture
by Celsus is easily understood, however, once both rhetorical convention
and the prejudices of the Greek cultural elite are taken into account.

Another sop to those prejudices is to be seen in the attribution of
Jesus's magical expertise to an Egyptian origin. Although the source of

22. She for being a peasant – literally, of the countryside (ἐγχώρια); he for originating from a Jewish village (ἐκ κώμης ἰουδαϊκῆς). In the gospels, as, for instance,
at Mt. 2:23 and Lk. 1:26, Bethlehem is described as a city (πόλις) but for rhetorical
purposes Celsus downgrades this to a village (κώμη). By translating the words for
Jesus's place of origin as 'a poor country town', Hoffmann misses the social and
cultural significance of Celsus's choice of vocabulary at this point.

23. She for being impoverished (πενιχρά); he for having to emigrate to Egypt 'on
account of penury' (διὰ πενίαν) – a phrase inexplicably left untranslated by Hoffmann.
Jesus's poverty was no incidental matter but an important element in Celsus's
denigration of him, as the repeated references to Jesus's beggarly, outcast existence
shows. See, for instance, 1.61 and 62.

24. See LSJ, *s.v.* χερνῆτις. Its only occurrence in the mainstream literature of
Celsus's day was at *Iliad* 12.433-35, where it is used to describe a pathetic widowed
mother who, by means of her wool-spinning, managed 'to win a grim subsistence
(ἀεικέα μισθόν) for her children'. For this translation of *Iliad* 12.435, see Robert
Fagles, *Homer: The Iliad* (New York: Penguin, 1998), 339.

25. LSJ, *s.v.* μισθαρνέω. On its use in this sense by Demosthenes and Aeschines,
see LSJ *ad loc.* The speeches of both these admired and widely studied Attic orators
will have been very familiar to Celsus's audience/readership. They were core educational texts.

26. On accusations, probably not meant to be taken seriously, but designed to
provoke amusement more than anything else, see Jones, *Culture and Society*, 120–1
and 135.

this allegation against Jesus is generally agreed to have been Jewish,[27] it will have had an instant appeal to a Greek readership too. Many Greek texts, some broadly contemporary with the *Alethes Logos*, attest to Greek suspicion of Egyptian magic/sorcery.[28] That belief had deep roots – the earliest surviving evidence goes as far back as Homer.[29]

So far, so predictable. Celsus is not interested, however, in conventional mud-slinging or indulging elite Greek cultural prejudices simply for amusement. His over-riding aim is to destroy the legitimacy of the Christian cult in the eyes of his readers. Consequently, it is imperative that he demonstrate not merely that its instigator was a low-class bastard but, far more importantly, that he was a liar and an impostor. We have already seen how much emphasis he has placed on Jesus's mendacity in his preamble, its opening words containing an allegation of fabrication (πλασαμένου).[30] No surprise, then, to discover in the torrent of abuse that Celsus now channels towards Jesus yet more allegations along those lines. To present here a full catalogue of those accusations and others is not necessary. Instead, by way of illustrating Celsus's modus operandi, we shall focus on two of the more substantial quotations taken by Origen from the first part of the speech put in the mouth of the anonymous Jew. While the first of these relates to Jesus's deceitful conduct at the time of his 'baptism' in the Jordan by John, the second is concerned with the bogus claims being made for Jesus's 'miracle-working'.

Celsus's knowledge of the synoptic gospels is such that he is fully aware of the significance that their respective authors place on Jesus's baptism in the river Jordan by John. It was then, so all three believe,[31] that Jesus's divine sonship was made public for the first time, the announcement coming from none other than God himself.[32] Determined to deprive this crucial incident of all credibility, Celsus treats it with sustained and

27. On the origins of the tradition that it was as an adult that Jesus went to Egypt and there acquired his skill in sorcery, see Schäfer, *Jesus in the Talmud*, 24–8 (a detailed analysis of *b. Shabbat* 104b, the principal piece of evidence).

28. See, for instance, Lucian, *Philopseudes* (Lover of Lies) 33-36. On the Greek identification of Egypt with magic/sorcery, see Daniel Ogden, *Magic, Witchcraft, and Ghosts in the Greek and Roman Worlds: A Sourcebook* (Oxford: Oxford University Press, 2002), 52–60 and 100.

29. *Odyssey* 4.219-39 (especially 228).

30. For the application of this verb by Celsus also to the disciples, see 2.13.10.

31. Mt. 3:16-17; Mk 1:10-11 and Lk. 3:21-22.

32. On the significance of this episode for Mark, who makes it the opening point of his gospel, see now Bond, *First Biography of Jesus*, 128–32.

undiluted contempt, scornfully suggesting that what Jesus *claimed* he had seen and heard on the occasion of that 'dip' in the river[33] was pure invention. Thus we find him putting these words into 'his' Jew's mouth:

> When you were bathing in the river with John, *you* say that *you* saw what *appeared* to be a bird (φάσμα ὄρνιθος)[34] flying towards you out of the sky. What witness worthy of credence (ἀξιόχρεως μάρτυς) saw this apparition (φάσμα)? Who heard the voice from heaven adopting you as son of God? There is only *your* word for it and that of one of your companions in punishment.[35]

Given the importance of the evidence for the baptism for asserting Jesus's divine status, Celsus's deliberate debunking of it was no small matter, as the length and elaborate nature of Origen's defence shows.[36] In displaying such scepticism towards this crucial evidence, Celsus was doing little more, however, than pointing out the obvious: the gospel accounts of the episode, *if read carefully and interpreted literally*, do indeed support his claims, as Origen is forced, albeit reluctantly, to concede (1.43). None of them makes clear who actually heard the voice: while the synoptics merely comment that 'a voice was heard',[37] the account in John contains no mention of the heavenly voice at all. Further, it is only in John's gospel that any witness to the 'bird' other than Jesus is mentioned, that witness being the baptist himself.[38] His testimony, however, is swiftly discounted by Celsus on the grounds that he, like Jesus, ended up being 'punished' – i.e., put to death by the authorities. As a convicted criminal, he cannot, therefore, be considered 'a witness worthy of credence' (ἀξιόχρεως μάρτυς).[39]

---

33. On the deliberately disrespectful tone of language here (*profanen Klang*), see Lona, *Die Wahre Lehre*, 106. At no point does Celsus actually mention the word baptism.

34. Literally, a phantom of a bird.

35. 1.41 (trans. Williams). The allusion at the end is to John the Baptist, whose clear-cut witness to the descent of the dove is mentioned only in John's account. See Jn 1:32-34.

36. See Chadwick, *Contra Celsum* 39-46 (= 1.42-48).

37. Mt. 3:17; Mk 1:11; Lk. 3:22.

38. Jn 1:32.

39. On Celsus's rhetorical strategy here, see Lona, *Die Wahre Lehre*, 106. The reference to the associated deaths of Jesus and John, an occurrence unattested in any of the gospels, is thought by some scholars to reflect Celsus's use here of a Jewish tradition. For discussion, see Carleton Paget, 'The Jew of Celsus', 221 n. 119.

No less important for asserting Jesus's divine stature than God's public adoption of him as his son are Jesus's well known 'miracles' – 'those cures and resurrections, or feeding the crowds with but a few loaves (and having some left over to boot!)'.[40] Deceitfully claimed by Jesus himself as proof that he was a god[41] and vigorously promoted as such by his equally mendacious disciples,[42] these tales nonetheless command widespread credence.[43] How is Celsus to deprive them of credibility?

Rather than attempting to dismiss the evidence out of hand, Celsus declares himself ready, for the sake of argument, to accept that Jesus really did heal the sick, raise people from the dead and manage to feed thousands of people with just a few loaves.[44] However, he rejects completely the claim that these miracles were accomplished through Jesus's divine powers. They could just as easily be explained, so he contends, as no more than magic tricks of the kind that any common-or-garden sorcerer (γόης) with a knowledge of Egyptian magic could perform. Thus he writes:

> The sorcerers at least, for a few pence make their magic available in the marketplace. They drive away demons, conquer diseases of all kinds, and make the dead heroes of the past appear – indeed sitting at long tables and eating imaginary cakes and dishes. They make things move about, as if they were alive – an illusion to be sure, but quite appealing to the average imagination. Now I ask you: As these men are able to do such wonderful things, ought we not to regard them as sons of God? Or ought we rather to say that they are contrivances of evil men who are themselves possessed of demons?[45]

For Celsus, the answer is so obvious that he does not bother to spell it out.[46] Instead he moves swiftly to bring down the curtain on this, the

40. 1.68 (trans. Hoffmann, *Celsus*, 59).

41. At least according to Celsus. See 1.28.

42. The verb used by Celsus at 1.68 to describe their promotion of Jesus's miracles – namely, τερατεύομαι, carries with it the implication of falsehood. See *CGL* under τερατεύομαι ('tell tall stories or fairy tales').

43. For their importance to Christian apologists, see the extract from the earliest of them, Quadratus, cited at Eusebius, *Hist. eccl.* 4.3.

44. See 1.68 – 'Come, let us believe that these things were done by you' (trans. Williams).

45. For this translation of 1.68, see Hoffmann, *Celsus*, 59–60.

46. From his knowledge of the gospel of Matthew, especially Mt. 12:24, Celsus will have been perfectly well aware that this was precisely the charge that Jesus's Jewish opponents regularly brought against him. For a thorough discussion of the evidence, see Graham Stanton, 'Jesus of Nazareth: A Magician and a False Prophet

first act, of 'his' Jew's performance. As far as Celsus is concerned, the arguments he has presented offer conclusive proof that Jesus, far from being divine, can be seen to have been no more than 'a wicked sorcerer/ impostor (μοθχηρὸς γόης)'.[47]

9.2. *Celsus's Jew Takes on Jewish Converts to Christianity*

The opening phase of his case now completed, Celsus's Jewish mouth-piece now turns his attention to those Jews who have fallen for Jesus's deceptions (2.1). Since his main aim now is to convince those apostates from Judaism that they have made a dreadful mistake in abandoning 'the law of our fathers (i.e., the Mosaic code)' and switching to 'another name and another way of life',[48] he now proceeds to present a series of arguments demonstrating that each of their newly acquired beliefs has no validity. Principal among those beliefs are, firstly, that Jesus is the long-awaited Davidic messiah; secondly, that he is God's precious son and so a divinity in his own right, and, thirdly, that his rising from the dead proves that eternal life is guaranteed to all those who believe in him. Celsus's aim now being to persuade rather than attack, he largely abandons the vituperation and rhetorical questioning that were such marked features of the previous part of his discourse and opts instead for more reasoned argumentation.[49]

By way of proving that Jesus cannot be the messiah long prophesied in the Hebrew scriptures, Celsus starts out by simply repeating an assertion made earlier – namely, that the messianic predictions contained in those texts are so unspecific that they 'could be applied to thousands of others far more plausibly than to Jesus'.[50] In reiterating this point, Celsus was

Who Deceived God's People?', in *Jesus of Nazareth: Lord and Christ – Essays on the Historical Jesus and New Testament Christology*, ed. Joel B. Green and Max Turner (Grand Rapids: Eerdmans, 1994), 164–80 (especially, 173–80).

47. For this description, see 1.71. For a succinct and useful discussion of the term γόης, see Feldman's note in the Loeb edition of Josephus at *Ant.* 20.97. Although in classical Greek literature the word originally had meant sorcerer, by Josephus's day (and that of Celsus) it had acquired the more general meaning of impostor, deceiver or cheat.

48. 2.1 (*ad fin.*) – εἰς ἄλλο ὄνομα καὶ εἰς ἄλλον βίον.

49. On the literary form adopted by Celsus in this section, see Lona, *Die Wahre Lehre*, 173–5.

50. 2.28 (trans. Chadwick). Cf. 1.50 – 'Why should you be the subject of these prophecies rather than the thousands of others who lived after the prophecy was uttered?'

being neither unreasonable nor particularly original: there were many contemporary Christians, most notably the Marcionites, who were as sceptical as he about the application of that prophetic material to Jesus.[51]

From this argument based on probability, Celsus moves on to one based on impossibility – a procedure recommended by writers of rhetorical handbooks.[52] Focusing on the prophecy found in various parts of the scriptures that the messiah was to be 'both a great ruler and lord of the whole earth and all its peoples and armies',[53] Celsus argues that there is no way that this prediction can apply to such a 'pestilential creature' (τοιοῦτον ὄλεθρον) as Jesus (2.29).[54] Far from being a great ruler and commander of armies, Jesus was little better than a beggar.[55] As for the support he could command, that consisted of a tiny coterie of men, *fewer than a dozen*,[56] whose lifestyle was as beggarly and disreputable as his own.[57]

Celsus's repeated refusal to concede to Jesus the symbolically significant cohort of twelve disciples,[58] a feature of all four canonical gospels, is very striking. Well informed about the messianic hopes of both Jews and Christians (3.1), he must have been aware of the widely held belief that, once the messiah had come to reign, twelve men would be needed to sit in

51. On the Marcionite repudiation of all attempts to see Jesus as the fulfilment of the Old Testament prophecies about the messiah, see *Encyclopedia of Early Christianity*, *s.v.* Marcion.

52. Kennedy, *Progymnasmata*, 101.

53. For this messianic idea, see, *inter alia*, 2 Sam. 7:11-14; Pss. 2; 110; 132:11-18. According to Lona (*Die Wahre Lehre*, 141), the words used by Celsus here do not correspond to any particular 'OT' passage but '*entspricht…einem messianischen Ideal*'.

54. On this hyperbolic use of ὄλεθρος, the common Greek word for destruction, see *CGL* under ὄλεθρος (4).

55. For this stock element in Celsus's invective against religious charlatans of every kind, see 1.9 (the beggarly lifestyle of the priests of Cybele); 7.9 (the beggarly false prophets he has seen in action in Phoenicia and Palestine); 1.61 and 62 (Jesus).

56. See 2.46, where Celsus claims that 'When he [Jesus] was alive he won over only ten sailors [*sic*] and tax-collectors *and not even all of these*'. Earlier (1.61) he had been prepared to be slightly more generous, describing Jesus's close associates as '*ten or eleven infamous men, the most wicked tax-collectors and sailors*'.

57. Alleged at 2.55 and 1.62. It is possible, given Celsus's knowledge of Matthew's gospel, that underlying his pejorative description of the disciples' lifestyle are Jesus's instructions to them when he dispatched them on their mission of healing and exorcism (Mt. 10:9-11). They were told to take no money, no pack for the road and no spare clothes but to go barefoot and live off the community.

58. To be seen at both 1.61 and 2.46.

judgment upon Israel's now ingathered tribes.[59] Matthew, whose gospel he knew particularly well, could not have articulated that belief more clearly: in words put in the mouth of Jesus, he writes, 'In the world that is to be, when the Son of Man is seated on his throne in heavenly splendour, you my followers will have thrones of your own, where you will sit as judges of the twelve tribes of Israel'.[60]

Since Celsus must have known this passage in Matthew (later in the *Alethes Logos* he actually cites verbatim a verse that occurs shortly before it[61]), why does he deliberately ignore it? There surely can be only one answer: it must be to deny Jesus messianic status. That Celsus fabricated evidence to achieve that end is highly improbable, given his generally acknowledged accuracy.[62] More likely, in insisting that the disciples were fewer than the canonical twelve, he was selecting and pressing into use a theme found in contemporary Jewish anti-Christian polemic.[63]

Of far greater importance to Celsus than undermining Jesus's messianic status, however, is strengthening the case against his being a god. If Jesus's divine nature is disproved, then there can be no possible justification for anyone, Jew or pagan, either to 'sign up' to his cult or for converts to remain attached to it.

In the previous section (9.1) we saw Celsus focusing on happenings in the pre-passion part of Jesus's life to argue that the claims to godhead made by both the disciples and Jesus himself are ill-founded. Turning now to the accounts of Jesus's final days on earth, a part of his life-story that up to now he has barely examined,[64] Celsus proceeds to produce a whole string of arguments based on Jesus's feeble behaviour from his arrest to his crucifixion to add weight to his case that he cannot have been a god. What were gods, after all, if not figures of power?

59. For this belief, see Fredriksen, *When Christians Were Jews*, 90 and 211 n. 24.
60. Mt. 19:28 (NEB).
61. See 6.16 for his citation of Mt. 19:24 – 'It is easier for a rich man to go through the eye of a needle etc.'.
62. Morton Smith, *Jesus the Magician*, 58–9. For Celsus's general accuracy, see above 156–7.
63. Of relevance here is Schäfer's discussion (*Jesus in the Talmud*, 65–9) of *b. Sanhedrin* 43a-b, a passage in which Jesus is credited with having only *five* disciples. Although this passage assumed a written form long after the second century, it could well be reflecting a feature of Jewish anti-Christian polemic already current by that time.
64. In the first part of Celsus's attack, as presented by Origen, there is only a single, very brief allusion to Jesus's passion. At 1.54 we read 'He was not helped by his Father, nor was he able to help himself' (trans. Chadwick).

Starting with Jesus's arrest in Gethsemane, a police action that he did nothing to oppose,[65] Celsus makes much of his inability to command the loyalty of the disciples who, at the critical moment, deserted him en masse.[66] Resorting to *synkrisis* to underline this lack of authority (2.12), Celsus jeeringly remarks that even the head of a robber band would have done better than Jesus – a comparison that manages simultaneously to belittle both Jesus and the disciples, here likened to brigands.[67] Nor was Jesus's lack of authority shown only by his failure to prevent their mass desertion. He had even been unable to prevent them from betraying him to the authorities,[68] notwithstanding their teacher–pupil relationship (2.9) and their table-fellowship (2.20) – shared experiences that should have ensured an enduring loyalty.

Following his arrest, Jesus continued to behave in a thoroughly unassertive and therefore ungodlike manner:[69] when brought before the Roman governor, he made no attempt to defend himself; kitted out like a king and mocked by the soldiery, he simply soaked up their abuse in silence; when nailed to the cross, he did not lift a finger to help himself, let alone stage some miraculous, eleventh-hour escape.[70] All he did was display a deplorable frailty, first, by greedily (χανδόν) guzzling the vinegar and gall,[71] 'not even bearing his thirst patiently as even an ordinary man often bears it (2.37)', and then, with his last breath, producing an anguished cry about his miserable fate.[72] To Celsus, such behaviour on the part of someone supposedly divine was simply incomprehensible: 'Why,

65. For Celsus's criticism of Jesus on this point and Origen's defence of Jesus, see, respectively, 2.9 and 2.11.

66. This charge, first made at 2.9, is repeated again and at greater length at 2.45.

67. See Lona, *Die Wahre Lehre*, 129–30 (comm. on 2.12).

68. For rhetorical effect, Celsus exaggerates the extent of his betrayal by the disciples, as Origen is quick to point out (2.11). There was only a single betrayer, Judas.

69. For the various episodes of the passion narrative mentioned in this paragraph, see 2.34-37, 2.55 and 2.68. In the interests of clarity, I have decided, in contrast to Celsus, to present them in the order in which they appear in the gospel narratives.

70. For this accusation, see 2.68.

71. The adverb used by Celsus here, χανδόν (lit. with the mouth wide open), recalls *Odyssey* 21.294 and carries with it clear implications of unbecoming drinking. For Jesus's drinking of vinegar and gall, things so 'abominable and impure' that no god could possibly have contemplated consuming them, see, in addition to 2.37, also 7.13 and, very briefly, 1.70.

72. On the importance in classical culture of a good and noble death, see Bond, *First Biography*, 230 – 'Jesus's cry of desolation signifies a bad death, a wretched and miserable exit, fully in keeping with his servile execution on a Roman cross'. For

if not before, does he not at any rate now show forth "something divine" (θεῖόν τι), and deliver himself from this shame, and take revenge on those who insult both him and his Father?' (2.35).

To drive home how ungodlike Jesus's behaviour was, Celsus resorts once again to comparison (*synkrisis*), this time inviting his readers to contrast the conduct of Jesus when mocked and maltreated by the Roman authorities with that of the god Dionysus when similarly abused by those in power – in his case, the young Theban king, Pentheus. Dionysus, as his audience will hardly have needed reminding,[73] had left his persecutor in no doubt about his power – notoriously, he had caused Pentheus to be driven mad and torn limb from limb (2.34). By contrast, Jesus had done nothing either to help himself or to punish the man who had condemned him to such an excruciating and deeply humiliating end.[74] That, in Celsus's opinion, was not how a real god would have behaved.

Powerful as is the case so far constructed by Celsus, he realizes that no refutation of Jesus's divine status will be complete until the matter of his resurrection has been dealt with. It was this event, presented in the gospels as the fulfilment of a prediction made by Jesus himself (2.54), that constituted for believers the principal proof of Jesus's divinity and the main reason for signing up to his cult.[75] Hence the attention that Celsus now gives this subject.

Reeling off a number of familiar cases from Greek literature and mythology in which individuals who supposedly had died had come back to life (e.g., Orpheus, Theseus, Pythagoras), Celsus briskly points

Celsus, the cry from the cross proved that Jesus could not be divine – it showed that he lacked the essential, godlike virtue of imperturbability in the face of adversity. See Hoffmann's comment at *Celsus*, 142 n. 188.

73. For the popularity of Euripides's plays throughout antiquity, see William H. Willis, 'A Census of Literary Papyri from Egypt', *GRBS* 9 (1968): 205–41 (esp. 212 and 215). For the familiarity of Celsus's readers with the *Bacchae* in particular, see Simon Perris and Fiachra Mac Góráin, 'The Ancient Reception of Euripides' *Bacchae* from Athens to Byzantium', in *Dionysus and Rome*, ed. F. Mac Góráin (Berlin: de Gruyter, 2019), 39–84 (esp. 62–3 and 74–5).

74. 2.34. The point is made again and more strongly at 8.41 – 'But the men who tortured and punished your God in person suffered nothing for doing it, not even afterwards for as long as they lived'. The tradition, first found in Eusebius, *Hist. eccl.* 2.7.1, that God exacted retribution through the suicide of Pilate probably represents a Christian attempt to counter this criticism of Celsus's. Origen himself knows nothing of this tradition. For full discussion, see Paul L. Maier, 'The Fate of Pontius Pilate', *Hermes* 99 (1971): 362–71 (369–70).

75. This point was also made by Lucian. See *Peregr.* 13.

out that not one of them provides hard evidence for bodily resurrection (2.55). Most are simply stories (*mythoi*) whose fictional character is not for a moment doubted by anyone.[76] Where legendary characters are not involved (Pythagoras's slave, Zamolxis, is one such instance), the alleged resurrection turns out to have been pure fabrication.[77] Why, Celsus asks (ibid.), should the case of Jesus be regarded as having been any different?

No more compelling than this classical evidence, so Celsus argues, is the testimony of the gospel writers for the resurrection of Jesus and his triumph over death (2.55). The witnesses both to the empty tomb and to Jesus's appearances in his resurrected body were in each case few and unreliable. In the case of the empty tomb, the earliest witness on the scene was, 'as you yourselves admit',[78] merely a hysterical woman.[79] As for the testimony of the disciple who turned up at the sepulchre slightly later,[80] how can that be regarded as unbiased, given the closeness of his relationship with Jesus? Although Celsus is prepared to concede that those early witnesses might have been either deluded by sorcery (γοητεία) or suffering from hallucinations, he thinks it far more likely, given the disciples' track-record of fabrication,[81] that they were once again lying – 'wanting to impress the others by telling this fantastic tale, they made up this cock-and-bull story to provide a chance for other beggars'.[82] Equally dubious is the testimony of those to whom Jesus allegedly revealed 'the marks of his punishment and how his hands had been pierced' (2.55). As members of Jesus's 'own confraternity' (θιασῶται),[83] they cannot be regarded as impartial witnesses.

76. For useful notes on the individuals listed by Celsus at 2.55, see Whittaker, *Jews and Christians*, 180–1. For exhaustive commentary, see Lona, *Die Wahre Lehre*, 159–61.

77. See Herodotus, *Histories* 4.95 for the details.

78. See 2.55. Celsus is here referring to the account in John's gospel of the discovery of the empty tomb. See Jn 20:1-18.

79. The woman presumably Mary Magdalene (Jn 20:1-2). For further discussion, see above 156.

80. The reference probably is to Peter. See Chadwick's note at 2.55.

81. For this, see 2.13 and 2.27.

82. 2.55 (trans. Chadwick).

83. For this term for the disciples of Jesus, see 2.70 and 3.22, where it is witherh ingly translated by Hoffmann (*Celsus*, 71) as 'members of his [Jesus's] little club'. For Lucian's use of comparable vocabulary, see *Peregr.* 11, where Peregrinus is mockingly described as, among other things, a θιασάρχης – leader of a (Christian) cult-group.

To prove that he really did possess divine powers, 'Jesus should have appeared to those who had abused him, to the man who had passed judgement on him and, in short, to everybody' (2.63). Both from the fact that Jesus did not do so and from all the other arguments set out above, Celsus triumphantly concludes that 'the truth makes obvious and reason shows that Jesus was simply a man' (2.79).

9.3. *Celsus Against Jesus in His Own Voice*

Having used the Jew as a mouthpiece for disputing Jesus's claims to be the long-prophesied messiah and a god, Celsus now dispenses with *prosopopeia*. It is in his own voice that he speaks during the remainder of the *Alethes Logos*. His main aims now being to reveal the inadequacies of Christianity as a philosophical-theological system and to point out the dangers that it poses to society and the state, the direct comments he makes about Jesus are comparatively few. Where they occur, they tend to repeat things said earlier. Celsus clearly does not want his readers, as they work their way through his wide-ranging critique of Christianity's Jewish roots and its many contemporary forms, to forget the reason for the critique itself – namely, the pernicious activities of a low-status sorcerer. This fellow, so Celsus continues to stress, has nothing whatsoever to recommend him: he has deceived many (7.35), conferred few tangible benefits on humankind[84] and his claims to be regarded as divine are disproved by both the ungodlike character of his conduct throughout his life[85] and the utterly shameful manner of his death (7.53).

Despite the repetitious character of most of the references to Jesus in the later books of the *Alethes Logos*, some new material about him, however, is to be found, as the remaining sections of this chapter show. These deal with, respectively, Jesus's ungodlike appearance, philosophical objections to his incarnation and resurrection and, finally, Jesus's unsuitability as a role model, given his revolutionary character.

At the climax of the Jew's personal attack on Jesus (1.69-70), Celsus had him producing a whole string of additional considerations to underline why his claims to be a god were bogus. The first of these related to his physical appearance – 'a god would not have had a body such as yours'. Precisely what the Jew had meant by that particular accusation is not explained. Now Celsus, speaking in his own voice, clears the matter up:

84. At 3.24, Jesus is compared very unfavourably on this score with the healing god, Asclepius.

85. Shown by, *inter alia*, his drinking of vinegar and gall (7.13). For Celsus's earlier references to that event, see above, n. 71.

If a divine spirit was in a body, that body must certainly have differed from other bodies in size or beauty or strength or voice or striking appearance or powers of persuasion. For it is impossible that a body which had something more divine than the rest should be no different from any other. Yet Jesus's body was no different from any other, but, as they say, was little and ugly and undistinguished.[86]

Although this argument might not cut much ice with us, to Celsus's educated readership it will have been quite appealing. Immersed in Homer from their early schooldays onwards and having the texts of his two great epics at their fingertips, they will have had a very clear mental picture of what a godlike man (θεοειδής) should look like. Homer describes these Apollo-like alpha males on numerous occasions. Their most distinguishing characteristics are height, good looks and an impressive physique.[87] On these criteria, Celsus's runty Jesus, described as tiny (μικρόν), unsightly (δυσειδές) and without distinction (ἀγεννές), would have been regarded by the elite readers of the *Alethes Logos* simply as a non-starter. Indeed, if his description of Jesus reminded them of any Homeric character at all, it surely would have been the extremely ugly, mis-shapen commoner, Thersites, who is brutally put in his place by Odysseus for speaking out of turn in the assembly of the Achaeans.[88]

But the clear mismatch between Jesus, as described by Celsus, and the archetypal god-like man of Greek literature would not have been the only reason for Celsus's readers to find his argument convincing. Physiognomic considerations are likely to have played a part too. By Celsus's day, this pseudo-science, which postulated an intimate connection between an individual's outer and inner nature, had become very popular in elite circles.[89] Consequently, it was widely believed that, if an individual looked undistinguished, it followed that internally s/he must be inferior too. Given the prevalence of such thinking,[90] it is not difficult

86. 6.75 (trans. Chadwick).

87. For a good example, see the description of the Greek commander, Agamemnon, at *Iliad* 2.477-82. For a satiric take on the godlike man, see Lucian, *Alex./False Prophet* 3.

88. *Iliad* 2.212-20 (216-19). The only common man to be given a role to play in the Iliad, he is also the only man to be described as ugly. See Willcock, *Homer*, 200 (comm. at *Iliad* 2.212).

89. E. C. Evans, 'Physiognomics in the Ancient World', *TAPS* 59, no. 5 (1969): 1–101 remains fundamental on this topic. For its popularity by Celsus's time, see M. Sassi at *OCD³*, *s.v.* physiognomy.

90. Sassi (previous note) attributes the popularity of physiognomy to the way in which it permitted the easy rationalization of everyday intuitions and social prejudices.

to see why Celsus chose to make an argument out of Jesus's physical deficiencies.

Celsus's description of Jesus's physical appearance has no parallel in classical literature.[91] This prompts the question of what his source is likely to have been. That his information was orally derived is suggested by the phrase, ὥς φασι ('as they say'). But if oral, from whom is Celsus likely to have acquired it? Taylor draws our attention to the fact that by the second half of the second century the practice had arisen in certain Christian circles of taking as a literal description of Jesus's physical appearance Isaiah's words at 53.2-3.[92] These, in my translation of the LXX, the version of the Hebrew scriptures that Christians at that time would have used, run as follows:

> He has no form (εἶδος) or magnificence (δόξα). And we saw him and he did not have either form (εἶδος) or beauty (κάλλος) but his form (εἶδος) was without distinction (ἄτιμον) and lacking (ἐκλεῖπον) in comparison with the sons of men (i.e., other human beings).

This development in Christian interpretation of Isaiah makes it more than likely that it was from Christians who thus interpreted this text (Carpocratians?) that Celsus had acquired this polemically useful nugget of information.[93] That he had gained it at first hand, through reading Isaiah himself, seems unlikely. There is no hard evidence in the *Alethes Logos*, at least as it has come down to us, that Celsus had read that text.

Jesus's ungodlike appearance was not the only new argument adduced by Celsus to undermine his claims to being a god. He also employs arguments from philosophy, specifically Platonism, to quash any notion that Jesus can be divine. Unsurprisingly, given the importance to Christians of the incarnation and the resurrection of Jesus in claiming divine status for him, it is on these two particular topics that Celsus focuses his attention. Whereas earlier, he had been content summarily to dismiss them as fabrications on the part of Jesus and his disciples (1.28 and 68), now he demonstrates why philosophically they are untenable concepts.

---

91. The gospel writers were equally unforthcoming about Jesus's physical appeareance. On the possible reasons for the silence of Mark on this subject, see Bond's speculations at *First Biography*, 161–6.

92. Joan E. Taylor, *What Did Jesus Look Like?* (London: T&T Clark, 2018), 141.

93. That Celsus's source was Carpocratian, as argued by Taylor (*What Did Jesus Look Like?*, 143–8), cannot be proved. However, given Celsus's knowledge of the sect (5.62 and 64) and their practice of using images of Jesus in their worship (Irenaeus, *Against the Heresies* 1.25.6-7), that remains a very attractive possibility.

As a Platonist, Celsus firmly believes that

> God is good and beautiful and happy, and in the highest degree of beauty and excellence. If, then, He comes down to men, He must undergo a change, a change from good to bad, from beautiful to ugly, from felicity to misfortune, and from the best to the most evil. Who would choose a change such as this? It is the nature of what is mortal to change and to re-fashion itself, whereas it is the nature of what is immortal to stay the same without alteration. God, therefore, could not be capable of undergoing this change.[94]

Given this conviction on Celsus's part, it follows that for him an incarnated supreme God is a contradiction in terms. For him, it was simply inconceivable that God would befoul himself by 'breathing into the womb of a woman' (6.73). This would represent an unconscionable violation of the gulf between the transcendent deity and the inferior material world.[95]

Celsus knows, however, that not all followers of Christ believe in the actual incarnation of the divine principle as articulated so eloquently in the opening section of John's gospel.[96] He is aware that there are those (he probably has certain Gnostics in mind) who have convinced themselves that God did no more than *appear* to assume a human form in the likeness of Jesus.[97] Such apparent incarnation, however, is no more acceptable to Celsus as a viable philosophical proposition than physical incarnation. To believe that the supreme God could behave in such a fashion would be tantamount to accepting that he was a deceiver. For Celsus, that is a theological impossibility (4.18).

No less impossible for him is the idea of resurrection as allegedly experienced by Jesus and promised to those who believe in him. For Celsus (as for Plato), human beings are composed of two distinct, contrasting parts – a physical body, subject to decay and 'full of things which it is not nice even to mention' (5.14), and a soul which is immortal. Since death means the release of the soul from this prison (8.53),[98] what sane person would long for a reversal of that process and yearn to live

---

94. 4.14 (trans. Williams). On the Platonic passages underlying Celsus's discussion here – namely, *Phaedrus* 246c and *Republic* 381b-c – see Lona, *Die Wahre Lehre*, 228–9.

95. Hargis, *Against the Christians*, 49.

96. Jn 1:1-14 - the 'word' (*logos*) became flesh etc.

97. On these Docetists, as they were later to be called, see *Encyclopedia of Early Christianity*, *s.v.*, Docetism.

98. For other ancient references to the body as the prison of the soul, see Borret, *Contre Celse*, 4:291 (comm. on 8.53).

for ever in a putrefying body, 'the hope of worms?' (5.14). For Celsus, the idea is not only deeply repugnant, 'an abominable blasphemy',[99] but utterly absurd (8.49).

As for the particular case of Jesus, even if, for the sake of argument, it were to be conceded that he was the incarnate son of God, 'he could not possibly have risen with his body, since God would not have taken back the spirit which he had given once it had been defiled by the nature of the body' (6.72).

Besides these philosophical objections to the beliefs generated by Jesus, Celsus also had concerns of a more practical nature. As 'a conservative intellectual',[100] he regarded the maintenance of the status quo as a matter of paramount importance. Essentially, this involved meeting two obligations. The first of these was the continuous acknowledgement of the supremacy of God: 'As for God, one should never forsake him in any way at all, neither by day nor by night, neither in public nor in private. In every word and action...let the soul be continually directed towards God' (8.63). Hardly less important was the performance of the time-honoured rituals in respect of the lesser gods, spirits (*daimones*) and 'rulers and emperors among men' whose powers are derived from God himself.[101] Christians, however, through their devotion to Jesus, can be seen to be failing on both counts. Although they acknowledge the existence of God, it is to his son that they clearly give primacy: 'When they call him Son of God, it is not to reverence God greatly, but to exalt him (i.e., Jesus) mightily (8.14)'. And by refusing to worship the lesser gods or acknowledge the emperor's divinity, they show themselves nothing less than seditious. Since it is Jesus who has inspired this behaviour, Celsus feels no hesitation in branding him 'the author of their sedition (τῆς στάσεως ἀρχηγέτης)'.[102] By encouraging his followers to 'worship him to an extravagant degree' (8.12) and to reject the forms of religious observance that have ensured social and political stability down the ages, Jesus is undermining the very state and society of which they are members. Hence the fervent plea with which Celsus brings his polemic to an end. His readers should abandon any flirtation with the cult of Christ, let alone membership of it. The very survival of the empire depends upon it.

99. Frede, 'Celsus philosophus Platonicus', 5211.

100. For this characterization, see Wilken, *Christians as the Romans Saw Them*, 94–125 (heading to Chapter 5).

101. The doctrine that Celsus is espousing here (8.63) and again at 8.67-68 is essentially the Divine Right of Kings. See the commentaries of Chadwick and Borret *ad loc.*

102. 8.14.

9.4. *Final Observations*

How persuasive Celsus's arguments proved to be, we have no means of knowing. MacMullen claims that Celsus was 'instantly forgotten'[103] and Frede attributes the long interval (roughly seventy years) between Celsus's composition of the *Alethes Logos* and Origen's refutation of it to its rather low quality: 'By Origen's time, Celsus's treatise must have seemed in many regards rather uninformed and unsophisticated.'[104] Such negative evaluations, however, seem completely at odds with the insistence of Origen's patron, Ambrose, that he produce a full-scale refutation of Celsus's polemic[105] and with the immense effort that Origen put into carrying out that clearly unwelcome and arduous task. Had Celsus's treatise commanded so little interest and been so lacking in merit, their actions would make no sense at all. Also implying the seriousness with which the work was taken is the fate of Origen's refutation: one of only three works from his vast oeuvre to survive in the original Greek and the longest by far of that trio,[106] it was held in the highest esteem by early Christian scholars. Indeed, it was regarded as the perfect manual for dealing with the various charges that continued to be made against both Christianity and Christ himself.[107] Although Celsus is the first surviving classical author to take on Jesus and the cult of which he was the originator, he was far from being the last, as the surviving fragments of the anti-Christian polemics of Porphyry, Sossianus Hierocles and the emperor Julian clearly demonstrate. An examination of that material, however, would take us beyond the scope of this monograph.

---

103. See 'Two Types of Conversion', 177.
104. Frede, 'Origen's Treatise against Celsus', 155.
105. *Praef.* 3.
106. Carleton-Paget, 'The Jew of Celsus', 202.
107. See Pseudo?-Eusebius, *Against Hierocles* 1. On the unlikelihood of the great Eusebius of Caesarea being the author of this fourth-century CE Christian apologetic tract, see Tomas Hägg, 'Hierocles the Lover of Truth and Eusebius the Sophist', *Symb. Osl.* 67 (1992): 138–50.

Chapter 10

OVERVIEW AND CONCLUSION

With Celsus's brutal, well-informed attack on Jesus, we have now reached the end of our study. What our in-depth examination of the surviving classical references to Jesus has shown is that in the course of the second century vast changes have occurred in the way in which Jesus is treated by classical authors. Merely a passive figure for the earliest of these writers, by the time we get to our final author Jesus has become the main protagonist in an entirely new literary genre – anti-Christian polemic. How and why this has come about will be the subject of the following overview.

At the start of our enquiry we found ourselves dealing with a pair of elite, Rome-based writers, neither of whom appears to have much interest in Jesus or, on the face of it, much knowledge about him either. If either Pliny or Tacitus did know that the man whom they held responsible for the creation of the so-called Christian superstition bore the name Jesus, they kept totally silent about it. Similarly, there is no hint in their writings, at least as they have come down to us, that they had the faintest idea as to the implications of their name for him – i.e., Christus.[1] In fact, the sum total of Pliny's belatedly acquired knowledge about (Jesus) Christus appears to amount to no more than that he was the object of a cult so extreme in its demands and yet commanding such loyalty from its devotees that the latter were prepared to die rather than deny Christ's name, supplicate any of the traditional gods or acknowledge the divinity of the reigning emperor (*Ep.* 10.96). Whether Pliny knew, as Tacitus most certainly did (*Annals* 15.44.3), that Jesus, a lowly subject of Rome, had suffered the supreme penalty at the hands of Tiberius's governor in Judaea is not revealed in his famous letter to Trajan about the Christians. But had he been aware of that fact, we may be sure that he would not have drawn

---

1. The first pagan writer to grasp that the 'name' Christus (= The Anointed One) underlined Jesus's messianic status is Celsus, who, therefore, consistently avoids using it.

that emperor's attention to it – Pliny's rhetorical strategy in that lengthy missive, as we saw in Chapter 3, required him to depict both Jesus himself and his erstwhile followers, the embarrassingly large number of irregularly charged Christian apostates whom he held for the moment under lock and key, as essentially harmless. To admit that Christ had ended his life as a condemned criminal would have been fatal to his case.

That Pliny and Tacitus should appear to have known so little about Jesus and to have so little to say about him is not at all surprising. Traditionally the Roman establishment, of which both were fairly recent members, viewed with the utmost distaste unauthorized cults of foreign origin. Convinced that they actively fostered immorality and criminality among the lower orders of society and could even become hot-beds of sedition, they regarded as meritorious any attempt to come down hard on their adherents.[2] Indeed, such was the suspicion in which those cults were held that even the slightest interest or involvement in them by members of the elite (or behaviour that might be construed as such) could lead to those individuals coming under suspicion[3] or investigation[4] and even incurring severe punishment. In the closing years of Domitian's reign, both Pliny and Tacitus had had ample opportunity to see for themselves the dangers of being suspected of involvement in such 'superstitions', especially those of a 'Jewish' and therefore an 'atheistic' character.[5]

Although with Domitian's assassination the likelihood of being accused and punished on such grounds receded, there was no guarantee that such a situation might not arise again, given the vicissitudes of political life at Rome.[6] Such accusations tended to be accorded a very favourable reception when a regime ran into trouble and there was a need to have

2. For some Republican examples of this traditional and long-standing attitude, see Valerius Maximus, *Memorable Deeds and Sayings* 1.3.1-4.

3. See, for instance, Seneca, *Moral Epistles* 108.22 (= Stern, *Greek and Latin Authors*, 1: no. 189), where he records how at the time when Tiberius was taking action against foreign cults (19 CE), he heeded his father's advice to abandon his vegetarianism, since the latter was being taken as proof of involvement in superstition (*inter argumenta superstitionis ponebatur quorundam animalium abstinentia*).

4. See Tacitus, *Annals* 13.32, for the case of Pomponia Graecina, wife of the Claudian general, Aulus Plautius. Her husband was ordered by the Senate in 57 CE to carry out an investigation into her alleged involvement in a 'foreign superstition' (*superstitionis externae*), thought by many scholars to have been Christianity. For full discussion, see Furneaux, *Annals*, note *ad loc.*

5. Dio, *Roman History* 67.14.1-2 and above 32–3.

6. On the ever-present danger for elite Romans of any seemingly irregular religious behaviour on their part being used politically against them, see Strunk, 'Domitian's Lightning Bolts'.

scapegoats to distract public attention.[7] Consequently, for either Pliny
or Tacitus to have displayed an untoward level of knowledge about the
Christian cult and its founder would have been extremely unwise. It
is surely not without significance that when these two writers do have
occasion to focus on the Christians and their superstition, both of them
seek to give authority to their words and/or actions by referencing Livy's
well-known account of the suppression of the devotees of Bacchus
(Dionysus) in 186 BCE. The firm action taken by Roman authorities on
that occasion against the so-called Bacchic conspiracy (*coniuratio*) not
only met with approval at the time but came to be regarded by the Roman
governing elite thereafter as paradigmatic.[8]

Given, then, the deep suspicion in which the foreign cults so popular
with the masses were held by the Roman establishment, it is hardly
surprising that throughout their writings both Pliny and Tacitus make only
minimal reference to them and stress instead their own unimpeachable
conduct in the area of cult. At no point in his carefully constructed
collection of personal correspondence, nine whole books, does Pliny
so much as mention the subject of foreign superstitions, let alone say
anything concrete about a particular one. Instead we find him drawing
attention to his patronage of traditional cults[9] and boasting about his life
appointment by the emperor to the college of augurs, an ancient priestly
body (*Ep.* 4.8.1). One of his aims at least in writing to Trajan about the
Christian problem in the Pontic part of his province, even if it was not
his main motive, was to draw that emperor's attention to the zeal and
thoroughness with which he was handling that illegal cult.

Nor is Tacitus's treatment of religious matters significantly different
from that of Pliny. Revealingly, his only autobiographical comment in
the whole of the surviving *Annals* relates to his membership of another
of Rome's four exclusive ancient priestly orders, the *Quindecimvirate
sacris faciundis* (*Annals* 11.11.1). Further, in his references to foreign
superstitions he is at pains to make clear that his views about them are
utterly conventional. With manifest satisfaction he endorses the callous
punishment meted out by the senate in 19 CE to four thousand adherents
of the Jewish superstition at Rome.[10] And in his 'Great Fire' narrative he

7. On the recurrence of this pattern of behaviour and imperial grandstanding over
superstitions, see Gruen, *Diaspora*, Chapter 1.

8. See above 40 n. 26 and 80–1.

9. Pliny, *Ep.* 3.6; 4.1.3-6; 9.39. For details of his actions on those occasions, see
Chapter 3 n. 11.

10. See Tacitus, *Annals* 2.85.4 with Stern's commentary at *Greek and Latin
Authors*, 2:284.

goes out of his way to put on record his conviction that Nero's Christian victims, notwithstanding their scapegoating by the latter, really did deserve 'the ultimate exemplary punishment'.[11] For theirs was a 'deadly' (*exitiabilis*) superstition, something only to be expected, so he implies, given its Judaean origin (*Annals* 15.44.3).

This pandering to the prejudices of the Roman establishment on the part of both Pliny and Tacitus[12] is no more than one would expect of them: dyed-in-the-wool traditionalists, as their respective oeuvres make absolutely clear, they knew that for 'new men' (*novi homines*) like themselves the key to their continuing social acceptance and political advancement was conspicuous conformity with establishment views and values.[13]

Following Tacitus's thumbnail sketch of the 'author' (*auctor*) of the Christian superstition at *Annals* 15.44.3, we have no indisputable mentions of Jesus in a classical text for over forty years, Suetonius's reference in his biography of Claudius to the urban rioter, Chrestus, almost certainly being to an entirely different individual.[14] During those silent decades, however, the cult of Christ did not remain static. Not only did it flourish mightily, particularly in the eastern half of the empire, but it began to acquire a social acceptability unimaginable in the days of Pliny, Tacitus and Suetonius. No longer was devotion to Jesus confined almost exclusively to the non-elite; his cult now began to attract serious attention from the well educated too, some of whom in due course became eloquent and prominent apologists for it.[15] Justin, for instance, openly taught 'Christianity' at Rome in the years before his martyrdom there sometime in the 160s CE.[16] With 'Christianity's' profile thus heightened, inevitably both Jesus and those who worshipped him began to attract far more attention than hitherto from pagan intellectuals also. The writings of both Lucian and Celsus demonstrate this very clearly, albeit in rather different ways – something that is only to be expected, given the differences between their respective agendas.

---

11. For this translation of the phrase *novissima exempla meritos* at *Annals* 15.44.5, see Woodman, *Tacitus*, 326.

12. For another Tacitean example, see *Annals* 11.15.

13. Syme, *Tacitus*, 2:582–3.

14. See Chapter 6 and Appendix 4.

15. For a useful survey of these early Christian apologists, starting with Quadratus under Hadrian and ending with several contemporaneous with Lucian and Celsus, see Eric Osborn, 'The Apologists', in Esler, ed., *The Early Christian World*, 1:525–51.

16. Osborn, 'Apologists', 527.

For Lucian, whose main concern was to provide his various audiences with lightweight but sophisticated escapist entertainment,[17] both the devotees of Jesus and Jesus himself represented welcome additions to his satirical repertoire. For who could fail to derive amusement from the ignorant Christian rank-and-file, so easily preyed upon and gulled by unscrupulous operators such as the elite Peregrinus? And who could fail to view the founder of the Christian cult as anything other than totally ridiculous? The sheer preposterousness of Jesus's claim to divine status is shown by way his life ended: despite claiming to be a god, and thus immortal, not only had he been put to death but he had been subjected to the most humiliating and contemptible form of public execution possible – namely, crucifixion (*anaskolopesis*).[18] As for his achievements as a teacher of wisdom (*sophistes*) and a dispenser of laws (*nomothetes*), these would appear to have amounted to little more than a few half-baked ideas and idiotic injunctions. How could anyone of intelligence and discrimination (i.e., the kind of people who comprised a typical Lucianic audience) take seriously Jesus's recommendations that his followers pool their private property, regard themselves as the equal members of one large family and abandon the worship of all the traditional gods in favour of himself, a self-appointed deity, alone?

This satirical take on the Christians and their founder shows not only how widespread public knowledge about them must have become but what the general opinion of Christians in elite circles is likely to have been. Since Lucian's prime aim was to amuse, his calculation clearly must have been that his send-up of contemporary Christians and their improbable deity, 'that fellow who was crucified in Palestine',[19] would play well with the wealthy, leisured, sophisticated individuals who paid to attend his performances. From this, we may deduce that the typical Lucianic audience did not regard either 'the crucified sophist' or his cult as remotely threatening.

But lightly as most of the educated elite almost certainly viewed the Christians and Christ, that attitude was not held by everybody. Conspicuous among the minority who regarded 'Christianity' with the greatest foreboding was Lucian's close contemporary, the minor Platonist, Celsus. A deeply conservative, conventionally pious man with an unexpectedly

17. On his 'understandable' omission of any reference to the major crises that occurred during the period when he was active as a writer and public performer, see Jones, *Culture and Society*, 18. Those crises included plague, barbarian invasion and internal rebellion.

18. Lucian, *Peregr.* 11 and 13.

19. *Peregr.* 11.

wide knowledge of Christian writings, he viewed with the greatest alarm the seemingly unstoppable proliferation of Christian believers throughout Graeco-Roman society. Even at the best of times these revolutionary cultists through their blanket refusal to worship the traditional gods posed a clear threat to that society's well-being. But now with the empire facing a perfect firestorm on account of the combined effects of plague, pressure from 'barbarians' and unrelenting frontier warfare, that threat had become existential.[20]

Convinced, therefore, that something had to be done to check this dangerous, upstart cult, Celsus decided to go on the offensive. Hence his 'bolt from the blue',[21] the virulent polemic against 'Christianity' and the unprecedented personal attack on Jesus himself preserved in large parts for us through Origen's generous citations from the *Alethes Logos* in his *Contra Celsum*. Drawing upon an impressively wide range of sources, Christian, Jewish and classical, Celsus set about the comprehensive destruction of Jesus's credibility. Maximizing the impact of his attack through the heavy use of the weapons he had been taught to wield in the course of his rhetorical training, he argued that Jesus, far from being the Supreme God's incarnate son by a human mother, had not even been the long-awaited Davidic messiah. A wicked, low-class impostor (1.71), he had simply tricked people into believing those things about him through a combination of braggadocio, lying and some very questionably acquired magical skills (1.28). The fact that the latter were of Egyptian origin made them particularly suspect.[22]

From this synopsis, we can see that the treatment of Jesus by pagan writers has undergone a complete transformation in the course of a couple of generations. In our earliest texts, very little direct attention is paid to Jesus himself. Instead, such interest as there is in the 'Christian superstition' is in its devotees. In the case of Pliny, this interest is mostly directed towards their regular cultic practices and their insane determination to lay down their lives rather than deny 'the name of Christ' (*nomen Christianum*). Tacitus and Suetonius meanwhile are more focused on the Christians' criminal behaviour, whether actual[23] or assumed.[24] When Jesus (or rather Christus) does get a mention in these early sources,

---

20. For Celsus's concerns, see Simmons, 'Graeco-Roman Philosophical Opposition', 2:859–60.

21. Carleton-Paget, Review of Horacio E. Lona, 299.

22. See above, 166–7.

23. Suetonius, *Nero* 16.2, where Nero's various punishments of assorted social miscreants are reported on approvingly.

24. Tacitus, *Annals* 15.44.2-3.

he is depicted as a totally passive figure – a mere object of either worship[25] or humiliating punishment.[26] What he has done to deserve either is not made clear.

However, in our two final texts, *On the Death of Peregrinus* and *Alethes Logos*, we find the situation completely reversed: in these, it is Jesus who is the driver of the action; his devotees, by contrast, are depicted as credulous nincompoops. In neither text do we find so much as a hint of immorality or criminality on their part – a surprising omission given the prevalence at that time of accusations against Christians of incest and cannibalism.[27] If, however, attention is paid to the literary aims of Lucian and Celsus, then their silence becomes entirely comprehensible. Since their priority is to show Jesus in a bad light, that goal is best attained by depicting his devotees as hapless victims. Such a characterization makes Jesus appear, at best, as unscrupulous and exploitative (Lucian), and, at worst, as an out-and-out deceiver (Celsus).

If we ask ourselves why this reversal has occurred, it is hard not to conclude that the main causative factor is most likely to have been the increasing seriousness with which the cult of Christ was being regarded in elite circles from the reign of Hadrian onwards. Whereas previously it had been the preserve largely of the non-elite, now the highly educated were not only converting to 'Christianity' but they were providing their newly adopted cult with considerable intellectual heft through their not inconsiderable literary endeavours. Starting as a trickle under Hadrian with a treatise by a certain Quadratus,[28] their apologetic writings, works in which the topics of Jesus's divinity, his messianic status and his bodily resurrection bulk large, had, by Lucian and Celsus's day, become a veritable flood.[29] Indeed so well-known had the literary activity of these elite converts become that Lucian treats the topic as grist for his satirical mill. Thus among the features of Peregrinus's career as a Christian at which Lucian pokes fun is the latter's composition of large numbers of Christian texts (*Peregr.* 11).

While Lucian appears to have taken 'Christianity's' growing intellectual respectability rather lightly, Celsus most clearly did not. For him, the cult of Christ represented nothing less than a revolutionary movement.

25. Pliny, *Ep.* 10.96.7.

26. Tacitus, *Annals* 15.44.3.

27. See Wagemakers, 'Incest, Infanticide, and Cannibalism: Anti-Christian Imputations in the Roman Empire'. For a contemporary defence of Christians against those charges, see *Encyclopedia of Early Christianity*, *s.v.* Athenagoras.

28. Eusebius, *Hist. eccl.* 4.3.1.

29. Hurtado, *Lord Jesus Christ*, 490.

Hence his constant harping on about its recent origins.[30] Even worse, it was also, so he thought, a massive confidence trick. Hence the relent-lessness with which throughout the *Alethes Logos* he attacks the cult's central claim – namely, that Jesus was God's incarnate son who by his rising from the dead had guaranteed eternal life to all those who believe in him.

But differently as our pagan authors depict Jesus/Christus, there is one thing that they do have in common. All take it for granted that Jesus was an historical figure. It simply does not occur to any of them to query his humanity.[31] That Jesus is no more than a fictional figure, the result of the imaginings and longings of certain inhabitants of Judaea around the middle of the first century CE, is a relatively modern idea and one that says more about modern preoccupations than ancient ones. The fact that it first surfaced in Revolutionary France, a time of great antagonism towards things ecclesiastical, is highly significant.[32] The ancient critics of the cult of Christ, however, had concerns of an entirely different order: their main worry throughout the period covered in this monograph was the seemingly unstoppable growth in the number of Jesus-worshippers, all of them, to their way of thinking, out-and-out atheists. For if, as a consequence of that atheism, the traditional gods were increasingly dishonoured, there was every chance that they would withdraw their protection and the empire would, as a result, suffer irreparable harm. Hence the opposition of all our authors, with the possible exception of Lucian,[33] to the cult and hence the various ways in which they sought to undermine its originator, Jesus, 'the man of Nazareth',[34] himself.

30. See Origen, *Contra Celsum* 1.26; 2.4; 6.10; 8.12 (each passage containing a quotation from Celsus's work).

31. Although Pliny refers to Christus only as an object of worship, the manner in which he does so suggests that he was aware that he had once been a human being. See above 43.

32. For a brief history of mythicism, the first proponent of which was Volney, see Ehrman, *Did Jesus Exist?*, 14–19.

33. On the difficulty of being certain about Lucian's views on anything, see above 125 and 142.

34. So referred to by Celsus at 8.71.

Appendix 1

INSCRIPTIONS RELATING TO PLINY, TACITUS AND SUETONIUS

As pointed out above, our knowledge and understanding of all three of our Latin authors, Pliny, Tacitus and Suetonius, have been greatly enhanced by a number of chance epigraphic finds made in various parts of the Roman Empire. Presented here are translations of those inscriptions to which reference has been in the main body of the monograph. Standard epigraphic conventions are used in the presentation of these texts. Words enclosed in square brackets indicate those places where the original text has undergone restoration. Material in curved brackets shows where expansions to the text have been made in order to facilitate comprehension.

(A) *Gaius Plinius Caecilius Secundus (*ca. *61–*ca. *111 CE)*

The inscriptions relating to Pliny the Younger, besides providing us with the richest material to date for an early imperial senatorial career, are important for several other reasons too. It is from inscriptions, and inscriptions alone, that we learn of Pliny's dedication in his home town of Comum of the elaborate temple begun by his father for the worship of Rome and the Emperors (no. 1). And it is only because of the chance survival of an honorific text in a small neighbouring town, Vercellae (now the village of Fecchio), that we learn of his subsequent appointment as a priest (*flamen*) of the deified emperor, Titus (no. 2). Clearly Pliny came from a family conspicuous for its 'empire-loyalty' – a tradition which he carried on. These facts help us to appreciate better his conduct vis-à-vis apostate Christians in Bithynia-Pontus – i.e., requiring them, in addition to praying publicly to the gods of Rome, to acknowledge the emperor's divinity through the pouring of a libation before his statue.

Inscriptions also act as an important corrective to the picture Pliny paints of his experiences under Domitian. In his letters, he makes great play of his allegedly close relationships with opposition figures, such as the Stoic martyrs, Helvidius Priscus, Junius Rusticus and Herennius Senecio.[1] Indeed, in some letters and the *Panegyricus* he even goes so far as to suggest that his own life likewise had been in danger from the tyrant.[2] The inscriptions give the lie to this attempted re-writing of history. They show that Pliny continued to prosper under Domitian, even when the latter's rule was at its most repressive (from 93 CE onwards). His tenure of the Prefectship of the Military Treasury, most likely held from 94–96 CE, constitutes the chief proof of this (nos. 2 and 3). In his letters, there is no mention at all of this Domitianic appointment.

The Inscriptions
1. Inscribed plaque from Comum on which are recorded (a) the inauguration by Pliny's birth father, Lucius Caecilius Secundus, of a temple for the worship of the goddess Roma and emperors past and present and (b) its subsequent dedication by Pliny himself.[3]

> (a) In the name of his daughter [Caeci]lia, Lucius Ca[eciliu]s Secundus, son of Gaius, of the Oufentine voting-tribe, *praefectus [fabrum]* on the nomination of the consul, *quattuorvir* for the administration of justice, *pontifex*, began the temple to the Eternity of Rome and of the Augusti together with its porticoes and ornamentation.

> (b) [...Caeci]lius Secundus, his son,[4] dedicated it.

2. Inscription containing the sole surviving reference to Pliny's priesthood in the cult of Titus.[5] Also of note is the prominence given in this text to his two most prestigious public appointments, those of consul and augur. Had a strict chronological order been observed throughout this text, they should have been placed *after* his curatorship of the channel and banks

1. See, for instance, *Ep.* 3.11.3 and 9.13.
2. *Ep.* 3.11.3 and 7.27.14; *Panegyricus* 90.5.
3. *CIL* 5, Add. 745 and 746 = *AE* (1983) no. 443. The interpretation followed here is that of Alföldi, 'Ein Tempel der Herrscherkultes in Comum'.
4. This is our Pliny. Before his adoption in 79 CE under the will of his maternal uncle, the Elder Pliny, our Pliny's name was [first name lost] Caecilius Secundus. On adoption, his name, in accordance with current onomastic practice, changed to Gaius Plinius Caecilius Secundus.
5. For the original Latin, see *CIL* 5.5667 = *ILS* 6727.

of the Tiber. However, so impressive was the attainment of those two positions by a first-generation senator, a so-called 'new man' (*novus homo*), that they are given priority in this virtual CV.

> To Gaius Plinius Caec[ilius] Secundus, [son of Lucius], of the Oufentine voting-tribe, consul, augur, curator of the channel and the banks of the Tiber and the sewers of Rome, p[refect of the Tr]easury of Saturn, prefect of the Mil[itary] Treasury, [praetor, tribune of the people], quaestor of the emperor, commissioner for the Roman knights, military tribune of the third Gallic legion, member of the Board of Ten for Judging Lawsuits, priest (*flamen*) of the deified emperor Titus, the people of Vercellae (have erected this monument).

3. Inscription now in Milan but originally from Comum.[6] Quite possibly composed by Pliny himself,[7] this text falls into two parts of which only the first is presented here. Starting with a comprehensive list of the offices Pliny had held in the course of his thirty-year senatorial career, the inscription ends with a catalogue of his many benefactions to Comum, both those conferred during his lifetime and those set out in his last will and testament. Of particular interest is the part of the text relating to his crowning achievement – i.e., his governorship of Bithynia-Pontus. Great emphasis is placed on the special nature of that appointment. Pliny is determined that his fellow-townsmen remember that he was head-hunted by the emperor, no less, for that post. The many restorations to be observed in this text have been made on the basis of other inscriptions relating to Pliny not reproduced here.

> Gaius Plinius Caecilius [Secundus], son of Lucius, of the Oufentine voting-tribe, [consul], augur, propraetorian governor with [pro]consular power of the province of Pon[tus and Bithynia, sent] to that province in accordance with a [decree of the senate] by the emperor Caesar Nerva Trajan Augustus, Conqueror of Germany, [Conqueror of Dacia, Father of the Fatherland], curator of the channel and the banks of the Tiber and [the sewers of the city (i.e., Rome)], prefect of the Treasury of Saturn, prefect of the Mil[itary] Treasury, [praetor, tribune of the people], quaestor of the emperor, commissioner for the Roman knights, military tribune of the third Gallic legion in the province of Syria, member of the Board of Ten for Judging Lawsuits......
> (details of his public benefactions and bequests follow).

6. *CIL* 5.5262. The translation here is based on the Latin text provided by Gibson and Morello at *Reading the Letters*, 271.

7. Eck, 'Rome and the Outside World', 98–9.

(B) *Publius (?) Cornelius Tacitus (ca. 56 CE to ?)*

About Tacitus, Pliny's slightly older contemporary, we have comparatively little firm information. If, as is generally assumed, the equestrian procurator, Cornelius Tacitus, to whom Pliny the Elder makes brief reference (*Nat.* 7.76), was the historian's father,[8] then the social position of our Tacitus can be seen to be virtually the same as that of Pliny – i.e., he was a first-generation senator, a so-called 'new man' (*novus homo*).

About his senatorial career, Tacitus has little specific to say. In the introduction to his *Histories* (1.1.3), a work covering the Flavian period, by way of protecting himself against allegations of pro-Flavian bias, he admits quite openly that he had enjoyed the favour of all three Flavian emperors: 'Nor can I deny that my senatorial career (*dignitatem*) was started by Vespasian, advanced by Titus, and taken (even) further by Domitian'. But about this steady upward progress, which saw him by the time of Domitian's assassination (18 September 96 CE) almost certainly designated by that emperor for a consulship in the following year,[9] he supplies almost no information. However, an extremely fragmentary inscription from Rome (no. 1),[10] helps to fill in some of the gaps in our knowledge. Previously nothing at all was known about Tacitus's career prior to his holding of the praetorship in 88 CE.[11] Thanks to this text, we can see that his early career was virtually identical to that of Pliny. Of especial note is that he, just like Pliny, had been 'a quaestor of the emperor' – an appointment that marked him out too as a régime-favourite.

Inscriptions also tell us something about his post-Flavian career. From a text inscribed on a column shaft found in a vineyard at Mylasa in south-west Asia Minor (no. 2), we know that he became proconsul of the province of Asia.[12] In this text Tacitus's tenure of that office functions as a dating device. Since the province of Asia at that time (c. 113 CE)[13] was home to many flourishing Christian congregations, it is highly likely that Tacitus will have had some interaction with their members – a matter of considerable relevance to us.

---

8. Birley, 'Life and Death of Cornelius Tacitus', 233.

9. Birley, 'Life and Death of Cornelius Tacitus', 238.

10. *CIL* 6.1574 = *AE* 2000, 160.

11. His tenure of this office, along with his membership of the priestly college, the *Quindecimviri sacris faciundis*, is mentioned by him at *Annals* 11.11.1.

12. *OGIS* 487 = Smallwood, *Documents*, no. 203.

13. For the date of Tacitus's proconsulate of Asia, see Syme, *Tacitus*, 2:664–5 (= Appendix 23), who shows that it must be dated to either 112/3 or 113/4 CE.

Translations of the Inscriptions

1. Inscription found in Rome, thought to be part of Tacitus's epitaph.[14] Although the name of the deceased is incomplete, the rarity of Roman names ending -citus have convinced many that the text does come from the historian's tomb.[15]

> To [...]citus Ca[...] Board of Ten for [Judging] Lawsuits [...quaest]or of Augustus, tribun[e of the people...]

2. Inscription from Mylasa in Asia Minor containing the names of the officials from various Ionian communities who had participated in a dedication ceremony to the local Mylasian deity, Zeus Osogos.[16] In the opening lines of the text, we find Tacitus's tenure of the proconsulship of Asia employed as a means of recording the date of that event.

> The Ionians of Asia. During the proconsulship of Cornelius Tacitus.... (the names of the various dedicators, not reproduced here, now follow).

(C) *Gaius Suetonius Tranquillus (*ca. *70 CE–?)*

Useful as inscriptions are for increasing our knowledge about Pliny and Tacitus, in neither case can their impact be said to have been substantially transformative. With Suetonius, the situation is entirely different: in his case, an honorific inscription from Hippo Regius (modern Annaba, formerly Bône, in Algeria)[17] has forced a total revaluation of his significance. Here I present, first, the Latin text as set out in the Clauss/ Slaby Epigraphic Database,[18] and then a translation of my own.

> C(aio) Suetoni[o] /... Tra[nquillo] / [f]lami[ni ...] / [adlecto] int[er selectos a di]vo Tr[a]/[iano Parthico] [p]ont(ifici) Volca[ni / [...a]studiis a b<i=Y>blio[thecis] / [ab e]pistulis / [Imp(eratoris) Caes(aris) Trai]ani Hadrian[i Aug(usti)] / [Hipponien]ses Regii d(ecreto) d(ecurionum) p(ecunia) p(ublica)

---

14. For full discussion, see Birley, 'Life and Death of Cornelius Tacitus', 230–1 building on a suggestion first made by Alföldi.

15. For a full and sober assessment of the question, see M. G. L. Cooley, *The Flavians*, LACTOR 20 (London: Association of Classical Teachers, 2015), 388 (commentary on entry U32b).

16. He was a Hellenized version of the local deity, Osogoa. See Revilo P. Oliver, 'The Praenomen of Tacitus', *AJP* 98, no. 1 (1977): 64–70 (67).

17. *AE* 1953, 73.

18. EDCS-13900062. The text, with a few slight variations, may also be found at Smallwood, *Documents*, no. 281.

To Gaius Suetonius Tranquillus, priest (*flamen*)…enrolled among the jurors by the deified Trajan Parthicus, priest of Vulcan…. Minister for Studies (*a studiis*), Minister for Libraries (*a b<i>bliothecis*), Minister for Correspondence (*ab epistulis*) for the emperor Caesar Trajan Hadrian Augustus. The citizens of Hippo Regius by a decree of the town council (have erected this) at public expense.

Notwithstanding the fragmentary state of the text,[19] enough survives to provide indisputable evidence for Suetonius's high public standing in the Hadrianic period. To have a statue erected *at public expense* in the main forum of a significant provincial town was a signal honour.[20] To be appointed Minister for Correspondence speaks volumes for the high opinion entertained of him in imperial circles.

19. That substantial portions of it have been lost admits of no doubt. For discussion as to what Suetonius's earlier appointments, probably listed in the missing parts of the text, might have been, see Townend, 'Hippo Inscription', 102.

20. The reason for this honour is unknown and disputed. Those who believe that Suetonius actually came from Hippo think that it was a case of a provincial town honouring a local boy who had made very good. For a recent articulation of this case, see D. Wardle, 'Suetonius as *ab epistulis*', *Historia* 51 (2002): 462–80 (465–70). Others, not convinced that Suetonius was a native of Hippo, think that in his capacity as *ab epistulis* he had won some significant benefit for the town from Hadrian. See, for instance, Crook, 'Suetonius *ab epistulis*', 21.

Appendix 2

SUETONIUS AND THE ARRANGEMENT OF MATERIAL *PER SPECIES* (BY CATEGORY)

One of the most distinctive features of Suetonius's Lives of the Caesars is the extensive presentation of material by category (*per species*), the purpose being 'to make the account clearer and more intelligible' (*quo distinctius demonstrari cognoscique possint*).[1] The categories themselves tend to be introduced with sign-post words or phrases, cues which in the scholarly literature are generally referred to as rubrics. These are then followed in each case by a bald list of illustrative examples. This presentational method is used exclusively in the core part of each biography, when the emperor's actual administration is the subject under consideration. Material relating to his life before his accession to power and his principal end-of-life experiences (usually downfall and death) are treated quite differently. In these curtain-raising and curtain-lowering sections, Suetonius adopts a chronological rather than a thematic approach. Hence Hurley's characterization of the Lives of the Caesars as 'rubric sandwiches'.[2]

The section in the life of Claudius containing Suetonius's comment about Chrestus provides an excellent illustration of his organization of material *per species* (by type). Opening with the sign-post words, *peregrinae condicionis homines* (individuals of peregrine – i.e., alien/ non-Roman status), Suetonius proceeds to set out eight examples of Claudius's dealings with foreign individuals and communities. Each of his actions is dealt with in a single, generally short, sentence. This aspect of his composition can get somewhat obscured in translation, when the need to produce 'good' English sometimes requires turning Suetonius's

1. Suetonius, *Div. Aug.* 9.1.
2. Donna W. Hurley, 'Suetonius' Rubric Sandwich', in Power and Gibson, eds, *Suetonius*, 21–37.

single Latin sentences into two sentences in our language.³ Information about each measure is largely kept to the minimum needed to illustrate the point at issue here – namely, that Claudius showed no less attentiveness in matters involving *peregrini* (aliens) than in those relating to the various status groups that comprised Roman society itself. These have been dealt with in descending order of prestige in the preceding sections of the life.⁴ No attempt is made to contextualize the measures listed or to supply much information about them. No attention whatsoever is paid to chronology, as that is irrelevant to Suetonius's purpose. His only concern is to provide his readers with a bald catalogue of Claudius's peregrine-related measures. It is important to note, as this is not always appreciated, that Suetonius is not concerned at this point in the biography with Claudius's handling of foreign cults. These are dealt with elsewhere in the life.⁵ Here the focus strictly is on those who, for one reason or another, do not possess Roman citizenship and so are classed as aliens. Several of the cases cited concern individuals who are punished by the emperor since their behaviour is at odds with their peregrine status.

It will be observed that, notwithstanding my comments about Suetonius's indifference to dating, some of the Claudian measures have been supplied with a date (in brackets) in the translation below. These dates are not part of the original text. Established through information supplied by Tacitus or Dio,⁶ they have been included primarily for interest. In those cases where no date is given, the reason is that Suetonius is our sole source of information and so no date can be established.

Suetonius: Divus Claudius *25.3-4 (trans. Margaret Williams)*

Individuals of alien status (*peregrinae condicionis homines*) Claudius forbade to use Roman names, at least Roman clan/family names (*gentilicia*).⁷ Those who usurped Roman citizenship he had beheaded in the Esquiline

---

3. A case in point is my translation of Suetonius's final example in the passage below, the anecdote about the German envoys.

4. For Suetonius's practice of organizing his material hierarchically, see Wallace-Hadrill, *Suetonius*, 101–3.

5. On this point, see the useful comments of both Hurley, *Divus Claudius*, 176 and Mottershead, *Claudius*, 149–50.

6. Full details can be found in the respective commentaries of Hurley and Mottershead.

7. It was the *gentilicium*, the second of the three names (*tria nomina*) traditionally borne by Romans, that signified the possession of Roman citizenship. See Mottershead, *Claudius*, 101.

Field. He restored to the Senate the provinces of Achaea and Macedonia (44 CE), which Tiberius had taken into his own charge. He deprived the Lycians of their independence because of their deadly intestinal feuds (43 CE). To the people of Rhodes he restored theirs since they had shown remorse for their former offences (53 CE). He granted to the people of Ilium (Troy) exemption in perpetuity from the payment of tribute on the grounds that they were the founding fathers of the Roman people (53 CE).[8] The Jews who were constantly disturbing the peace on account of Chrestus's incitement he expelled from Rome. He allowed the envoys of the Germans to sit in the orchestra because he was moved by their naïveté and self-confidence. For when they had been conducted to the seats occupied by the common people and had seen the Parthian and Armenian envoys sitting in those reserved for the Senate, they had moved of their own accord to the same place, protesting that their worth and rank were not inferior.

8. I have omitted here Suetonius's longish description of the public ceremony involving the reading of an ancient (possibly forged) document in which this benefit was conferred. The ceremony is described elsewhere by both him (*Nero* 7.2) and Tacitus (*Annals* 12.58). The unusually generous treatment accorded this measure by Suetonius probably arises from its antiquarian features. Given his strong antiquarian bent, he will have found these inherently interesting.

Appendix 3

SUETONIUS'S SKILL IN SOURCE-EVALUATION

As we saw in Chapter 6 above, the widely accepted identification of the Chrestus of *Div. Claud.* 25.4 with (Jesus) Christ rests principally on the assumption that Suetonius himself was a sloppy and incompetent operator who 'had neither the interest nor the inclination' to carry out serious research in the manner of Tacitus.[1] That such a view of Suetonius bears no relationship whatsoever to reality can be demonstrated very easily. Here I present by way of proof a large part of the famous passage from his life of Gaius (Caligula) in which he discusses that emperor's place of birth and 'establishes beyond doubt'[2] that it was neither on the Rhine frontier nor at Tibur (modern Tivoli) but at Antium (modern Anzio on the west coast of Italy south of Rome).

Suetonius, Gaius *8.1-5 (trans. Margaret Williams)*

Gaius Caesar was born the day before the Kalends of September (i.e., 31 August) in the year when his father (Germanicus) and Gaius Fonteius Capito were consuls (i.e., 12 CE). Where he was born the differences between our sources/authorities (*diversitas tradentium*) render uncertain. Gnaeus Lentulus Gaetulicus writes that he was born at Tibur (modern Tivoli), Pliny (the Elder) that it was among the Treveri[3] in a place called Ambitarvio-above-the-Confluence.[4] And he adds, by way of proof, that altars are on display there inscribed *OB AGRIPPINAE PVERPERIVM* ('For the Safe Delivery of Agrippina'). Verses circulated soon after Gaius became emperor indicate that he was conceived in the winter-quarters of the legions:

1. Bruce, 'Christianity under Claudius', 316.
2. Wallace-Hadrill, *Suetonius*, 89.
3. A Gallic tribe from whom the present day city of Trier takes its name.
4. This was in the vicinity of modern Koblenz, just above the confluence of the Rhine and Moselle.

'Born in the camp, reared with his father's troops; it was a sign (*omen*) that already he was destined to be an emperor (*princeps*)'. I myself find in the public records (*acta*) that he was born at Antium [modern Anzio].

Pliny rebuts Gaetulicus on the grounds of his being a flattering liar [a long explanation, here omitted, now follows]. A calculation of dates proves Pliny wrong, since those who entrust to memory the deeds of Augustus (i.e., the historians of his reign) are in agreement that Gaius had already been born (*iam nato Gaio*) when Germanicus was despatched to Gaul at the close of his consulship. Nor does the inscription on the altar support at all Pliny's view of the matter, since Agrippina twice gave birth to daughters in that region and any birth may be termed a *puerperium* regardless of (the child's) sex (*sexus*), because the ancients used to call girls *puerae*, just as they called boys *puellae*. Further, there survives a letter of Augustus to his grand-daughter, Agrippina, written just a few months before he died (19 August 14 CE) in which he writes thus of this Gaius, no other infant of the name being alive at the time – 'Yesterday I arranged with Talarius and Asillius that they should serve as escorts for the child Gaius on the fifteenth day before the Kalends of June (i.e., 13 May), if the gods be willing. Moreover, with him I am sending one of my slaves who is a doctor and I have written to Germanicus that he may keep him if he wishes. Farewell, my own Agrippina and take care that you reach your Germanicus safely'.

I think it is abundantly clear that Gaius could not have been born in a place to which he was first taken from the city (of Rome) when he was almost two. These same considerations undermine also the trustworthiness of the verses and the more so since they are anonymous. Therefore, the authority of a public document (*publici instrumenti auctoritas*), the one thing that remains, must be accepted, especially since Gaius always preferred Antium to all other locations and places of retreat for no other reason than that it was his birthplace and since it is said that he even intended, through boredom with Rome, to transfer to that place the seat of empire (*sedem ac domicilium imperii*) itself.

Quite why Suetonius needed to go to such lengths to establish Gaius's place of birth must remain a matter of speculation. Possibly his main purpose was to correct Tacitus who at *Annals* 1.41.2 had claimed that Gaius had been born in the camp (*in castris genitus*)[5] and thus to demonstrate that his own mastery of documentary sources was superior to that of his more illustrious contemporary.[6] This is not the only place, as we saw above, where he seeks to do this.[7]

---

5. Goodyear, *Tacitus*, 1:286 n. 3.

6. For Suetonius's point-scoring at Tacitus's expense, see Wallace-Hadrill, *Suetonius*, 10 n. 15 and Hurley, *Divus Claudius*, 9 n. 33.

7. For discussion of *Tiberius* 21.4-7 and *Nero* 52, see 115 above.

CHRESTUS, THE UNKNOWN (AND UNKNOWABLE?) CLAUDIAN AGITATOR

About the identity of the Chrestus characterized at *Div. Claud.* 25.4 as an agitator (*impulsor*), Suetonius has nothing specific to say. That should not surprise. Throughout his Lives of the Caesars Suetonius's main concern is always with the emperor. Consequently it is on him that the spotlight is relentlessly trained.[1] Non-elite individuals make few appearances in these biographies. Even important actors in the imperial drama such as leading courtiers and principal advisers (*amici*) receive, at most, only minimal attention. Lucius Vitellius, a key figure at the court of Claudius, for instance, does not rate so much as a mention in the biography of that emperor.[2] Seneca, one of Nero's two principal advisers, figures only fleetingly in the life of Nero. Even then, it is as the teenage Nero's tutor (*praeceptor*) that we see him,[3] not as the man who virtually ran Nero's government for the better part of his reign. On those relatively rare occasions when Suetonius does happen to mention individuals other than the emperor and his immediate family, he takes it for granted that his readers either know or can easily inform themselves about their identity.[4] In the case of Claudius's reign, several contemporary accounts were still available for them to consult.[5] Consequently, although the Claudian agitator, Chrestus, is unknown *to us*, it does not follow that he was equally unknown to an early second-century CE readership. Far more resources, both written and oral, were available to Suetonius's readers than there are

---

1. Hurley, *Divus Claudius*, 9.
2. Mottershead, *Claudius*, xii.
3. *Nero* 7.1; 35.5; 52.
4. Wallace-Hadrill, *Suetonius*, 13.
5. This is shown by Tacitus's explicit use of, for instance, the histories of Pliny the Elder, Cluvius Rufus and Fabius Rusticus. See above, 64.

to us.[6] It should never be forgotten that we have no complete, continuous narrative history of Claudius's reign. The only ones to survive, those of Tacitus and Cassius Dio, exist only in parts.[7]

However, even if Chrestus eludes precise identification by us, that does not mean that nothing of substance can be inferred from Suetonius's brief reference to him. In the first place, the application to him of the word *impulsor* clearly implies, as was noted in Chapter 6 above, that he must have been physically present in Claudian Rome and actively engaged in the Jewish disturbances for which Claudius issued his edict of expulsion.[8] Secondly, the context suggests that Chrestus almost certainly was not a local Jew but a resident alien. Suetonius opens the section in which Chrestus appears (*Div. Claud.* 25.3-4) with the signpost words 'of peregrine condition' (*peregrinae condicionis*) – i.e., of non-citizen status. Since all the other communities and individuals listed under that virtual rubric demonstrably are foreigners, the implication must be that both Chrestus himself and the *Iudaei* stirred up by him are foreigners too. The punishment that Claudius inflicts upon them confirms that: had they been other than *peregrini* they could not have been summarily expelled from the city. Members of the Roman Jewish community who enjoyed full Roman citizen status (and certainly there were some, possibly quite a large number, in that situation[9]) will have had to be tried formally.[10]

Generally, as noted earlier, Suetonius's Christus sentence is taken to be a somewhat muddled reference to inter-communal Jewish rioting between Jews who believed in the messiahship of Jesus and those who did not.[11] But this interpretation does not appear in our sources before the fifth century CE, when it crops up as an add-on to Orosius's somewhat

6. For Suetonius's own use of oral reminiscences, see Wallace-Hadrill, *Suetonius*, 65.

7. See Tacitus, *Annals* 11 and 12 and Dio, *Roman History* 60.

8. See Cook, *Roman Attitudes*, 20 for a full discussion of the evidence.

9. See E. Mary Smallwood, *Philonis Alexandrini Legatio ad Gaium* (Leiden: Brill, 1961), 235 (comm. on *Leg.* 156).

10. Max Radin, *Jews Among the Greeks and Romans* (Philadelphia: The Jewish Publication Society of America, 1915), 314; Rutgers, 'Roman Policy toward the Jews', 98.

11. See, for instance, Smallwood, 'The Diaspora in the Roman Period before CE 70', 176; Botermann, *Das Judenedikt*, 57–71; Lane, 'Social Perspectives', 204–5; Jakob Engberg, *Impulsore Chresto: Opposition to Christianity in the Roman Empire c. 50–250 AD*, trans. Gregory Carter (Frankfurt am Main: Peter Lang, 2007), 99–104.

inaccurate citation of Suetonius's testimony.[12] If our focus is concentrated, as surely it ought to be, solely on what Suetonius originally wrote in this section of his life of Claudius,[13] then an entirely different interpretation of his Chrestus testimony is possible. What Suetonius makes abundantly clear by both the structure of the life at this point (i.e., his choice of the rubric, *peregrinae condicionis*) and his list of illustrative examples is that this section is not about 'foreign religions', which are treated elsewhere in the life, but 'foreign populations'.[14] Consequently, it is not the cultic practices of those individuals and communities that are the issue with him at this point but their legal status.[15]

With regard to Chrestus and his fellow, peace-disrupting Jews, then, what may well have lain at the root of their disturbances was their disadvantaged status. They will have belonged to the least privileged section of Rome's Jewish population.[16] Unlike those Jews who were fully enfranchised Roman citizens, peregrine Jews were not only liable to summary ejection but, even more significantly, they were denied the all-important privilege of access to the *annona*, the system under which free corn was made available to the poor.[17] Was this issue the cause of the persistent unrest of Chrestus and his followers? If we accept Dio's statement that at the start of his reign Claudius closed down the synagogues,[18] that would

---

12. Orosius, *Historiae adversum paganos* 7.6.15-16. For a brief treatment of the inaccuracy of this passage, see Levinskaya, *Book of Acts*, 172.

13. On the methodological impropriety of using fifth-century CE evidence as an interpretive tool for an early second-century text, see Levinskaya, *Book of Acts*, 177.

14. On this point, see Mottershead, *Claudius*, 149 and 154 n. 5; Hurley, *Divus Claudius*, 176.

15. The whole of this data-rich part of Suetonius's life of Claudius (*Div. Claud.* 22-25) is organized, as is so often the case with this writer, largely on hierarchical principles (Wallace-Hadrill, *Suetonius*, 101–3), the discussion commencing with Rome's highest social stratum, the senatorial order, and proceeding thereafter, first, downwards and then outwards. Thus this section on non-citizens (*peregrini*) forms a natural bridge between the major constituent groups of Roman society and the world outside. So, perceptively, Hurley, *Divus Claudius*, 174.

16. For a brief discussion of the various legal categories into which a Jew at Rome might fall, see Rutgers, 'Roman Policy toward the Jews', 97–8. Besides being a full Roman citizen or a resident alien (*peregrinus*), s/he might be a Junian Latin. For this poorly understood intermediate category, see J. A. Crook, *Law and Life of Rome* (London: Thames & Hudson, 1967), 43–5.

17. On the importance of this to its Jewish recipients, see Philo, *Legatio ad Gaium* 158.

18. Dio, *Roman History* 60.6.6. For defence of the traditional date for this action – namely, 41 CE – see Levinskaya, *Book of Acts*, 174. The likelihood of the historicity

seem quite likely. Charitable food-giving was a notable feature of Jewish community life.[19] With the closure of the synagogues, that life-line would have become unavailable to impoverished urban Jews whose lowly status made them ineligible for food-aid from the state.[20]

In this particular section of the life of Claudius (25.3-4), several of the cases presented by Suetonius concern *peregrini* claiming privileges not consonant with their status. In one instance we see foreign envoys bagging seats reserved for the elite in ignorance and contravention of the *Lex Iulia Theatralis*; in another, we have individuals being forbidden to appropriate Roman family names (*gentilicia*) and thus to give the false impression that they possessed full Roman citizenship with all its concomitant benefits. Might we not have a similar case with Chrestus and his fellow peregrines – i.e., individuals trying to improve their lot by laying claim to what was not, as things stood, legally theirs?

A final matter to be pondered is why Chrestus himself is singled out for naming in the section Suetonius devotes to Claudius's dealings with those of 'peregrine condition'. It is of note that he is the only individual to be so treated in that passage, the rest of the cases mentioned there either being left in anonymity or referred to collectively – e.g., as the Rhodians, the Lycians, the people of Ilium (Troy). Was the very similarity of his name to that of Christ the motivating factor here?[21] Given the latter's fascination with onomastics, the coincidence of two early imperial Jewish challengers of the Roman status quo having such similar names, one very common and the other unique, may have intrigued (and amused?) him.[22] But a more substantial reason surely is supplied by the clear structural function performed by its inclusion: the name serves to define very neatly which members of Rome's large, several thousand-strong Jewish

of this action is strengthened by Claudius's simultaneous disbanding of clubs and closure of taverns. For these various security measures, see Dio, *Roman History* 60.6.6-7.

19. For a negative take on this, see Juvenal, *Satires* 3.296 and Artemidorus, *Onirocritica* 3.53 (= Stern, *Greek and Latin Authors* 2: no. 395), where synagogues (prayer-houses) are described as the haunts of beggars.

20. On the persistent problems with the food supply at Rome throughout Claudius's reign and the extensive measures he took to improve the situation, see Levick, *Claudius*, 109–11 and Hurley, *Divus Claudius*, 141. For hunger as the principal cause of serious rioting at Rome, see Mottershead, *Claudius*, 71 (comm. on *Div. Claud.* 18.1).

21. For this attractive suggestion, see Mottershead, *Claudius*, 155 n. 10.

22. On the popularity of the name Chrestus in early imperial Rome, especially among the non-elite, see Heikki Solin, *Die griechische Personennamen in Rom: Ein Namenbuch* (Berlin: de Gruyter, 2003), *s.v.* Chrestus.

population actually were expelled. Clearly it was not, so Suetonius's Latin encourages us to infer, the community as a whole. Rather it was only those who rioted persistently, led on by Chrestus.[23] How many Jews were expelled by Claudius on that account is, of course, impossible to determine. Although Radin argued that the numbers were probably fairly limited,[24] the impact made by these riots (they were still worth mentioning nearly a century after their occurrence) suggests that they could have been quite substantial.[25]

What happened to Chrestus himself, the champion, as I have argued, of some of Rome's hungriest and most frustrated peregrine Jews, is unknown. As the actual instigator of their rioting, he may well have received from Claudius a rather harsher penalty than expulsion from the imperial capital. Certainly the officials who governed Judaea on his behalf, procurators such as Cuspius Fadus (44–*ca.* 46 CE) and Tiberius Julius Alexander (*ca.* 46–48 CE), were not slow to put to death those who had the temerity to threaten or to disturb the *pax Augusta*.[26]

23. For a succinct and compelling analysis of Suetonius's Latin here, see Lampe, *Christians at Rome in the First Two Centuries*, 13–14.

24. Radin, *Jews among the Greeks and Romans*, 314–15 ('some relatively small group').

25. Gruen's apologetically driven contention that Chrestus probably did not even exist and the riots were a figment of Suetonius's imagination (*Diaspora*, 39, 41 and 272 n. 171) is not to be taken seriously. It goes against everything that we know about Suetonius and his scholarly ways.

26. Josephus, *Ant.* 20.97-98 and 102.

BIBLIOGRAPHY

Alföldi, Géza. 'Ein Tempel der Herrscherkultes in Comum'. Pages 211–19 in *Städte, Eliten und Gesellschaft in der Gallia Cisalpina: Epigraphisch-historische Untersuchungen*. Stuttgart: Franz Steiner, 1999. An update of 'Ein Tempel der Herrscherkultes in Comum'. *Athenaeum* 61 (1983): 362–73.

Ameling, Walter. 'Pliny: The Piety of a Persecutor'. Pages 271–99 in *Myths, Martyrs, and Modernity. Studies in the History of Religions in Honour of Jan N. Bremmer*. Edited by Jitse Dijkstra, Justin Kroesen and Yme Kuiper. Leiden: Brill, 2010.

Anderson, G. *The Second Sophistic: A Cultural Phenomenon in the Roman Empire*. London: Routledge, 1993.

Andresen, Carl. *Logos und Nomos. Die Polemik des Kelsos wider das Christentum*. Berlin: de Gruyter, 1955.

Ash, Rhiannon. *Tacitus*. London: Bristol Classical, 2006.

Ash, Rhiannon, ed., *Tacitus, Annals Book XV*. Cambridge: Cambridge University Press, 2018.

Baldwin, Barry. *Suetonius*. Amsterdam: Hakkert, 1983.

Baldwin, Barry. 'Suetonius: Birth, Disgrace and Death'. *Acta Classica* 18 (1975): 61–70.

Bammel, C. P. 'Die erste lateinische Rede gegen die Christen'. *ZKG* 104 (1993): 295–311.

Barclay, John M. G. 'Jews and Christians in the Eyes of Roman Authors c. 100 CE'. Pages 313–26 in *Jews and Christians in the First and Second Centuries: How to Write Their History*. Edited by P. J. Tomson and J. Schwartz. Leiden: Brill, 2014.

Barclay, John M. G. *Jews in the Mediterranean Diaspora*. Edinburgh: T&T Clark, 1996.

Barnes, T. D. 'Legislation Against the Christians'. *JRS* 58 (1968): 32–50.

Barnes, T. D. Review of the second, revised edition of R. Freudenberger, *Das Verhalten der römischen Behörden gegen die Christen im 2. Jahrhundert* (Munich: C. H. Beck'sche, 1969), *JRS* 61 (1971): 311–12.

Barrett, Anthony A., Elaine Fantham and John C. Yardley, eds. *The Emperor Nero: A Guide to the Ancient Sources*. Princeton: Princeton University Press, 2016.

Beale, G. K. *The Book of Revelation: A Commentary on the Greek Text*. Grand Rapids: Eerdmans, 1999.

Beard, Mary, John North and Simon Price. *Religions of Rome*. 2 vols. Cambridge: Cambridge University Press, 1998.

Behr, C. A. *Aristides and the Sacred Tales*. Amsterdam: Hakkert, 1968.

Benario, Herbert W. 'The Annals'. Pages 101–22 in *A Companion to Tacitus*. Edited by Victoria Emma Pagán. Chichester: Wiley-Blackwell, 2012.

Benko, Stephen. 'Pagan Criticism of Christianity during the First Two Centuries A. D.'. Pages 1055–1118 in *ANRW* 23.2. Berlin: de Gruyter, 1980.

Benko, Stephen. 'The Edict of Claudius of A.D. 49 and the Instigator Chrestus'. *TZ* 25 (1969): 406–18.

Benko, Stephen. *Pagan Rome and the Early Christians*. London: Batsford, 1985.

Bennett, Julian. *Trajan: Optimus Princeps*. London: Routledge, 1997.

Bettenson, Henry. *Documents of the Christian Church*. London: Oxford University Press, 1943.

Bettenson, Henry. *Documents of the Christian Church*. Revised by Chris Maunder. 3rd edn. Oxford: Oxford University Press, 1999.

Birley, Anthony R. *Garrison Life at Vindolanda: A Band of Brothers*. Stroud: Tempus, 2002.

Birley, Anthony R. 'The Life and Death of Cornelius Tacitus'. *Zeitschrift für Altegeschichte* 49, no. 2 (2000): 230–47.

Birley, Anthony R. 'Pliny's Family, Pliny's Career'. Pages 51–66 in *The Epistles of Pliny*. Edited by Roy K. Gibson and Christopher Whitton. Oxford: Oxford University Press, 2016. Originally printed in pages 1–17 of A. R. Birley, *Onomasticon to the Younger Pliny: Letters and Panegyric*. Munich: K. G. Saur, 2000.

Birley, Anthony R. *Septimius Severus: The African Emperor*. London: Eyre & Spottiswoode, 1971.

Bloch, René S. *Antike Vorstellungen vom Judentum. Der Judenexkurs des Tacitus im Rahmen der griechisch-römischen Ethnographie*. Historia Einzelschriften 160. Stuttgart: Franz Steiner, 2002.

Blumell, Lincoln. 'A Jew in Celsus' *True Doctrine*? An Examination of Jewish Anti-Christian Polemic in the Second Century C. E.'. *SR* 36, no. 2 (2007): 297–315.

Blundell, Sue. *Women in Ancient Greece*. London: British Museum Press, 1995.

Boman, Jobjorn. 'Inpulsore Cherestro? Suetonius' Divus Claudius 25.4 in Sources and Manuscripts'. *SBFLA* (2011): 355–76.

Bond, Helen K. *The First Biography of Jesus: Genre and Meaning in Mark's Gospel*. Grand Rapids: Eerdmans, 2020.

Bond, Helen K. *The Historical Jesus: A Guide for the Perplexed*. London: Bloomsbury, 2012.

Bond, Helen K. *Pontius Pilate in History and Interpretation*. Cambridge: Cambridge University Press, 1986.

Borret, Marcel. *Origène: Contre Celse*. 5 vols. Paris: CERF, 1967–76.

Botermann, Helga. *Das Judenedikt des Kaisers Claudius: Römischer Staat und Christiani im 1. Jahrhundert*. Stuttgart: F. Steiner, 1996.

Bovon, François, and John M. Duffy. 'A New Greek Fragment from Ariston of Pella's "Dialogue of Jason and Papiscus"'. *HTR* 105, no. 4 (2012): 457–65.

Bowersock, G. W. *Greek Sophists in the Roman Empire*. Oxford: Clarendon, 1969.

Bowie, E. L. 'Greeks and Their Past in the Second Sophistic'. Pages 166–209 in *Studies in Ancient Society*. Edited by M. I. Finley. London: Routledge & Kegan Paul, 1974.

Bowie, E. L. 'The Importance of Sophists'. *YCS* 27 (1982): 29–59.

Bradley, Keith R. 'Introduction'. Pages 11–34 in *Suetonius*. Translated by J. C. Rolfe. 2 vols. Cambridge, MA: Harvard University Press, 1998.

Bradley, Keith R. 'Review Article: The Rediscovery of Suetonius', *CPh* 80, no. 3 (1985): 254–65.

Bradley, Keith R. *Suetonius' Life of Nero: An Historical Commentary*. Collection Latomus 157. Brussels: Latomus, 1978.

Bradley, Keith R. 'Suetonius, *Nero* 16.2: "afflicti suppliciis Christiani"'. *CR* 22 (1972): 9–10.

Bremmer, Jan N. *Maidens, Magic and Martyrs: Collected Essays*, 1. Tübingen: Mohr Siebeck, 2017.

Bremmer, Jan N. 'Peregrinus' Christian Career'. Pages 729–47 in *Flores Florentino: Dead Sea Scrolls and Other Early Jewish Studies in Honour of Florentino García Martínez*. Edited by Anthony Hilhorst, Émile Puech and Eibert J. C. Tigchelaar. Leiden: Brill, 2007.

Bremmer, Jan N. 'Why Did Jesus's Followers Call Themselves "Christians"?'. Pages 3–12 in *Maidens, Magic and Martyrs: Collected Essays*, 1. Tübingen: Mohr Siebeck, 2017.

Bruce, F. F. 'Christianity under Claudius'. *BJRL* 44 (1961/62): 309–26.

Bruce, F. F. *Jesus and Christian Origins Outside the New Testament*. London: Hodder & Stoughton, 1974.

Burke, Gary T. 'Celsus and Justin: Carl Andresen Revisited'. *ZNW* 76 (1985): 107–16.

Burke, Gary T. 'Celsus and the Old Testament'. *VT* 36, no. 2 (1986): 241–5.

Butcher, Kevin. *Roman Syria and the Near East*. London: British Museum Press, 2003.

Campbell, J. B. *The Roman Army 31 BC–AD 337: A Sourcebook*. London: Routledge, 1994.

Carleton Paget, James N. Review of Horacio E. Lona, *Die* Wahre Lehre *des Kelsos. Übersetzt und erklärt* (Freiburg: Herder, 2005), *JEH* 58 (2007): 297–9.

Carleton Paget, James N. 'The Jew of Celsus and *adversus Judaeos* Literature'. *ZAC* 21, no. 2 (2017): 201–42.

Carleton Paget, James N., and Simon Gathercole, eds. *Celsus in his World: Philosophy, Polemic and Religion in the Second Century*. Cambridge: Cambridge University Press, 2021.

Carrier, Richard. *On the Historicity of Jesus: Why We Might Have Reason for Doubt*. Sheffield: Sheffield Phoenix, 2014.

Carrier, Richard. 'The Prospect of Christian Interpolation in Tacitus, Annals 15.44'. *VC* 68 (2014): 264–83.

Carter, John M. *Suetonius Divus Augustus*. Bristol: Bristol Classical, 1982.

Casson, Lionel. *Libraries in the Ancient World*. New Haven: Yale University Press, 2001.

Chadwick, Henry. *Origen: Contra Celsum*. Cambridge: Cambridge University Press, 1953.

Champlin, Edward. *Fronto and Antonine Rome*. Cambridge, MA: Harvard University Press, 1980.

Champlin, Edward. *Nero*. Cambridge: Belknap, 2003.

Chapman, David W. *Ancient Jewish and Christian Perceptions of Crucifixion*. WUNT 2/244. Tübingen: Mohr Siebeck, 2008.

Charlesworth, Martin P. 'Some Observations on the Ruler-Cult, Especially in Rome'. *HTR* 28 (1935): 5–44.

Chilver, G. E. F. *Cisalpine Gaul: Social and Economic History from 49 B. C. to the Death of Trajan*. Oxford: Clarendon, 1941.

Clay, Diskin. 'Lucian of Samosata: Four Philosophical Lives (Nigrinus, Demonax, Peregrinus, Alexander Pseudomantis)'. Pages 3406–50 in *ANRW* 2.36.5. Berlin: de Gruyter, 1992.

Clay, Diskin. *Paradosis and Survival: Three Chapters in the Epicurean Philosophy*. Ann Arbor: University of Michigan Press, 1998.

Coleman, K. M. 'Fatal Charades: Roman Executions Staged as Mythological Enactments'. *JRS* 80 (1990): 44–73.

Cook, John Granger. 'Celsus'. Pages 3:3–29 in *The Reception of Jesus in the First Three Centuries*. Edited by Chris Keith, Helen K. Bond, Christine Jacobi and Jens Schröter. 3 vols. London: Bloomsbury T&T Clark, 2020.

Cook, John Granger. '*Chrestiani, Christiani,* Χριστιανοί: A Second Century Anachronism?' *VC* 74 (2020): 237–64.

Cook, John Granger. *The Interpretation of the New Testament in Greco-Roman Paganism.* STAC 3. Tübingen: Mohr Siebeck, 2000.

Cook, John Granger. *Roman Attitudes Toward the Christians.* WUNT 261. Tübingen: Mohr Siebeck, 2011.

Cooley, Alison E. *Res Gestae Divi Augusti: Text, Translation, and Commentary.* Cambridge: Cambridge University Press, 2009.

Cooley, M. G. L., ed. *The Flavians.* LACTOR 20. London Association of Classical Teachers, 2015.

Corke-Webster, James. 'Trouble in Pontus: The Pliny-Trajan Correspondence on the Christians Reconsidered'. *TAPA* 147, no. 2 (2017): 371–411.

Cornell, T. J. 'The Citing Authorities. 4.2. Individual Sources: Suetonius'. Pages 1:125–9 in *The Fragments of the Roman Historians.* Edited by T. J. Cornell. 3 vols. Oxford: Oxford University Press, 2013.

Costa, C. D. N. *Lucian: Selected Dialogues.* Oxford World Classics. Oxford: Oxford University Press, 2006.

Cribiore, Raffaella. *Gymnastics of the Mind: Greek Education in Hellenistic and Roman Egypt.* Princeton: Princeton University Press, 2001.

Crook, J. A. *Consilium Principis: Imperial Councils and Counsellors from Augustus to Diocletian.* Cambridge: Cambridge University Press, 1955.

Crook, J. A. *Law and Life of Rome.* London: Thames & Hudson, 1967.

Crook, J. A. 'Suetonius "ab epistulis"'. *PCPhS* 184 (1956–57): 18–22.

Cross, F. L., ed. *The Oxford Dictionary of Christian Church.* Revised by E. A. Livingstone. 3rd edn. Oxford: Oxford University Press, 2005.

Cureton, William, ed. and trans. *Spicilegium Syriacum: Containing Remains of Bardesan, Meliton, Ambrose and Mara Bar Serapion.* London: Rivington, 1855.

de Sélincourt, Aubrey, trans. Livy, *The Early History of Rome.* Harmondsworth, Penguin, 1960.

de Ste Croix, G. E. M. 'Why Were the Early Christians Persecuted?'. Pages 210–49 in *Studies in Ancient Society.* Edited by M. I. Finley. London: Routledge & Kegan Paul, 1974.

Dickie, Matthew W. 'Lucian's Gods: Lucian's Understanding of the Divine'. Pages 348–61 in *The Gods of Ancient Greece: Identities and Transformations.* Edited by J. N. Bremmer and A. Erskine. Edinburgh: Edinburgh University Press, 2010.

Drews, Arthur. *The Christ Myth.* Translated by C. Delisle Burns. 3rd edn. London: T. Fisher Unwin, 1910.

Duff, John Wight. *A Literary History of Rome in the Silver Age, from Tiberius to Hadrian.* London: Unwin, 1927.

Duncan-Jones, Richard P. 'The Finances of a Senator'. Pages 89–106 in *The Epistles of Pliny.* Edited by Roy K. Gibson and Christopher Whitton. Oxford: Oxford University Press, 2016.

Dunderberg, Ismo. 'Valentinian Teachers in Rome'. Pages 157–74 in *Christians as a Religious Minority in a Multicultural City.* Edited by Jürgen Zangenberg and Michael Labahn. JSNTSup 243. London: T&T Clark, 2004.

Dunn, J. D. G. *Jesus Remembered.* Grand Rapids: Eerdmans, 2003.

Dunn, J. D. G. *Romans 1–8.* WBC 38A. Waco: Word, 1988.

Eck, Werner. 'Provincial Administration and Finance'. Pages 266–92 in *The Cambridge Ancient History, XI: The High Empire, AD 70–192.* Edited by Alan K. Bowman, Peter Garnsey and Dominic Rathbone. Cambridge: Cambridge University Press, 2000.

Eck, Werner. 'Rome and the Outside World: Senatorial Families and the World They Lived In'. Pages 73–99 in *The Roman Family in Italy: Status, Sentiment, Space*. Edited by Beryl Rawson and Paul Weaver. Oxford: Oxford University Press, 1997.

Eddy, Paul, and Gregory A. Boyd. *The Jesus Legend*. Grand Rapids: Baker Academic, 2007.

Edwards, Catharine, trans. *Suetonius: Lives of the Caesars*. OWC. Oxford: Oxford University Press, 2000.

Edwards, Mark. 'Lucian of Samosata in the Christian Memory'. *Byzantion* 80 (2010): 142–56.

Edwards, Mark. 'Satire and Verisimilitude: Christianity in Lucian's Peregrinus'. *Historia* 38, no. 1 (1989): 89–98.

Ehrenberg, Victor, and A. H. M. Jones. *Documents Illustrating the Reigns of Augustus and Tiberius*. 2nd edn. Oxford: Clarendon, 1955.

Ehrman, Bart D. *Did Jesus Exist? The Historical Argument for Jesus of Nazareth*. New York: Harper Collins, 2012.

Engberg, Jakob. *Impulsore Chresto: Opposition to Christianity in the Roman Empire c. 50–250 AD*. Translated by Gregory Carter. Frankfurt am Main: Peter Lang, 2007.

Evans, Craig A. 'Jesus in Non-Christian Sources'. Pages 443–78 in *Studying the Historical Jesus: Evaluations of the State of Current Research*. Edited by Bruce Chilton and Craig A. Evans. NTTS 19. Leiden: Brill, 1994.

Evans, E. C. 'Physiognomics in the Ancient World'. *TAPS* 59, no. 5 (1969): 1–101.

Fabia, Philippe. 'Les ouvrages de Tacite réussirent-ils auprès des contemporains?' *Rev. Phil.* 19 (1895): 1–10.

Fagles, Robert. *Homer: The Iliad*. New York: Penguin, 1998.

Feldman, Louis H. *Jew and Gentile in the Ancient World: Attitudes and Interactions from Alexander to Justinian*. Princeton: Princeton University Press, 1993.

Feldman, Louis H. *Josephus and Modern Scholarship (1937–1980)*. Berlin: de Gruyter, 1984.

Feldman, Louis H. 'Reflections on Jews in Graeco-Roman Literature'. *JSP* 16 (1997): 39–52.

Feldman, Louis H., and Meyer Reinhold, eds. *Jewish Life and Thought Among Greeks and Romans*. Edinburgh: T&T Clark, 1996.

Ferguson, Everett, ed. *Encyclopedia of Early Christianity*. 2nd edn. New York: Garland, 1998.

Ferris, Iain. *Cave Canem: Animals and Roman Society*. Stroud: Amberley, 2018.

Fornara, Charles William. *The Nature of History in Ancient Greece and Rome*. Berkeley: University of California Press, 1983.

Foster, Paul. 'The Epistles of Ignatius of Antioch'. Pages 81–107 in *The Writings of the Apostolic Fathers*. Edited by Paul Foster. Edinburgh: T&T Clark, 2007.

France, R. T. *The Evidence for Jesus*. London: Hodder & Stoughton, 1986.

Frank, Tenney. 'The Carmen Saeculare of Horace'. *AJP* 42 (1921): 324–9.

Frede, M. 'Celsus' Attack on the Christians'. Pages 218–40 in *Philosophia Togata II*. Edited by Jonathan Barnes and Miriam Griffin. Oxford: Clarendon, 1997.

Frede, M. 'Celsus philosophus Platonicus'. Pages 5183–5213 in *ANRW* 2.36.7. Berlin: de Gruyter, 1994.

Frede, M. 'Origen's Treatise Against Celsus'. Pages 131–55 in *Apologetics in the Roman Empire: Pagans, Jews and Christians*. Edited by M. Edwards, M. Goodman and S. Price. Oxford: Oxford University Press, 1999.

Fredriksen Paula. *When Christians Were Jews: The First Generation*. New Haven: Yale University Press, 2018.

Freese, J. H., trans. *Photius, Biblioteca. Vol. I*. London: SPCK, 1920.

Frend, W. H. C. *Martyrdom and Persecution in the Early Church*. Oxford: Blackwell, 1985.

Frend, W. H. C. *The Rise of Christianity*. Philadelphia: Fortress, 1984.

Fuchs, Harald. 'Tacitus über die Christen'. *VC* 4, no. 2 (1950): 65–93.

Furneaux, Henry, ed. *The Annals of Tacitus*. Revised by H. F. Pelham and C. D. Fisher. Oxford: Clarendon, 1907.

Galand-Hallyn, P. 'Bibliographie Suétonienne (les "Vies des XII Césars")'. Pages 3576–3622 in *ANRW* 2.33.5. Berlin: de Gruyter, 1991.

Gallagher, Eugene V. *Divine Man or Magician? Celsus and Origen on Jesus*. SBL Dissertation Series 64. Chico: Scholars Press, 1982.

Gibbon, Edward. *The History of the Decline and Fall of the Roman Empire*. Edited by J. B. Bury. 7 vols. London: Methuen, 1906.

Gibson, Roy K., and Ruth Morello. *Reading the Letters of Pliny the Younger: An Introduction*. Cambridge: Cambridge University Press, 2012.

Goldhill, Simon. 'Rhetoric and the Second Sophistic'. Pages 228–41 in *The Cambridge Companion to Ancient Rhetoric*. Edited by E. Gunderson. Cambridge: Cambridge University Press, 2009.

González, Julián. 'Tacitus, Germanicus, Piso, and the Tabula Siarensis'. *AJP* 120, no. 1 (1999): 123–42.

Goodyear, F. R. D. *Tacitus*. New Surveys in the Classics 4. Oxford: Clarendon, 1970.

Goodyear, F. R. D., ed. *The Annals of Tacitus: Books 1–6*. 2 vols. Cambridge: Cambridge University Press, 1972 and 1981.

Grant, Michael, trans. *Tacitus: The Annals of Imperial Rome*. Harmondsworth: Penguin, 1956.

Green, Peter, trans. *Juvenal: The Sixteen Satires*. Harmondsworth: Penguin, 1967.

Griffin, Miriam T. *Nero: The End of a Dynasty*. London: Batsford, 1984.

Griffin, Miriam T. 'Pliny and Tacitus'. *Scripta Classica Israelica* 18 (1999): 139–58 = Pages 355–77 in *The Epistles of Pliny*. Edited by Roy K. Gibson and Christopher Whitton. Oxford: Oxford University Press, 2016.

Griffin, Miriam T. Review of Helga Botermann, *Das Judenedikt des Kaisers Claudius: Römischer Staat und Christiani im 1. Jahrhundert* (Stuttgart: F. Steiner, 1996). *Latomus* 59, no. 3 (2000): 693–5.

Griffiths, Mark. *The Authenticity of Prometheus Bound*. Cambridge: Cambridge University Press, 1977.

Gruen, Erich S. *Diaspora: Jews Amidst Greeks and Romans*. Cambridge, MA: Harvard University Press, 2002.

Gruen, Erich S. *Rethinking the Other in Antiquity*. Princeton: Princeton University Press, 2012.

Hägg, Tomas. *The Art of Biography in Antiquity*. Cambridge: Cambridge University Press, 2012.

Hägg, Tomas. 'Hierocles the Lover of Truth and Eusebius the Sophist'. *Symb.Osl.* 67 (1992): 138–50.

Halliwell, Stephen. *Greek Laughter: A Study of Cultural Psychology from Homer to Early Christianity*. Cambridge: Cambridge University Press, 2008.

Hardy, E. G. *Studies in Roman History*. London: Swan Sonnenschein, 1910.

Hargis, Jeffrey W. *Against the Christians: The Rise of Early Anti-Christian Polemic*. New York: Peter Lang, 1999.

Harmon, A. M., et al., trans. *Lucian*. LCL. 8 vols. London: William Heinemann, 1936–67.

Harris, Murray J. 'References to Jesus in Early Classical Authors'. Pages 343–68 in *Gospel Perspectives: The Jesus Tradition Outside the Gospels* 5. Edited by David Wenham. Sheffield: JSOT, 1984.

Harvey, Sir Paul, ed. *The Oxford Companion to Classical Literature*. 1st edn. Oxford: Clarendon, 1937.

Heemstra, Marius. *The Fiscus Judaicus and the Parting of the Ways*. WUNT 2/277. Tübingen: Mohr Siebeck, 2010.

Hengel, Martin. *Crucifixion*. Translated by John Bowden. London: SCM, 1977.

Henten, J. W. van. 'Testimonium Flavianum'. Pages 1:365–70 in *The Reception of Jesus in the First Three Centuries*. Edited by Chris Keith, Helen K. Bond, Christine Jacobi and Jens Schröter. 3 vols. London: T&T Clark, 2020.

Hermann, L. 'Les interpolations de la lettre de Pline sur les chrétiens'. *Latomus* 13, no. 3 (1954): 343–53.

Heubner, H., ed. *P. Cornelii Taciti libri qui supersunt, I: Ab excessu divi Augusti*. Stuttgart: Teubner, 1994.

Hochart, Polydore. *Études au sujet de la persécution des Chrétians sous Néro*. Paris: Ernest Leroux, 1885.

Hoffmann, R. Joseph. *Jesus Outside the Gospels*. Buffalo: Prometheus, 1984.

Hoffmann, R. Joseph, trans. *On the True Doctrine: A Discourse Against the Christians*. New York: Oxford University Press, 1987.

Hopkinson, Neil, ed. *Lucian: A Selection*. Cambridge: Cambridge University Press, 2008.

Horbury, William. *Jewish War Under Trajan and Hadrian*. Cambridge: Cambridge University Press, 2014.

Horbury, William. *Jews and Christians in Contact and Controversy*. Edinburgh: T&T Clark, 1998.

Horrell, David G. 'The Label Χριστιάνος: 1 Peter 4:16 and the Formation of Christian Identity'. *JBL* 126, no. 2 (2007): 361–81.

Horst, Pieter W. van der. 'Consolation from Prison: Mara bar Sarapion and Boethius'. Pages 209–19 in *Studies in Ancient Judaism and Early Christianity*. Leiden: Brill, 2014.

Horst, Pieter W. van der. Review of Pilhofer et al., *Lukian: Der Tod des Peregrinos*. *BMCR* 200511.16.

Householder, F. W. *Literary Quotations and Allusion in Lucian*. New York: King's Crown, 1941.

Howatson, M. C., ed. *The Oxford Companion to Classical Literature*. 2nd edn. Oxford: Oxford University Press, 1989.

Hurley, Donna W. *Suetonius: Divus Claudius*. Cambridge: Cambridge University Press, 2001.

Hurley, Donna W. 'Suetonius' Rubric Sandwich'. Pages 21–37 in *Suetonius the Biographer: Studies in Roman Lives*. Edited by Tristan Power and Roy Gibson. Oxford: Oxford University Press, 2014.

Hurley, Donna W., trans. *Suetonius: The Caesars*. Indianapolis: Hackett, 2011.

Hurtado, Larry W. *Destroyer of the Gods: Early Christian Distinctiveness in the Roman World*. Waco: Baylor University Press, 2016.

Hurtado, Larry W. *Lord Jesus Christ: Devotion to Jesus in Earliest Christianity*. Grand Rapids: Eerdmans, 2003.

Isaac, Benjamin, and Israël Roll. 'Judaea in the Early Years of Hadrian's Reign'. *Latomus* 38, no. 1 (1979): 54–66. Re-printed with Postscript in pages 182–97 of Benjamin Isaac, *The Near East Under Roman Rule: Selected Papers*. Mnemosyne Supp. 177. Leiden: Brill, 1998.

Jackson, Howard M. 'The Setting and Sectarian Provenance of the Fragment of the "Celestial Dialogue" Preserved by Origen from Celsus's Ἀληθὴς Λόγος'. *HTR* 85, no. 3 (1992): 273–305.

James, M. R. *The Apocryphal New Testament*. Oxford: Clarendon, 1953.

Janne, H. 'Impulsore Chresto'. Pages 531–53 in *Mélanges Bidez: Annuaire de l'Institut de philosophie et d'histoire orientales* 2. Brussels: Secrétariat de l'Institut, 1934.

Johnson, Gary J. 'De conspiratione delatorum: *Pliny and the Christians Revisited*'. *Latomus* 47, no. 2 (1988): 417–22.

Jones, A. H. M. *A History of Rome Through the Fifth Century. Vol. I: The Republic. Vol. II: The Empire.* New York: Harper & Row, 1968 and 1970.

Jones, Brian W. *The Emperor Domitian*. London: Routledge, 1992.

Jones, C. P. *Culture and Society in Lucian*. Cambridge, MA: Harvard University Press, 1986.

Jones, C. P. 'The Historicity of the Neronian Persecution: A Response to Brent Shaw'. *NTS* 63 (2017): 146–52.

Jones, C. P. *The Roman World of Dio Chrysostom*. Cambridge, MA: Harvard University Press, 1978.

Just, Roger. *Women in Athenian Law and Life*. London: Routledge, 1989.

Kaster, Robert A. *C. Suetonius Tranquillus: De Grammaticis et Rhetoribus*. Oxford: Clarendon, 1995.

Keim, Theodor. *Celsus's Wahres Wort. Aelteste Streitschrift antiker Weltanschauung gegen das Christentum, vom Jahr 178 n. Chr. Wiederhergestellt, aus dem Griechischen übersetzt, untersucht und erläutert, mit Lucian und Minucius Felix verglichen.* Zürich, 1873.

Kennedy, George, A. *A New History of Classical Rhetoric*. Princeton: Princeton University Press, 1994.

Kennedy, George A. *Progymnasmata: Greek Textbooks of Prose Composition and Rhetoric*. Writings from the Greco-Roman World 10. Atlanta: SBL, 2003.

Kenney, E. J. 'Small Writing and Less Reading'. *CR* 41, no. 1 (1991): 168–9 = review of William V. Harris, *Ancient Literacy*. Cambridge, MA: Harvard University Press, 1989.

Kidd, B. J. *Documents Illustrative of the History of the Church*. 2 vols. London: SPCK, 1920 and 1923.

Kinzig, Wolfram. 'Pagans and the Bible'. Pages 752–74 in *The New Cambridge History of the Bible 1: From the Beginnings to 600*. Edited by James Carleton Paget and Joachim Schaper. Cambridge: Cambridge University Press, 2013.

Koestermann, E. *Cornelius Tacitus Annalen, Band 4. Buch 14–16*. Heidelberg: Winter, 1968.

Koestermann, E. 'Ein folgenschwerer Irrtum des Tacitus (Ann. 15, 44, 2ff.)?' *Historia* 16 (1967): 456–69.

König, Jason. 'The Cynic and Christian Lives of Lucian's *Peregrinus*'. Pages 227–54 in *The Limits of Ancient Biography*. Edited by Brian C. McGing and Judith Mossman. Swansea: Classical Press of Wales, 2006.

König, Jason. *Greek Literature in the Roman Empire*. London: Bristol Classical / Duckworth, 2009.

Kraus, C. S., and A. J. Woodman. *Latin Historians*. New Surveys in the Classics 27. Oxford: Oxford University Press for the Classical Association, 1997.

Lampe, Peter. *Die stadtrömischen Christen in den ersten beiden Jahrhunderten: Untersuchungen zur Sozialgeschichte*. Tübingen: Mohr, 1989 = *From Paul to Valentinus: Christians at Rome in the First Two Centuries*. Translated by Michael Steinhauser. London: T&T Clark International, 2003.

Lane, William L. 'Social Perspectives on Roman Christianity during the Formative Years from Nero to Nerva: Romans, Hebrews, *I Clement*'. Pages 196–244 in *Judaism and Christianity in First-Century Rome*. Edited by Karl P. Donfried and Peter Richardson. Grand Rapids: Eerdmans, 1998.

Lane Fox, Robin. *Pagans and Christians*. London: Viking, 1986.

Leon, Harry J. *The Jews of Ancient Rome*. Philadelphia: The Jewish Publication Society of America, 1960; updated edn, Peabody: Hendrickson, 1995.

Levick, Barbara. *Claudius*. London: Batsford, 1990.

Levinskaya, Irina. *The Books of Acts in Its Diaspora Setting*. Grand Rapids: Eerdmans, 1996.

Lewis, Naphtali, and Meyer Reinhold, eds. *Roman Civilization: Selected Readings*. 2 vols. 3rd edn. New York: Columbia University Press, 1990.

Lightfoot, J. L. *Lucian: On the Syrian Goddess. Edited with Introduction, Translation, and Commentary*. Oxford: Oxford University Press, 2003.

Lindsay, Hugh. 'Suetonius as *ab epistulis* to Hadrian and the Early History of the Imperial Correspondence'. *Historia* 43, no. 4 (1994): 454–68.

Lona, Horacio E. *Die Wahre Lehre des Kelsos. Übersetzt und erklärt*. Freiburg: Herder, 2005.

Macleod, Matthew D. *Luciani Opera*. 4 vols. Oxford: Clarendon, 1972–87.

MacMullen, Ramsay. 'Two Types of Conversion to Early Christianity'. *VC* 37 (1983): 174–92.

Magie, David. *Roman Rule in Asia Minor*. 2 vols. Princeton: Princeton University Press, 1950.

Maier, Paul L. 'The Fate of Pontius Pilate'. *Hermes* 99 (1971): 362–71.

Marcovich, Miroslav. *Origenes Contra Celsum: libri VIII*. Leiden: Brill, 2001.

Marec, E., and H. G. Pflaum. 'Nouvelle inscription sur la carrière de Suétone'. *CRAI* (1952): 76–85 = *AE* 1953, no. 73.

Martin, R. H., and A. J. Woodman, eds. *Tacitus: Annals Book IV*. Cambridge: Cambridge University Press, 1989.

Mason, Steve. 'Griechische, römische und syrische Quellen über Jesus'. Pages 159–65 in *Jesus Handbuch*. Edited by Jens Schröter and Christine Jacobi. Tübingen: Mohr Siebeck, 2017.

McVey, Kathleen E., 'The Letter of Mara bar Serapion to His Son and the Second Sophistic: Palamedes and the "Wise King of the Jews"'. Pages 305–25 in *Syriac Encounters: Papers from the Sixth North American Syriac Symposium*. Edited by Maria Doerfler, Emanuel Fiano and Kyle Smith. Leuven: Peeters, 2015.

McVey, Kathleen E. 'Mara bar Serapion'. Pages 3:71–88 in *The Reception of Jesus in the First Three Centuries*. Edited by Chris Keith, Helen K. Bond, Christine Jacobi and Jens Schröter. 3 vols. London: Bloomsbury T&T Clark, 2020.

Meier, John P. *A Marginal Jew: Rethinking the Historical Jesus*. 5 vols. New York: Doubleday, 1991.

Mellor, Ronald. *Tacitus*. New York: Routledge, 1993.

Michie, James. *The Odes of Horace*. Harmondsworth: Penguin, 1964.

Millar, Fergus. *The Emperor in the Roman World (31 BC–AD 337)*. London: Duckworth, 1977.

Millar, Fergus. *The Roman Near East 31 BC–AD 337*. Cambridge, MA: Harvard University Press, 1993.

Millar, Fergus. *A Study of Cassius Dio*. Oxford: Clarendon, 1964.

Millar, Fergus. 'Trajan: Government by Correspondence'. Pages 419–41 in *The Epistles of Pliny*. Edited by Roy K. Gibson and Christopher Whitton. Oxford: Oxford University Press, 2016.

Moll, Sebastian. *The Arch-Heretic Marcion*. WUNT 250. Tübingen: Mohr Siebeck, 2010.

Momigliano, Arnaldo. *Claudius: The Emperor and His Achievement*. Cambridge: Heffer, 1961; repr. with corrections of the 1934 Clarendon edn.

Momigliano, Arnaldo. *Studies in Historiography*. London: Weidenfeld & Nicolson, 1969.

Mottershead, J. *Suetonius: Claudius*. Bristol: Bristol Classical, 1986.

Nickelsburg, George W. E. 'Enoch, Books of'. Pages 2:249–53 in *Encyclopedia of the Dead Sea Scrolls*. 2 vols. Edited by Lawrence H. Schiffman and James C. VanderKam. Oxford: Oxford University Press, 2000.

Nicolai, Roberto. 'The Place of History in the Ancient World'. Pages 13–26 in *A Companion to Greek and Roman Historiography*. Edited by John Marincola. Malden, MA: Wiley-Blackwell, 2011.

Niehoff, Maren R. 'A Jewish Critique of Christianity from Second-Century Alexandria: Revisiting the Jew Mentioned in *Contra Celsum*'. *JECS* 21, no. 2 (2013): 151–75.

North, John. 'The Development of Religious Pluralism'. Pages 174–93 in *The Jews Among Pagans and Christians in the Roman Empire*. Edited by Judith Lieu, John North and Tessa Rajak. London: Routledge, 1992.

Ogden, Daniel. *Magic, Witchcraft, and Ghosts in the Greek and Roman Worlds: A Sourcebook*. Oxford: Oxford University Press, 2002.

Ogilvie, R. M. *The Romans and Their Gods*. London: Chatto & Windus, 1969.

Ogilvie, R. M., and Ian Richmond, eds. *Cornelii Taciti De Vita Agricolae*. Oxford: Clarendon, 1967.

Oliver, Revilo P. 'The Praenomen of Tacitus'. *AJP* 98, no. 1 (1977): 64–70.

Osborn, Eric. 'The Apologists'. Pages 1:525–51 in *The Early Christian World*. Edited by Philip F. Esler. 2 vols. London: Routledge, 2000.

Osgood, Josiah. *Claudius Caesar: Image and Power in the Early Roman Empire*. Cambridge: Cambridge University Press, 2011.

Paterson, J. J. Review of Andrew Wallace-Hadrill, *Suetonius: The Scholar and His Caesars*. *G&R* 31 (1984): 218–19.

Patterson, L. 'Origin of the Name Panthera'. *JThS* 19 (1917): 79–80.

Penella, Robert J. 'The "Progymnasmata" in Imperial Greek Education'. *CW* 105, no. 1 (2011): 77–90.

Perris, Simon, and Fiachra Mac Góráin. 'The Ancient Reception of Euripides' *Bacchae* from Athens to Byzantium'. Pages 39–84 in *Dionysus and Rome*. Edited by Fiachra Mac Góráin. Berlin: de Gruyter, 2019.

Pichler, K. *Streit um das Christentum. Der Angriff des Kelsos und die Antwort des Origenes*. Frankfurt-am-Main, 1980.

Pilhofer, Peter, Manuel Baumbach, Jens Gerlach and Dirk Uwe Hansen. *Lukian: Der Tod des Peregrinos*. SAPERE IX. Darmstadt: Wissenschaftliche Buchgesellschaft, 2005.

Porter, Roy. *Gibbon: Making History*. London: Phoenix, 1995.

Potter, David S. 'Tacitus's Sources'. Pages 125–40 in *A Companion to Tacitus*. Edited by Victoria Emma Pagán. Chichester: Wiley-Blackwell, 2012.

Power, Tristan. 'Introduction: The Originality of Suetonius'. Pages 1–18 in *Suetonius the Biographer: Studies in Roman Lives*. Edited by Tristan Power and Roy Gibson. Oxford: Oxford University Press, 2014.

Pucci Ben Zeev, M. *Diaspora Judaism in Turmoil, 116–117 CE: Ancient Sources and Modern Insights*. Leuven: Peeters, 2005.

Pucci Ben Zeev, M. 'The Uprisings in the Jewish Diaspora, 116–117'. Pages 93–104 in *The Cambridge History of Judaism, vol. 4: The Late Roman-Rabbinic Period*. Edited by S. T. Katz. Cambridge: Cambridge University Press, 2006.

Quasten, Johannes. *Patrology*. Westminster: Christian Classics, 1983–88.

Radice, Betty, trans. *Pliny the Younger: Letters and Panegyricus*. LCL. 2 vols. London: William Heinemann, 1969.

Radin, Max. *The Jews Among the Greeks and Romans*. Philadelphia: The Jewish Publication Society of America, 1915.

Rajak, Tessa. *Josephus: The Historian and his Society*. London: Duckworth, 1983. 2nd edn. 2002.

Rees, Roger. 'Afterwords of Praise'. Pages 175–88 in *Pliny's Praise: The Panegyricus in the Roman World*. Edited by Paul Roche. Cambridge: Cambridge University Press, 2011.

Renahan, Robert. 'Christus or Chrestus in Tacitus?' *La Parola del Passato* 23 (1968): 368–70.

Robinson, Christopher. *Lucian and His Influence in Europe*. London: Duckworth, 1979.

Roche, Paul. 'Pliny's Thanksgiving: An Introduction to the Panegyricus'. Pages 1–28 in *Pliny's Praise: The Panegyricus in the Roman World*. Edited by Paul Roche. Cambridge: Cambridge University Press, 2011.

Rolfe, J. C., trans. *Suetonius*, 2 vols. Cambridge, MA: Harvard University Press, 1913–14. Revised with an introduction by K. R. Bradley, 1998.

Rosenbaum, H.-U. 'Zur Datierung von Celsus' ΑΛΗΘΗΣ ΛΟΓΟΣ'. *VC* 26 (1972): 102–11.

Rougé, Jean. 'L'incendie de Rome en 64 et l'incendie de Nicomédie en 303'. Pages 433–41 in *Mélanges d'histoire ancienne offerts à William Seston*. Paris: Boccard, 1974.

Rudd, Niall, trans. Juvenal, *The Satires*. OWC. Oxford: Oxford University Press, 1992.

Rutgers, Leonard Victor. 'Roman Policy Toward the Jews: Expulsions from the City of Rome During the First Century C. E.'. Pages 93–116 in *Judaism and Christianity in First-Century Rome*. Edited by Karl P. Donfried and Peter Richardson. Grand Rapids: Eerdmans, 1998.

Sartre, Maurice. *The Middle East Under Rome*. Translated by Catherine Porter and Elizabeth Rawlings. Cambridge, MA: Harvard University Press, 2005.

Schäfer, Peter. *Jesus in the Talmud*. Princeton: Princeton University Press, 2007.

Schäfer, Peter. *Judeophobia: Attitudes Toward the Jews in the Ancient World*. Cambridge, MA: Harvard University Press, 1997.

Schmitt, T. 'Des Kaisers Inszerierung: Mythologie und neronische Christenverfolgung'. *ZAC* 16 (2012): 487–515.

Schürer, Emil. *The History of the Jewish People in the Age of Jesus Christ*. Revised and edited by Geza Vermes, Fergus Millar and Martin Goodman. 3 vols. Edinburgh: T&T Clark, 1973–87.

Schwartz, Jacques. 'Celsus Redivivus'. *RHPhR* 53 (1973): 399–405.

Schwartz, Jacques. 'Du Testament de Lévi au Discours véritable de Celse'. *RHPhR* 40 (1960): 126–45.

Shaw, Brent D. 'The Myth of the Neronian Persecution'. *JRS* 105 (2015): 73–100.

Sherwin-White, A. N. *The Letters of Pliny: A Historical and Social Commentary*. Oxford: Clarendon, 1966.

Shotter, David, ed. *Suetonius: Lives of Galba, Otho and Vitellius*. Warminster: Aris & Phillips, 1993.

Simmons, Michael B. 'Graeco-Roman Philosophical Opposition'. Pages 2:840–68 in *The Early Christian World*. Edited by Philip F. Esler. 2 vols. London: Routledge, 2000.

Slingerland, H. Dixon. *Claudian Policymaking and the Early Imperial Repression of Judaism at Rome*. Atlanta: Scholars Press, 1997.

Slingerland, H. Dixon. 'Suetonius, *Claudius* 25.4, Acts 18, and Paulus Orosius' *Historiarum adversum paganos libri VII*: Dating the Claudian Expulsion(s) of Roman Jews'. *JQR* 83 (1992): 127–44.

Smallwood, E. Mary. 'The Diaspora in the Roman Period Before CE 70'. Pages 168–91 in *The Cambridge History of Judaism III: The Early Roman Period*. Edited by W. Horbury, W. D. Davies, and J. Sturdy. Cambridge: Cambridge University Press, 1999.

Smallwood, E. Mary. *Documents Illustrating the Principates of Nerva Trajan and Hadrian*. Cambridge: Cambridge University Press, 1966.

Smallwood, E. Mary. *The Jews Under Roman Rule from Pompey to Diocletian*. SJLA 20. Leiden: Brill, 1976.

Smallwood, E. Mary. *Philonis Alexandrini Legatio ad Gaium*. Leiden: Brill, 1961.

Smith, Morton. *Jesus the Magician*. Wellingborough: Aquarian, 1985.

Solin, Heikki. *Die griechische Personennamen in Rom: Ein Namenbuch*. 3 vols. Berlin: de Gruyter, 2003.

Solin, Heikki. 'Juden und Syrer im westlichen Teil der römischen Welt'. Pages 590–789 and 1222–49 in *ANRW* II.29.2. Berlin: de Gruyter, 1983.

Sommerstein, Alan H. *Aeschylus: The Persians and Other Plays*. London: Penguin, 2009.

Sommerstein, Alan H., trans. *Aristophanes: Lysistrata and Other Plays*. London: Penguin, 2002.

Stanton, Graham. 'Jesus of Nazareth: A Magician and a False Prophet Who Deceived God's People?' Pages 164–80 in *Jesus of Nazareth: Lord and Christ – Essays on the Historical Jesus and New Testament Christology*. Edited by Joel B. Green and Max Turner. Grand Rapids: Eerdmans, 1994.

Stauffer, Ethelbert. *Die Pilatusinschrift von Caesarea*. Erlanger Universitätsreden, N.F. 12. Erlangen, 1966.

Steidle, Wolf. *Sueton und die antike Biographie, Zetemata 1*. Munich: Beck, 1951; repr. 1963.

Stern, Menahem. *Greek and Latin Authors on Jews and Judaism*. 3 vols. Jerusalem: Israel Academy of Sciences and Humanities, 1974–84.

Stevenson, J. *A New Eusebius: Documents Illustrating the History of the Church to AD 337*. Revised by W. H. C. Frend. London: SPCK, 1987.

Strunk, Thomas E. 'Domitian's Lightning Bolts and Close Shaves in Pliny'. *CJ* 109, no. 1 (2013): 88–113.

Strunk, Thomas E. 'Pliny the Pessimist'. *G&R* 59, no. 2 (2012): 178–92.

Syme, Ronald. 'Pliny the Procurator'. *HSCP* 73 (1969): 201–36.

Syme, Ronald. 'Pliny's Less Successful Friends'. *Historia* 9, no. 3 (1960): 362–79.

Syme, Ronald. *Tacitus*, 2 vols. Oxford: Clarendon, 1958.

Syme, Ronald. 'The Travels of Suetonius Tranquillus'. *Hermes* 109 (1981): 105–17.

Taillardat, Jean. *Suétone: Περὶ βλασφημιῶν. Περὶ παιδιῶν. extraits byzantins*. Paris: Les Belles Lettres, 1967.

Taylor, Joan E. *What Did Jesus Look Like?* London: T&T Clark, 2018.

Theissen, Gerd, and Annette Merz. *The Historical Jesus: A Comprehensive Guide*. London: SCM, 1998.

Thurn, Ioannes, ed. *Ioannis Malalae Chronographia*. Berlin: de Gruyter, 2000.

Townend, G. B. 'The Date of Composition of Suetonius' Caesares'. *CQ* 9 (1959): 285–93.

Townend, G. B. 'The Hippo Inscription and the Career of Suetonius'. *Historia* 10 (1961): 99–109.

Townend, G. B. 'Introduction'. Pages vii–xv in *Suetonius: Divus Julius*. Edited by H. E. Butler and M. Cary. Bristol: Bristol Classical, 1982.

Townend, G. B. 'Suetonius and his Influence'. Pages 79–111 in *Latin Biography*. Edited by T. A. Dorey. London: Routledge & Kegan Paul, 1967.

Turner, Paul, trans. *Lucian: Satirical Sketches*. Harmondsworth: Penguin, 1961.

Van der Lans, Birgit, and Jan N. Bremmer. 'Tacitus and the Persecution of the Christians: An Invention of Tradition?' *Eirene. Studia Graeca et Latina* 53 (2017): 299–331.

Van Voorst, Robert E. *Jesus Outside the New Testament*. Grand Rapids: Eerdmans, 2000.

Wagemakers, Bart. 'Incest, Infanticide, and Cannibalism: Anti-Christian Imputations in the Roman Empire'. *G&R* 57 (2010): 337–54.

Walker, B. *The Annals of Tacitus*. Manchester: Manchester University Press, 1952.

Wallace-Hadrill, Andrew. *Suetonius: The Scholar and His Caesars*. London: Duckworth, 1983. Repr. with minor corrections, 1995.

Walsh, P. G., trans. *Pliny the Younger: Complete Letters*. OWC. Oxford: Oxford University Press, 2006.

Wardle, D. 'Suetonius as *ab epistulis*'. *Historia* 51 (2002): 462–80.

Warmington, B. H. *Suetonius: Nero*. Bristol: Bristol Classical, 1977.

Warner, Rex, trans. *Thucydides. History of the Peloponnesian War*. Harmondsworth: Penguin, 1954.

Weaver, P. R. C. *Familia Caesaris: A Social Study of the Emperor's Freedmen and Slaves*. Cambridge: Cambridge University Press, 1972.

Welburn, A. J. 'Reconstructing the Ophite Diagram'. *NovT* 23 (1981): 261–87.

Wellesley, Kenneth. *Cornelius Tacitus 1.2, Annales XI–XVI*. Leipzig: Teubner, 1986.

Wells, G. A. *Did Jesus Exist?* 2nd edn. London: Pemberton, 1986.

Wells, G. A. *The Historical Evidence for Jesus*. Buffalo: Prometheus, 1982.

Whitmarsh, Tim. *Battling the Gods: Atheism in the Ancient World*. London: Faber & Faber, 2016.

Whitmarsh, Tim. *The Second Sophistic*. New Surveys in the Classics 35. Oxford: Oxford University Press, 2005.

Whittaker, John. 'Celsus no. 70'. Pages 2:255–6 in *Dictionnaire des philosophes antiques*. Edited by Richard Goulet. 5 vols. Paris: CNRS 1994–.

Whittaker, Molly. *Jews and Christians: Graeco-Roman Views*. Cambridge: Cambridge University Press, 1984.

Whitton, Christopher. *The Arts of Imitation in Latin Prose: Pliny's Epistles/Quintilian in Brief*. Cambridge: Cambridge University Press, 2019.

Whitton, Christopher. '"Let us tread our path together": Tacitus and the Younger Pliny'. Pages 345–68 in *A Companion to Tacitus*. Edited by Victoria Emma Pagán. Chichester: Wiley-Blackwell, 2012.

Whitton, Christopher. *Pliny the Younger: Epistles Book II*. Cambridge: Cambridge University Press, 2013.

Wilken, Robert L. *The Christians as the Romans Saw Them*. New Haven: Yale University Press, 1984.

Willcock, M. M. *Homer – Iliad I–XII*. London: Bristol Classical, 1996.

Williams, Margaret H. 'Domitian, the Jews and the "Judaizers": A Simple Matter of *Cupiditas* and *Maiestas*?', *Historia* 39 (1990): 196–211 = pages 95–110 in *Jews in a Graeco-Roman Environment*. Tübingen: Mohr Siebeck, 2013.

Williams, Margaret H. 'Latin Authors on Jews and Judaism'. Pages 870–75 in *The Eerdmans Dictionary of Early Judaism*. Edited by John J. Collins and Daniel C. Harlow. Grand Rapids: Eerdmans, 2010.

Williams, Margaret H. 'Pliny the Younger'. Pages 3:41–50 in *The Reception of Jesus in the First Three Centuries*. Edited by Chris Keith, Helen K. Bond, Christine Jacobi and Jens Schröter. 3 vols. London: Bloomsbury T&T Clark, 2020.

Williams, Margaret H. 'Prefects and Procurators'. Pages 2:686–7 in *Encyclopedia of the Dead Sea Scrolls*. 2 vols. Edited by Lawrence H. Schiffman and James C. VanderKam. Oxford: Oxford University Press, 2000.

Williams, Margaret H. 'Tacitus'. Pages 3:61–70 in *The Reception of Jesus in the First Three Centuries*. Edited by Chris Keith, Helen K. Bond, Christine Jacobi and Jens Schröter. 3 vols. London: Bloomsbury T&T Clark, 2020.

Williams, Wynne, *Pliny the Younger: Correspondence with Trajan from Bithynia*. Warminster: Aris & Phillips, 1990.

Willis, William H. 'A Census of Literary Papyri from Egypt'. *GRBS* 9 (1968): 205–41.

Wilson, A. N. *Paul: The Mind of the Apostle*. London: Sinclair-Stevenson, 1997.

Wirszubski, C. *Libertas as a Political Idea at Rome during the Late Republic and Early Empire*. Cambridge: Cambridge University Press, 1950.

Wood, Jamie. 'Suetonius and the *De vita Caesarum* in the Carolingian Empire'. Pages 273–91 in *Suetonius the Biographer: Studies in Roman Lives*. Edited by Tristan Power and Roy Gibson. Oxford: Oxford University Press, 2014.

Woodman, A. J. *Rhetoric in Classical Historiography*. London: Croom Helm, 1988.

Woodman, A. J. 'Tacitus and the Contemporary Scene'. Pages 31–43 in *The Cambridge Companion to Tacitus*. Edited by A. J. Woodman. Cambridge: Cambridge University Press, 2009.

Woodman, A. J., trans. *Tacitus: The Annals*. Indianapolis: Hackett, 2004.

Woodman, A. J., ed., with contributions from C. S. Kraus. *Tacitus: Agricola*. Cambridge: Cambridge University Press, 2014.

Woolf, Greg. 'Pliny's Province'. Pages 442–60 in *The Epistles of Pliny*. Edited by Roy K. Gibson and Christopher Whitton. Oxford: Oxford University Press, 2016.

Wright, Brian J. 'Ancient Rome's Daily News Publication with Some Likely Implications for Early Christian Studies'. *TynBul* 67, no. 1 (2016): 145–60.

Wuilleumier, P. *Tacite: Annales Livres XIII–XVI*. Paris: Société d'édition 'Les Belles Lettres', 1978.

Yardley, J. C., trans. *Tacitus: The Annals*. OWC. Oxford: Oxford University Press, 2008.

INDEX OF AUTHORS

INDEX OF SUBJECTS

education (*paideia*) (*see also*
    progymnasmata)
    core Greek texts 138, 139, 140, 166
        n. 25
    core Latin texts (Livy) 80–1
    paramouncy of Homer 140, 165,
        166 n. 24, 167, 177
    pepaideumenoi (educated elite)
        125, 138, 140, 145, 186
    rhetorical training 159–61

incarnation
    a fabrication by Jesus 162
    Platonic arguments against 179–80

Jesus, depictions of
    as a charlatan 136
    as a common criminal 81, 95
    as a god 43, 90, 169
    as a liar and impostor/sorcerer (*goes*)
        167, 169, 170, 187
    as a revolutionary leader 122, 176,
        180
    as a teacher (sophist) and lawgiver
        130, 135, 136, 138, 143, 186
Jesus, life-events (*see also* crucifixion,
    incarnation, Panthera, resurrection,
    ungodlike behaviour)
    baptism 167–8
    birth, parentage and upbringing
        162–3, 164, 165–6
    death 5, 83, 173–4
    sojourn in Egypt 163, 165 n. 21, 166
Jesus, negative features
    bastardy 162, 164
    beggarly life-style 171
    expertise in Egyptian-style magic
        163, 166–7, 169, 187
    ungodlike appearance 176–8
    ungodlike behaviour 172–4, 176
    un-messianic conduct 170–2
Jesus, positive aspects
    a 'founder-hero' 43, 44, 49
    a god 90
    a positive role model 44, 49
Jewish anti-Christian polemic
    denigration of Mary 158 n. 89, 164
    Jesus's bastardy 164 n. 10
    Jesus's sojourn in Egypt 167
    non-messianic status of Jesus 172

Josephus
    on Jesus 1 n. 4, 39 n. 22, 54, 103
    as an historian of provincial origin
        10

Mara bar Serapion 4
mythicism 5–6, 16–17, 54–5, 68, 189
    n. 32
mythicists
    Carrier, R. 6 n. 21, 17 n. 80, 55
        n. 25, 67, 69 n. 98, 119 n. 114
    Drews, A. 5 n. 21, 17 n. 81, 68 n. 96
    Wells, G. A. 6 n. 21, 55 n. 24, 60
        n. 48, 61 n. 51, 119 n. 114

Panthera 164–5
Pontius Pilatus
    dates of governorship 54 n. 20
    official title 60 n. 47, 87
    treatment by Tacitus 87–92
progymnasmata (*see also* education and
    rhetorical training)
    comparison (*synkrisis*) 160–1, 173,
        174, 176 n. 84
    encomium 126
    invective (*psogos*) 133, 160, 163–4,
        165–6
    personification (*prosopopeia*) 126,
        160, 176
    refutation (*anaskeue*) 160, 171

resurrection
    fabrication by the disciples 175, 178
    implausibility 174–5
    lack of hard evidence 175
    lack of impartial witnesses 175
    philosophical arguments against
        179–80
rhetorical exercises (*see* education and
    progymnasmata)
rhetorical ploys
    exaggeration 59 n. 43, 171 n. 54
    generalising plurals 110 n. 70
    calculated misuse of words
        (*catachresis*) 78, 92, 157
    use of names for denigration or
        eulogy 165 n. 17
rhetorical textbooks
    Latin 31
    Greek 159

Made in the USA
Thornton, CO
06/20/24 20:47:21